DEMONSTRATIONS IN
PHYSICAL EDUCATION

DEMONSTRATIONS IN
PHYSICAL EDUCATION—

by

WILLIAM ALBERT HEALEY, Pe.D.

Professor of Physical Education
Northern Illinois University
DeKalb, Illinois

- **Organization**
- **Supervision**
- **Administration**

Danville, Illinois:

THE INTERSTATE
Printers & Publishers, Inc.

This book is one of the Interstate Series in Physical Education,
Athletics, and Recreation.

TO MY CHILDREN

Judith, John, and Robert

PREFACE

The purpose of this book is to present material which will be of help to the individuals responsible for conducting a physical education demonstration. Only those activities that could be used in the regular physical education curriculum and that are applicable for use in a demonstration which is to be viewed by the general public are considered. This book is concerned primarily with the details confronting the administrator of the demonstration; it is an attempt to be helpful in better organizing and conducting the demonstration of those activities which are being taught in the regular physical education classes and presenting them to the general public in an enjoyable and yet forceful manner.

While many individuals are skilled in the teaching of physical education activities, they are wholly unprepared, both experience-wise and talent-wise, to present the results of their teachings in an organized and systematic manner to an interested public. This book is an attempt to present this needed information in detailed form, and in such a manner that it is easily understood. Examples of every administrative detail—as well as examples of school administrative procedure which, with slight alteration, can be applied to almost every situation—are fully outlined for immediate use.

The last chapter discusses in detail many of the activities which can be used in the demonstration and how they are used.

Finally it is the author's hope that the material presented in this book will serve as an incentive for the physical education teacher to do a better job in the teaching of physical education and that the information contained within the pages will provide him with the techniques which will enable him to present to the general public a "new look" at the physical education program. It is hoped it will provide an effective means of placing the activities taught in a program of physical education before the general public in their true light and provide a helpful guide for those persons engaged in teaching physical education to accomplish this task. This book gives the why and how of physical education demonstrations. So it is that the book is primarily directed toward making clear the process of putting on a physical education demonstration, stressing both the author's deep concern for the improvement of physical education programs for American youth and his firm conviction that we are morally obligated to give to the youth the experiences gained in a good physical education program, these experiences being invaluable and an essential part of our educational structure.

CONTENTS

CHAPTER I

The Philosophy, Planning, and Outcomes of the Physical Education Demonstration

Physical education is an integral part of the total education process. It is occupying an increasingly important place in the school curriculum. Its objectives are closely associated with those of general education.

THE PLACE OF PHYSICAL EDUCATION IN THE SCHOOL CURRICULUM

Since physical education is a segment of the whole system of education, it should not be thought of as a thing apart. It is not the education of the physical body alone. Physical courage, quick thinking, sportsmanship, character, and fair play are best learned on the athletic field and in the gymnasium as a part of the program. This fact should be brought before the public, and there is not a better or more interesting way than through a physical education demonstration.

For many years the physical educator has been trying to justify his program. Now that physical education is recognized as occupying an important place in the educational system, everything should be done to keep it there.

World War II taught us the value of physical education. The various governmental agencies gave their recognition and support to

programs of physical education which were scientifically constructed, taught, and evaluated. It is necessary to carry the program forward. It is imperative to "educate" the parents of our boys and girls
as to the value of a well rounded program in physical education.

UNDERSTANDING PHYSICAL EDUCATION

In recent years more and more people have come to a better
understanding of physical education because of the efforts of trained
instructors to enlighten the general public as to the benefits of a
good program in the form of a more enriched life. Physical fitness
is now a household term, and people are more conscious than ever
before of their own physical conditions. Much has been written concerning the benefits of a regular and sustained amount of
physical exercise. The value of such exercise cannot be overlooked,
but continued effort on the part of physical educators to establish
good programs should always be forthcoming. The physical education demonstration is one way in which the importance of good
training can be brought before the general public.

There are laws in many states which provide for a definite amount
of time to be spent in physical education. Programs must meet the
standards set up by the various state agencies. Too often programs
do not meet these standards. A great deal can be done toward bringing physical education to the front and showing the general public
its value through demonstrations, as too few people really know much
about the school program. It should be brought to their attention
that physical fitness for effective living does not require the same
program as physical fitness for athletic competition. It is possible
through the demonstration to place the program of physical education before the public in such a way that it is both entertaining and
educational.

CHANGES IN PHYSICAL EDUCATION

Physical education has undergone great changes during the past
25 years. Schools are now giving training in activities that can be
maintained throughout life. They are giving training in skills that
have a carry-over value in order that people may spend their leisure
time more advantageously.

SELLING THE COMMUNITY ON
PHYSICAL EDUCATION

The physical education demonstration will help to sell the community as well as the student on physical education. For many students it will afford an opportunity to appear before an audience for the first time. It may be just walking across the gym floor but it will mean a great deal to the individual who has not had such an opportunity before. It will afford the people in the community an opportunity to see first-hand the activities which are being offered in the physical education program and of which they, in many cases, are totally unaware. The only other activities which the general public has an opportunity to see are in athletic areas, which they believe make up the entire program.

Physical education is boredom to many boys and girls because they do not possess the skill necessary to enjoy the activity, whether it be basketball or weight lifting. It is important that boys and girls like physical activity; therefore, every effort should be made to provide the means by which the student can be motivated. Being a part of a group attempting to show the general public what is being done in the classroom can be instrumental in appealing to the younster to participate (to become better skilled in the activity) and to improve in his ability to perform the skills necessary to become more proficient in the activity. A physical education demonstration will provide this opportunity and, at the same time, give the general public a good hard look at what is being accomplished in the teaching and learning of physical skills other than those taught and learned in the athletic program. There are many special physical skills displayed in physical education activities which are particularly adapted to individuals who may not be adept at the skills required in interscholastic athletics. Therefore, it gives these individuals an opportunity to perform such skills before an appreciative audience and one that is especially interested in seeing them perform.

The general public tends to support the things it sees and believes in. That is one reason it endorses and supports interscholastic athletics for the very few; it can observe first-hand what the coach has taught and how well the student has learned. The public almost never is given the opportunity of seeing a good physical education program for the vast majority of students. Here is its chance to do so and the physical educator, overworked though he might be, should be quick to grasp this opportunity and use it for the advancement of his program and his profession.

The physical education teacher who attempts to put on a demonstration is accepting a challenge. The world is full of critics, and some of the worst ones are in the field of physical education and athletics. The teacher must realize this and therefore must be careful that the activities selected to demonstrate will fit the occasion and can be justified as the kind to be offered in a physical education program. Care should be taken that the public demonstration does not become a public spectacle and exhibition. It should not give the impression that the entire class time is being used in preparation for the demonstration.

PURPOSE OF THE DEMONSTRATION

Sponsoring a demonstration will be well worth the time and effort of all concerned, as it will result in increased interest and enthusiasm by both parents and students. It will make the physical educator's job much easier in the days to follow and serve as an added incentive to both student and teacher so that both may look forward to the next year and the next demonstration.

The purpose of the demonstration should be the same as that of any other school function. The goals should compare with those set up for the entire school curriculum because the demonstration will educate the student the same as will any other agency within the school. Because the demonstration gives an opportunity for every student to participate in an activity that is educational in every respect, it should therefore, be included in the same category and be given as much time and attention as are given the other extracurricular activities. The aims and objectives of the demonstration compare with those of the school curriculum and supply an opportunity for the education of the whole child because emphasis will be placed on good relationships, upon a sharing, and an experiencing of "togetherness." The problems which boys and girls must solve are those centered in their relationships with others. Failure to solve them may bring about in an individual insecurity, inadequacy, emotional disturbance, or even disintegration of personality. Many schools have realized the importance of this and have evaluated all activities on the basis of how much these activities contribute to the establishment of satisfying relationships with students within the same age groups, both male and female.

The demonstration is an activity that will help the students make this social adjustment. It will be a means by which boys and girls may work out their social relationships in satisfactory ways. The need for programs that will help solve the problems of adolescents in this crucial area has been uppermost in the minds of many educators for some time. They need guidance and experience so that they may become socially well adjusted, responsible, cooperative citizens. The young person must learn to get along with others so that he may live harmoniously and work cooperatively in society. The demonstration may be used as one instrument for teaching him how to do this. He learns that he is a part of a team and that the success of the demonstration depends upon how well he does his job, and how he cooperates with others in doing this job. He must do these things if he is to live in a democratic society.

There are then three general purposes of the demonstration:

1. It helps to inform the general public and create a better feeling toward physical education by the average layman as well as the student.
2. It provides an opportunity for the students to have the experience of working toward a common goal. They learn to share responsibilities and end up by seeing what they have created.
3. It provides an opportunity for the instructor to gain recognition of the need for and value of physical education for every student. The student and parent alike will benefit from the participation in the activities presented in the demonstration.

VALUE OF THE DEMONSTRATION

There are many individuals—and this may include the students themselves—who can see little value in the learning of physical skills that do not relate directly to the students' ways of living. The value of participation may be brought out in the demonstration, for each student—because of engaging in the activities demonstrated—will learn to enjoy it, and he will feel part of the group that associates itself with physical activities. He will learn more about physical fitness and its place in physical education and he will be made more aware of the value of and need for this fitness as a result of the demonstration.

The demonstration will also afford opportunities for students and teachers to work together cooperatively, democratically, and creatively on a group project. Students who heretofore had little opportunity to be team members working for a common goal—that of winning—find themselves involved in a group project the result of which is to make the demonstration a success. The students will tend to take more and more responsibility, thereby lessening the teacher's load. If given the opportunity, and the proper incentive and motivation, students will literally perform miracles and will unselfishly work long hours to put the demonstration over. Many students have the ability to help in ways other than those needed for the performance of the physical skills used in the activities. The work crews that are needed for the many tasks to be done are all important parts of the demonstration. Thus, the demonstration provides a laboratory situation where the development of socially acceptable behavior patterns, including cooperation and sportsmanship, is encouraged. This cooperation with others will not be overlooked by the spectators and will at least partially answer the question: Why physical education?

The demonstration also provides the instructors with ways to gain recognition which they would not be able to do in any other way. The athletic coach is afforded the opportunity each week to show the public what he is teaching and how well it is being learned. His work is constantly in the public eye and, while he is often under severe criticism, he at least has the opportunity to display his teachings. He is not always judged on games won or lost. The physical education teacher does not have this opportunity, yet he may be doing an outstanding job of teaching Johnny how to tumble, rather than kick a football, shoot a basket, or hit a baseball. He may also be providing Johnny in a smaller way with the opportunity to derive the satisfaction of performing a physical skill in front of an audience —something almost every boy craves to do, yet few have the opportunity because they are not good enough to be a member of an athletic team.

DETERMINING THE THEME FOR THE DEMONSTRATION

The demonstration should be given in the evening and should portray the activities which are an outgrowth of the regular physical education classes. The program should be built around a general theme such as seasons, holidays, the good old days, the Deep South, Wild West, other sections of the country, etc.

This is important because the demonstration must have justification other than the fact that the administration wishes to sell the program to the public. It must have a guiding purpose and preferably be a direct outgrowth of the curriculum. If this is not the case, the demonstration will deteriorate to the point that it becomes an exhibition where only the better students perform difficult feats of skill to the detriment of those students who really need the experience which would be gained from a performance of this kind before an audience. This also will result in an attempt to outdo each preceding demonstration with better and better performances until all the educational benefits have disappeared. The results cannot be measured by outstanding performances, but by the experiences gained by all the students from the time the demonstration was first being planned. The selection of a few students who are able to perform skills better than others should be avoided. Everyone should be included in the demonstration; otherwise, a commercial production will result, accompanied by outside pressures to have a professional-type production. This, in turn, will bring about jealousies among the participants and friction concerning who is going to perform in different activities. Likewise, parents of the individual participants may feel that their child is better than someone else. Under such circumstances long periods of practice should be engaged in to perfect the skills and show off the abilities of all participating students, and a demonstration should not be thought of as a professional production.

REHEARSALS

All rehearsals should be held after school so that they do not interfere with the regular school program. This is important because other faculty members may object if time is taken from their classes or the classes are disrupted in any way. Extreme care should be taken that this does not happen. It is possible to rehearse many of the numbers during the regular class periods because they will include only those students within a particular class. Several mass rehearsals will be necessary before the actual demonstration takes place. There will be many details that will need to be worked out. The timing of each event in its relationship to the other events is important. The moving of the students from place to place is of major consideration and will take careful planning. Each student should be given a program and printed instructions so that he may study them. This will cut down the practice time and avoid a great deal of confusion during the actual demonstration. The rehearsals will give all of the students an opportunity to see all of the demonstration; they probably will not be able to do this during the performance.

Rehearsals give each participant an opportunity to go through the exact movements he will be required to go through at the time of the demonstration. This gives him a feeling of quiet confidence and overcomes any fear he may have that he will make a mistake and make a fool of himself. He will familiarize himself with the equipment, costumes, and other things directly connected with the activity. It will do much to quell any fears the participant may have of doing something wrong.

The rehearsal will also offer an opportunity for picture taking, an activity which is rather difficult during the actual performance for anyone except, perhaps, a professional photographer. It will afford an opportunity to make any costume or equipment changes. Some costumes may not fit certain individuals and will require alteration.

Rehearsal times should be worked out so that each group will have the required amount of time. To begin with, the schedule should be flexible enough for changes to be made as needed. Some of the activities will not need so much time as others; therefore, a change of scheduling will be necessary. Others may take more time and the schedule will need to be rearranged in order to fit the activity into the revised schedule. (It may need to be frequently revised.) More time will be needed if the demonstration is held only once a year; this, of course, will almost always be the case.

No more than four or five weeks should be allotted for preparing and producing the demonstration. Careful use of this time should be made so that it is not wasted. The first week will be used for a general discussion, selection of the general theme, and a consideration of ideas. The next week will be used for organizing the participants into specific working groups. These groups in turn discuss and plan, to the last detail, the specific activities to which they have been assigned. The groups will then use approximately two weeks in planning, practicing, and rehearsing. The making of needed costumes and special equipment will be included in these two weeks, with the last week used in group rehearsal with the participants in other activities and in bringing the entire group together in final rehearsals. A demonstration such as is described in this book will need several "dress rehearsals" to coordinate the entire program and bring all the loose ends together. This in itself requires advance planning and organization.

The rehearsals should be carried out exactly as planned for the demonstration. The same amount of time should be used for the activity as well as that for between activities. The exact time needed for the demonstration may be determined in this way. Two mass rehearsals are required.

PRINTED INSTRUCTIONS TO PARTICIPANTS

Printed instructions should include the procession and recession order, all the large numbers, the grand finale, and the specific responsibilities of certain persons in the entire program. All of the information should be printed in sequence so that one event or duty follows another in order of occurrence. In this way there is no mix-up and things will be run off in smooth and orderly fashion with few, if any, mistakes. The instructions should be in the hands of the students before the first rehearsal. The students should be assigned rooms, stations, or seats, during the time they are not performing. These places should preferably be outside of the gymnasium in adjoining rooms to avoid noise and confusion. Each group should be assigned a leader who will be partly responsible for their conduct. Enough time should be allowed in between activities to enable the participants to move from area to area and take down the equipment.

INSTRUCTIONS FOR THE TUMBLING GROUP

Leader—Fred Jones

7:15 Report to room 110 dressed for activity.
7:20 Make necessary costume arrangements.
7:23 Be seated and read instruction sheet.
7:25 Line up and prepare to enter gymnasium in single file as rehearsed.
7:30 As group marches into gymnasium, Bill Green, Mark Johnson,

and Bob Block place mats in correct position for tumbling.

7:35 Go through routine as rehearsed and, after finishing, line up in position ready to leave gymnasium.

7:45 As group is lining up, the equipment will be removed from the gymnasium by same boys that set it up.

7:50 March out of gymnasium as leader gives the command.

7:51 Go to room 110 and wait until demonstration is over, unless you are in another activity. If this is true, go to room assigned for this activity.

PLANNING FOR THE DEMONSTRATION

Care should be taken that the planning for the demonstration does not take precedence over the actual teaching of the physical education class. Too much class time must not be taken in practicing for the demonstration; otherwise, the instructor will find himself using the instructional time preparing for the demonstration. Class work should come first and the objectives set up for the physical education program should be adhered to. Class time should not be taken for practicing demonstrational routines and skills. This defeats the purpose of the demonstration. The regular physical education curriculum should be followed throughout the year, and care should be taken that activities which are to be used in the demonstration are not substituted. This can easily be done because certain activities are particularly adaptable to a demonstration. These activities should not be emphasized at the expense of others. The regular program must not be upset, and students should not be taken from other classes for rehearsals.

As one of the primary objectives of the demonstration is to give the general public an opportunity to see the physical education program in action, everyone should be given an opportunity to perform; otherwise, it will not give a true picture of the actual program. Every parent should be given the opportunity to see his or her child perform, even though the part may be a very minor one. The objectives of the program should be clearly stated beforehand and should be used as a guide line for the entire demonstration. The program will, therefore, meet the objective of the emotional-social growth aspect as well as that of development of physical skills.

There is no objection to inserting special activities where the better students may be used in the performance of specialized skills.

It will be the duty of the instructor to select the students that are able to do these skills best and to avoid too much duplication of personnel in the activities; otherwise, one student might be in several activities and this would defeat the purpose of the demonstration.

However, it is important that each student contribute as much as possible to the success of the demonstration without deviating too far from the main objective. It is justifiable, therefore, to make use of any special skills that certain students may have in order to "dress up" the program and make it more presentable. The end result will justify the means and, in the long run, make for a better and more interesting program without sacrificing the original objectives. The student also needs to know that he is being selected for the activities that he can do best as his contribution to the program. In this way, he will work harder to perfect his skills and to do a better job in his specific contribution to the demonstration. This, in turn, will help in the development of the social-emotional growth, which can be an important aspect of the demonstration and one which cannot and should not be overlooked.

There is no substitute for good planning. The demonstration depends upon both well selected activities and the method used in presenting them. Nevertheless, there is no magic formula. There are many ways to add variety to the demonstration in order to keep it alive and flexible and to prevent lag of spectator interest. The activities should be spaced in the program so that all of the same types of activities do not follow one another; the program should offer variation.

For example, a trampoline or tumbling act should follow a dance act so that a contrast may be seen. The audience will react to this contrast because the trampoline act will be more spectacular and sensational after watching a milder act like the dance. The active games should follow the quiet games. The entire program should be worked out so that the spectators are wondering what is coming next. Their interest is thus kept at a high pitch, and there is no let down feeling which comes from a program that drags.

The time in between acts will determine to a large extent whether or not the program will drag. As the entire program usually will take place in the gymnasium, all changes of scenery and equipment will take place in full view of the audience. This, of course, can take a great deal of time and, unless some expert planning is done, will do much to slow down the program and result in periods of non-activity. Such a situation brings on a feeling of restlessness in the audience.

The activities should also be placed in the program so that the moving of equipment would not present a major problem. It is sometimes possible to use one-half of the gym for the activity which is being demonstrated while the equipment is being removed from the other half or moved on for the next activity showing. This, of course, is not an ideal situation but does speed up the demonstration and prevents dragging of the in-between acts, which should be prevented if at all possible. The location of the audience and the accessibility of the equipment will determine to a large extent the use of the above plan. If the equipment can be removed while an activity is being demonstrated, it will result in the program's moving along a great deal faster and with more precision. This is important as some of the people will not like certain activities that are being demonstrated and will be anxious to have them completed and to move on to the next activity. This can be done if the equipment is set up and the participants are ready.

It must be remembered in planning a demonstration that the purpose is to show the general public what is being taught in the regular classroom. It is, therefore, important that the public not only see the end results of the teaching of an activity but also see the actual teaching situation. It must be made known that all participants will not be and need not be experts in the performance of the skills shown. If the purpose of the demonstration is to be accomplished, a clear distinction should be made between the technique of the activity and the technique of teaching the activity. It should be pointed out that learning comes about only through the activity of the learner. The student must learn by doing, and the skill and knowledge possessed by the teacher cannot, by some miracle, be transmitted from the teacher to the student. The teacher can only demonstrate the correct form; the student must acquire the skill through his own efforts.

In planning the demonstration, therefore, an attempt should be made to present this theme to the public: The function of the teacher is to promote the learning of the physical skills presented in the demonstration.

The administration should be vitally concerned with having every student in school participate. In planning the demonstration, the following points should be emphasized:

1. The program must be varied enough to offer activities which will include skills represented by the entire student body. Failure to do this may induce the general public to believe that only activities which are conducive to a program of competitive sports and athletics are being offered. It is necessary, therefore, to present activities such as table tennis, golf, horseshoe pitching, and corrective exercises in order to show that overall participation is not only possible but required.

2. The physical education department should make every effort to obtain the good will and interest of parents, administrators, and teachers of other departments, regarding the demonstration. These people must be made to realize that the physical education department is appreciative of any cooperation or thoughtfulness exhibited when and if the demonstration causes inconvenience to them in any possible way.

3. There should be an accurate procedure for determining the proper placement of boys and girls in the different activities. No boy or girl should be embarrased because he or she is unable to perform the skill required in the activity with a reasonable amount of success. This situation can be avoided if proper planning takes place. If the student cannot perform a specific skill, he should be placed in another activity in such a way that it will not be conspicuous. This should be done as a matter of course.

4. A plan should be prepared to discourage the excusing of students from participating in the demonstration. In case of an excuse from the family physician, the physical education department, in cooperation with the principal, should send a letter to the physician explaining the provisions under which the student will be participating and the type of activity in which the student will be engaged. The letter should explain that the student will not be subjected to performing in any activity that will be more vigorous than he is accustomed to. Usually a letter of this type will result in the physician's giving permission or a suggestion as to the type of activity in which the student may participate. Another practice which is rather effective in discouraging excuses is refusing to permit participation in other extracurricular activities such as dramatics, music, etc., if the student wishes to be excused from the demonstration for anything other than a physical reason.

5. Pleas for excuses from individuals who do not wish to appear and perform in public should be met by an explanation of the social-emotional values gained from this experience. Most people are required at some time or other to appear before an audience and the demonstration affords them an opportunity for this experience. It should be pointed out to them that here is an opportunity to gain the poise and confidence that come only with experience. Some administrators show little concern over the failure of any program to include all students. They take the attitude that the program will function more effectively and efficiently when unencumbered by nonconformists and subnormal individuals who are not interested in physical activity. This is an unfortunate attitude because it does not consider the welfare of all the students and is contradictory to the philosophy that physical education is valuable to everyone and therefore it is the responsibility of the school to see that all students participate.

6. The other departments should be included in the planning of the demonstration. The physical education demonstration affords a wonderful integrating force for the entire school if planned and conducted properly. Usually the staff of other departments will be happy to cooperate if they are asked and are more than willing to donate their services if they are made to feel that they are part of the demonstration. Many other persons belong to the physical education department by virtue of being active participants—the doctor, the nurse, counselors, psychiatrists—whether or not they are officially listed as staff members. Custodians, matrons, and others responsible for the maintenance of the plant and its equipment are part of the department. Including these people in making plans builds their understanding of reasons for certain procedures, brings greater cooperation on their part, utilizes these persons as valuable sources of information, and gains the contribution of their opinions and suggestions. There is, admittedly, a disadvantage in cooperative planning. It is a slower process. Even though cooperative planning does take longer, it is the only way in which common goals are felt and understandings met. It results in a growth process for students and teachers alike.

7. The students should be given an opportunity to help plan

the demonstration. It should not be a teacher-only production. There should be cooperation between students and teachers in planning the demonstration. The leadership is provided by the physical education teachers, who are in turn led by the department chairman. In addition to student participation in specific activities along with the teacher in charge, ways must be sought to bring student groups into the overall planning. There are a number of ways this may be done. Class representatives, selected by the students, may meet with the staff on occasions to present students' views and choices and problems. Joint committees of staff members and students may work on specific problems pertaining to various aspects of the demonstration. Executive boards and officials of student organizations such as activity clubs, honor societies, and athletic associations may share in the planning. Student assistants and student leaders, those especially selected and prepared to act as official leaders and the like, may share in planning the various aspects of the program.

8. The demonstration should begin on time and end on time. This is important. The demonstration should not attempt to be the tail that wags the dog. It should not attempt to overshadow the other activities within the school and it should not expect more time than the other activities. It must not be overemphasized at the expense of other activities in the school curriculum. The scheduling of the demonstration in relation to the other activities is important. The director of the demonstration should not expect top priority regarding dates. He should expect to take his turn with the other departments. He must learn to cooperate in this respect. Rehearsal dates must be worked out with other departments which may wish to use the same facilities. The determination of a date for the demonstration will need to be worked out with the principal and in cooperation with other departments which may also have demonstrations, such as the music and dramatics departments. The date for the demonstration should be set far enough in advance so that other activities may be scheduled also.

9. The demonstration should have variety and unity. "Variety is the spice of life." There is a great deal of truth in this old adage, but it should not overshadow the objectives set up for the program. As has been said, a general theme should be

followed and enough variety should be added so that the program does not border on boredom. Each activity should tie in, in some way or another, with the general theme, to assure continuity.

10. The demonstration should not take too much time and effort. It is understandable that a certain amount will have to be spent, for there is always the desire to put on a better demonstration than the preceding one. If care is not taken, much of the teaching time of the instructor is taken in preparing for the demonstration, both in planning and practicing. If the teacher does a good job of teaching, his energy will be expended and he has very little left for extra duties. The demonstration could be a good example of this situation. There is also the danger that the pressure of putting on a good demonstration will tire and fatigue both students and teacher. Constant practice and pressure will add to their already heavy burden. This will defeat the purpose of the demonstration and create a distasteful situation for both students and teachers. Every effort should be made to avoid this situation and create a feeling of satisfaction and enjoyment for all concerned in working on the demonstration.

11. The demonstration should be well organized. Organization is the secret to success. There must be a leader, but he must not dominate the entire production. He should delegate responsibility wherever possible. The leader needs the cooperation of the other departments. Every detail should be worked out in advance and put down on paper. Nothing should be left to chance. All of these things are absolutely necessary, due to the fact that there is such a large number of participants involved in the demonstration. Poor organization can be detected immediately by the general public; this, in turn, will be a direct reflection upon the school.

12. The demonstration should not be too costly. It should not be the purpose of the demonstration to raise money; therefore, a great deal of money should not be spent in putting it on. Even a small admission fee can be too much for many families, and the very ones that should see the demonstration are thereby excluded. A money-making scheme will do more to defeat the purpose of the demonstration than any other one thing. Expensive costumes and equipment should be a-

voided. Remember that the purpose of the demonstration is to show the general public what is being taught in the physical education classes. It should never be anything else.

13. The demonstration should be curriculum-centered. As has been stated, the main purpose of the demonstration is to show the general public what is being taught in physical education. There is no other reason. One way to sell the program to the people is to show it to them. If they understand it, they will like and support it. The public has no other way of finding out about the program except through the students themselves. The physical education department should bring this idea forcefully before the public. They should understand that only activities which are being taught and used in the regular physical education classes are being shown to them in the demonstration with the exception of a few to highlight the program and bring forth certain ideas in keeping with the general theme.

OUTCOMES OF THE DEMONSTRATION

A good demonstration:

1. Reflects the work of the entire school program in physical education.
2. Does a great deal to create good public opinion and good will.
3. Gives the parents and general public information relative to the physical education program being offered.
4. Promotes a better feeling and working agreement between parents and teachers.
5. Motivates both students and teachers to do better work in the future.
6. Furthers democracy, citizenship, sportsmanship, and loyalty in all participants.
7. Develops social equality among students.
8. Does much to help the delinquency problem.
9. Can promote a better understanding among parents, teachers, and students.
10. Teaches democracy within the school by placing all participants on an equal basis.

11. May show the public the specific needs of the department.
12. May show definite curriculum needs.
13. May show how physical education builds physical fitness.
14. Provides good entertainment.
15. Makes the parent feel more a part of the school and will encourage parent participation in future school activities.
16. Does a great deal to interpret physical education to the public in a forceful manner.
17. Makes parents feel that they are sharing the experience with their child.
18. Provides means of audience participation.
19. Is student-centered.
20. Does a great deal to educate the students.
21. Provides opportunities for pupils' social adjustment by giving students the chance to work together toward a common goal.
22. Provides opportunities for democratic thinking and planning in a group.
23. Motivates the student in his desire to participate in physical education activities.
24. Builds pupil and school morale.
25. Brings focus on the year's activities.
26. Helps to create a closer working relationship between departments.
27. Furthers the objectives of education.
28. Provides an opportunity for other teachers to see what is being done in physical education.
29. Promotes better faculty relationships.
30. Results in the professional growth of the physical education teacher.
31. Provides an incentive to both student and teacher.
32. Draws student and teacher closer together in a better understanding.
33. Provides an avenue for motivation and the creation of new ideas.
34. Gives training in individual versus group conflicts.
35. Provides the teacher with a better understanding of school problems.
36. Provides opportunities for social contacts among students and faculty.
37. Offers all students the experience of performing before an audience.

38. Results in a feeling of satisfaction for a job well done.
39. Serves as an agency for acquiring the objectives of physical education.
40. Gives the student valuable experience in everyday living.
41. Provides the climate for learning.
42. Places physical education in its rightful place within the school curriculum.
43. Helps the student to be self-sufficient.
44. Improves the student's attitude toward the school.
45. Provides the student with a better understanding of school problems.

SUMMARY

The demonstration should provide students the opportunity to develop skills and have enjoyable educational experiences. It will help to formulate opinions and attitudes in regard to physical education. Students should receive joy and satisfaction from participating in the demonstration and these experiences will have a great deal to do with his overall attitude toward physical education. He will enjoy participation to the point where he will never have to be forced to take part.

The demonstration should show improvement from year to year. Different activities should be presented to show progress and give variety. The demonstration should always display to the general public just what is being done in the physical education class.

The demonstration cannot be conducted in a "hit and miss" fashion. It must be planned and organized so that it will accomplish the purpose for which it is intended. Some of the considerations in planning a demonstration are suggested here:

1. The demonstration should represent important aspects of the program. The activities must remain in proper balance with the regular physical education program and be geared to the needs and interests of the students.
2. A sound philosophy as to the purpose and objectives of the demonstration should be established as a basis.
3. The needs of the student now and in later life, as reflected in the objectives of the demonstration, represent a main consideration for promoting the demonstration.

4. The social-emotional aspects and contributions should be kept in mind.
5. The demonstration should recognize the importance of co-educational activities for social growth and include them in the program.
6. The health aspect should be of prime importance in putting on a demonstration.
7. The demonstration should include all the students in all the physical education classes.
8. The demonstration should receive equal consideration with other extracurricular activities.
9. Joy and satisfaction should be an outgrowth of the demonstration.
10. Qualified leaders are necessary in all activities that are used in the demonstration.
11. The demonstration should be planned with educational objectives of the entire school in mind.
12. The demonstration should be planned to include a variety of activities.
13. The demonstration should contribute to democratic living.
14. A complete record of the demonstration should be kept so that improvement can be made with each succeeding year.
15. The demonstration should be enjoyed by the participants to such an extent that they will look forward to the next one.

CHAPTER II

Arranging the Date for the Demonstration

SELECTING THE DATE

The administration and organization of the demonstration are of very great importance. They contribute more to the success of the demonstration than anything else. While it is not necessary that a great deal of work be done in putting on a demonstration, as almost all the activities are regular parts of the school's physical education program, it is important that the demonstration move along smoothly and easily. All the details should be worked out in advance so that nothing is left to chance. Perfect cooperation should be expected and insisted upon. If the school is large enough to require more than one physical education teacher, then the director should take full charge and full responsibility. He should not dominate, but should delegate and organize. He should solicit the help of every department within the school, as the success of the demonstration depends upon their cooperation.

The director has two important tasks to perform—he must organize or set up the demonstration and he must administer it or see that it functions properly. He must cooperate with other departments in order to create harmony. It is the director's responsibility to delegate authority and responsibility. He should also place responsible people in key positions.

In order to follow the chain-of-command in establishing policies and procedures, it will be necessary to formulate and send a request to the superintendent of schools for permission to put on the demonstration. This letter should contain all the necessary information pertaining to the demonstration in order that the superintendent may have a clear picture of what is to be done and be able to pass judgment on the demonstration for approval or disapproval. The purpose of the demonstration should be clearly stated in the letter, as well as anything else which will affect the operation of the school in general. The superintendent must take an overall viewpoint of the entire school program before he can make any decisions. No plans should be made until official approval is given.

APPROVAL OF THE SELECTED DATE

The date selected for the demonstration should be one which will not conflict with other school activities. Other departments will have certain scheduled events that are significant and important to them, and the director of the demonstration should, insofar as possible, avoid conflicts with these events and their purposes. It is always the best policy to cooperate with other departments, as this creates a feeling of good will with the entire faculty. By demonstrating cooperation rather than contention as a characteristic of the people in the physical education department, there will be a feeling of good will with other faculty members. This, in turn, will result in a better response from other departments when they are asked to help with the demonstration. It is, therefore, important that other department heads be contacted and consulted before a date for the demonstration is selected. Before this is done, however, the school calendar should be checked for possible available dates. The selected dates should then be given clearance by the principal or the person in charge of this procedure. After consultation with other department heads and members of the physical education department, a date should be selected and placed on the school calendar. Extreme care should be exercised in the selection of the date for the demonstration so that circumstances which might exist at the selected time will not result in a change of the date. This situation could bring about changes in the plans of many people; therefore, the date should not be selected haphazardly nor without a great deal of forethought. A change of date might be unavoidable but everything possible should be done to avoid this and a change made only as a last resort.

There are many avenues that should be checked before the date is selected. Civic organizations, public officials, parents, students, and P.T.A., as well as school officials, should be contacted to make sure there will be no conflict of major proportion.

After careful consideration, the date selected should be sent to

---

LEROY J. KNOEPPEL
SUPERINTENDENT

EDWARD W. STUBBS
ASSISTANT SUPERINTENDENT
PRINCIPAL

PROVISO WEST HIGH SCHOOL

HILLSIDE, ILLINOIS

ARTHUR E. VALLICELLI
ADMINISTRATIVE ASSISTANT

HUBERT A. PITT
DEAN OF STUDENTS

September 15, 19__

Dr. John Jones
Principal, High School
Hillside, Illinois

Dear Dr. Jones:

    The Physical Education Department respectfully requests permission to stage a physical education demonstration on a date to be selected in accordance with the accepted procedure for scheduling school events.

    The purpose of the demonstration is to afford an opportunity for the general public to gain a better understanding of the physical education program as it is being offered at the high school. It will tend to enlighten them as to the benefits derived from a good program in physical education, and we feel that it will go far in correcting any misunderstanding of the program as an integral part of the curriculum. At the same time, it will give every student an opportunity to participate in an activity which will help him adjust to every day living.

    This program can be conducted without any expense to the school. All aspects of the demonstrations will be handled by our own personnel.

    We greatly appreciate your kind attention to this request.

                Sincerely yours,

                John Smith
                Director of Physical Education

rw

Fig. 2-1

OFFICE OF THE PRINCIPAL

Memorial
High
School

EAU CLAIRE
WISCONSIN

September 21, 19__

To: Mr. William Tonkin, Adm. Asst.

From: Mr. William Brown, Director of Physical Education

Subject: Date of Physical Education Demonstration

     The Physical Education Department has requested and received approval from Dr. R. Plath to conduct a physical education demonstration in the Field House in March of this school year.

     The school calendar has been checked and Friday, March 26, is open at the present time. Please enter the Physical Education Department's demonstration on this date and give us confirmation of the entry.

                 Sincerely,

                 William Brown
                 Director of Physical Education

ab

Fig. 2-2

the school official in charge of this particular area with the request that it be placed on the school calendar. This notification should be in the form of a letter, with a request that the date be confirmed. A copy of the letter should be placed on file for future reference if needed. After confirmation of the date has been received, the first step in the long list of details which accompany the presentation of a physical education demonstration has been accomplished and work may proceed with other details and plans. This is also the first step in the long list of preparations necessary in the administration of the successful demonstration. (See Figs. 2-1 and 2-2.)

DECATUR HIGH SCHOOL

ATHLETIC DEPARTMENT
DECATUR, GEORGIA
March 23, 19___

To: All Faculty and School Personnel

From: Mr. E. E. Hall, Director of Physical Education

Subject: Announcement of Physical Education Demonstration

The Physical Education Department is conducting a Physical Education Demonstration in the Gymnasium on Friday evening, March 26, at 7:30 P. M.

The program will involve all the students in the physical education classes and will attempt to show the general public just what is being taught in these classes. It will afford an opportunity for the people in the community to observe first hand the activities which are being offered and which they, in many cases, are totally unaware of. The Physical Education Department is anxious to give the general public a good hard look at what is being accomplished in the teaching and learning of physical skills other than those taught and learned in the athletic program. The general public is seldom given the opportunity of observing a good physical education program for the vast majority of students. The demonstration will afford this opportunity.

The Physical Education Department wishes everyone to be made aware of the fact that the demonstration is not being given for the express purpose of selling the physical education program, but rather to explain the program in terms of its contribution to the education of the whole child.

The Physical Education Department hopes that the demonstration will afford a wonderful opportunity for students and teachers to work together cooperatively, democratically, and creatively on a group project.

The Physical Education Department solicits your help as all of you will be affected in one way or another. We ask your patience and understanding and will appreciate the help you can give us.

Sincerely,

Eugene E. Hall
Director of Physical Education

de

Fig. 2-3

ANNOUNCEMENT OF THE DATE
TO THE SCHOOL STAFF

The faculty of the school will be directly affected by the demonstration. This will be brought about in various ways. It is, therefore, important that the faculty be notified of the demonstration in a courteous and dignified manner. This should be done by sending a letter to each faculty member. (See Fig. 2-3.) After this has been done, the announcement may be made over the P.A. system and also placed in the daily bulletin. The letter should ask the cooperation of the faculty and impress upon each member that the department is depending upon him for much-needed help and understanding in order to make the demonstration a success.

This letter should also state the purpose of the demonstration and present any other details that would help the faculty member obtain a better understanding of the demonstration and how it will affect the inner workings of the school in general and the faculty member in particular. The letter should explain that the demonstration will involve all the students taking physical education. It should point out to them that the demonstration will be conducted on the same basis as any other school function and that the goals compare with those set up for the entire curriculum. It should indicate the values received by the students from participating in the demonstration and the contribution it makes to the education of the whole child.

This letter to the faculty is very important because it is necessary that the faculty favor the demonstration and be willing to put up with some inconveniences to help assure its success. Nevertheless, it should make clear that any inconveniences do not include calling a student from another teacher's class.

This letter should also be sent to all the non-teaching school personnel, as their help is also necessary. The clerical help, custodians, and other school personnel will be asked to contribute in various ways in putting on the demonstration. The clerical help will be asked to mimeograph programs, send out notices, and make announcements over the P.A. system to homerooms at various times in order that information may be given to the students immediately. They will also act as a "go-between" from the director of the demonstration to the principal and various faculty members. It is very important that these people be well-informed on all the details in the administration of the demonstration.

The custodians are "VIP's" in the conducting of the demonstration, and their help should be solicited. The custodian has access to all the rooms in the building, various implements, tools, ladders, and any equipment that may be needed. His help is invaluable.

Other letters which may be sent are an invitation to parents to at-

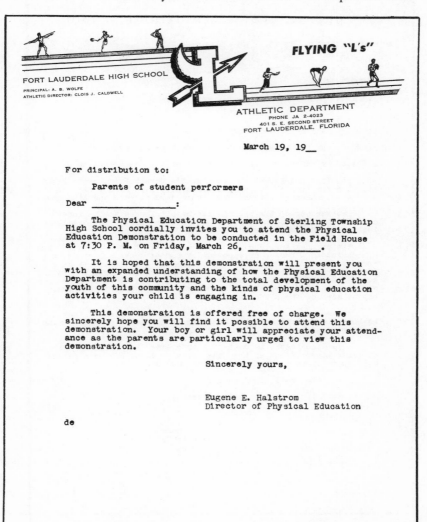

FORT LAUDERDALE HIGH SCHOOL
PRINCIPAL: A. B. WOLFE
ATHLETIC DIRECTOR: CLOIS J. CALDWELL

FLYING "L's"

ATHLETIC DEPARTMENT
PHONE JA 2-4023
401 S. E. SECOND STREET
FORT LAUDERDALE, FLORIDA

March 19, 19__

For distribution to:

    Parents of student performers

Dear _____:

    The Physical Education Department of Sterling Township High School cordially invites you to attend the Physical Education Demonstration to be conducted in the Field House at 7:30 P. M. on Friday, March 26, _____.

    It is hoped that this demonstration will present you with an expanded understanding of how the Physical Education Department is contributing to the total development of the youth of this community and the kinds of physical education activities your child is engaging in.

    This demonstration is offered free of charge. We sincerely hope you will find it possible to attend this demonstration. Your boy or girl will appreciate your attendance as the parents are particularly urged to view this demonstration.

                Sincerely yours,

                Eugene E. Halstrom
                Director of Physical Education

de

Fig. 2-4

tend, a thank you to participants, and a final report. (See Figs. 2-4, 2-5, and 2-6.)

NEW BRUNSWICK SENIOR HIGH SCHOOL

NEW BRUNSWICK   NEW JERSEY

Willard W. Lindstrom, Principal   Samuel M. Gordon, Vice Principal

April 30, 19___

To: All Personnel Concerned

From: Mr. A. B. Brown, Director of Physical Education

Subject: Final Report on Physical Education Demonstration

The Physical Education Department's Physical Education Demonstration was carried out very successfully last Friday evening before an estimated five hundred interested parents and students.

The success of the program can be attributed to the inter-department cooperation of personnel involved and to the committee leadership provided by staff members.

The program involved all but a very few of the students. The demonstration afforded an opportunity for teachers and students to work together cooperatively, democratically and creatively on a group project. The Physical Education Department feels that the educational benefits derived from the demonstration have been many and that it did a great deal in contributing to the educational experiences of the students.

The response to this year's demonstration indicates that serious consideration should be given to a similar program during the next year.

I feel our basic objective of informing the public of what is being accomplished at the local area in terms of the physical well being of their children has been accomplished.

A sincere "well done" to all.

Sincerely,

A. B. Brown
Director of Physical Education

Fig. 2-5

C. R. INGILS, SUPERINTENDENT
ASSISTANT SUPERINTENDENTS
A. DARREL BECKMAN,
PERSONNEL AND ADMINISTRATIVE
LOYD D. CRANE, INSTRUCTION
J. O. REED, BUSINESS AND PLANT

CHEYENNE PUBLIC SCHOOLS

District Administration   •   School District No. 1   •   Cheyenne, Wyoming, 82002   •   Telephone 632-0591

March 29, 19__

For distribution to:
    All committee chairmen
    All student performers
    Press and radio personnel

Dear _____:

        On behalf of the Physical Education Department of Sterling
High School, I would like to thank you for your contribution toward
the successful presentation of the Physical Education Demonstration
held on April 26, _____.

        I am sure that many people benefited from this demonstration
because it was the sincere desire of the Physical Education Department that it should be an all-school production and that it should
incorporate the educational aims and objectives of the entire curriculum. I am sure that everyone worked toward this goal and the
Physical Education Department is grateful for this opportunity to
contribute to the overall development of the youth of our community.

        May I express my sincerest appreciation to you for your
cooperation with me and the members of my staff in the preparation
and presentation of this demonstration. It was indeed a pleasure
working with you.

                                Gratefully yours,

                                Richard S. Pickney
                                Director of Physical Education

de

Fig. 2-6

CHAPTER III

The Role of the Director, the Supervisor, and the Announcer

THE DIRECTOR

The director of any student demonstration of physical education activities must assume the ultimate responsibility for all decisions made relative to the demonstration. As these demonstrations are a primary source of good public relations for the physical education program, the preparation for them is vital. The selection of the material to be presented and the selection of the personnel who are to carry out the various phases of the demonstration are the two major responsibilities of the director.

Selection of Material

If the program of physical education offered is of good quality, the selection of material is simply one of choosing that part which is to be presented. A poor program can not really be enhanced by the addition of specialties. The material should reflect what is going on in the classes. It should be varied and present an opportunity for many students to participate.

Selection of Personnel

The selection of personnel, however, could provide a more difficult task. Choosing the right people, making sure they are instructed properly as to their assigned duties and responsibilities, and generally directing their efforts constitute the bulk of the director's duties. As the staff is generally available and their abilities known to the director, assignment should be made by matching that ability with the job to be assigned. The director must detail the responsibility and recognize the effort and work done by each individual in carrying out that assignment.

Determination of the Central Theme

The director should take the initiative in the selection of a central theme. He should do this in cooperation with students, instructors, and committee chairmen. Suggestions from everyone are encouraged and a list should be made of these suggestions. After a discussion, the theme is selected by vote of the committee and student chairmen. It should then be the determining factor in the selection of many of the activities.

Determination of Activities

The director should have the responsibility of making the final determination of the activities to be presented. He should follow the planning committee's suggestions; it should be a rare occasion when a deletion would need to be made. However, the director has the opportunity of visualizing the entire production in relation to the general theme and is better able to determine whether or not a certain activity will be appropriate.

Appraisal of Activities

The fact that an activity has been selected for the demonstration does not mean that it cannot be deleted from the program. Sometimes an activity just does not fit in; it does not harmonize with the other activities or with the general theme. If, in the opinion of the director, this is true, the activity should be removed and replaced by another.

The director, supervisor and instructors should be constantly appraising each activity as it is being practiced and as progress is made toward the final rehearsal of all the activities.

Establishing the Order of Events

The order of events is important because of the equipment needed for the activity. It would be well to have certain activities follow each other if the same type of equipment is needed for both. The director should check the activities to see if it is possible to avoid the moving in and out of equipment.

Directing the Demonstration

The director's main duty is to be responsible for the preparation and success of the entire program. Long-range planning is the key to any successful endeavor, and the demonstration is no exception. The director should have a plan worked out so that each part of the program falls into place. He then can place the responsibility and production of each part in the hands of the most capable personnel. The director is the person who "pulls the strings" and makes the decisions which make the demonstration run smoothly and successfully.

Personnel Responsibilities

The demonstration will be no better than the personnel in charge of it. It is necessary that the director organize and direct the personnel in such a way as to obtain the best results. This entails appointment of chairmen, formation of committees, holding of planning conferences, delegation of authority, and general overall supervision of all personnel directly or indirectly associated with the demonstration. The director is ultimately responsible for the smooth operation of all the personnel.

Cooperation Between the School and the Community

The director must act as a liaison between the school and community. It is his responsibility to coordinate the efforts of the school personnel and the various agencies throughout the community as well as parents and citizens. He should interpret the objectives and purposes of the demonstration to the public, educate the public concerning these objectives and purposes, and try to create an image of the curriculum through the demonstration. This mutual understanding between the public and the school is essential to both parties.

Obtaining Facilities

Usually the demonstration will be held in the gymnasium. This solves the problem of space in the majority of cases; however, other rooms will be needed for a dressing room, cloak room, waiting room, etc. Provisions should be made for the use of these rooms. Facilities needed for the night of the performance are not so much a problem as are those needed for rehearsals for various events. The better the facilities, the fewer the problems that will be encountered. The director, in cooperation with the principal, is responsible for supplying all the facilities. The personnel working for the demonstration should not be expected to waste precious time and energy in trying to procure facilities. Their time should be spent in other areas of endeavor more directly associated with the demonstration itself.

Financial Responsibility

The director should establish, along with the school administration, a definite policy concerning the financing of the demonstration. There is no need for the expenditure of a great deal of money in producing a demonstration. To do this will defeat its purpose. A great deal of the expense can be taken care of by charging a small admission fee. It is better, however, to obtain the necessary money through the regular school channels. One way would be to include the demonstration admission in the activity fee that is charged every student in most schools. The director must establish a plan for payment of all expenses before going ahead with any plans for the demonstration. He then should set up a budget for each activity being presented.

Determination of Purpose

The director should determine whether the demonstration is required to pay its own expenses or whether it is an educational experience and a part of the school program with outcomes similar to those received from other courses and extracurricular subjects. He should make the decision as to whether or not the demonstration represents the work of the school and whether the educational values to the participants or entertainment of the audience comes first.

Scheduling of Facilities and Time

The director must take the responsibility of keeping the demonstration in its proper place within the framework of the school's activity program. It should not be overemphasized to the point where it takes precedence over other school activities. It must be kept in the right relationship to the school as a whole. This means that the director must work closely with other departments in scheduling and with the principal whose duty it is to see that events are evenly distributed throughout the school year. Other departments should be given an equal opportunity to schedule their events.

Organization of the Demonstration

If the director is responsible for the organization of the demonstration it will have a much better chance of success. It should be a cooperative enterprise with other organizations within the school as well as with all the various committees involved. The demonstration should reflect the organizational ability of the school personnel. The entire school administration is sometimes judged and criticized because of one poorly-organized activity.

Follow-up Letters

The follow-up letters and communications are not only an act of courtesy but also a gesture which will be a build-up for the next year's demonstration. Many people will have given a great deal of time and effort without monetary compensation to assure the success of the demonstration; therefore, the least the director can do is to send letters of thanks and appreciation.

Committee Chairmen Appointments

The director should make all committee chairmen appointments. The importance of the chairmen cannot be over-emphasized, so this selection should be given careful and serious thought and consideration. Each prospective chairman should be contacted and his duties explained by the director before he is asked to undertake this task. He should fully understand these responsibilities before he accepts the position.

Organization

The responsibility of organizing the entire demonstration falls directly upon the shoulders of the director. He can delegate a great deal of this responsibility and shift many of the tasks involved, but in the final analysis he must make the decisions. He should formulate a plan of attack which will encompass the work of each committee and result in a final workable, well-planned and well-organized demonstration. The time element is important, and a workable schedule should be formulated and adhered to. The demonstration should not be too time-consuming and drawn-out. This shows poor organization.

Provision of Facilities

It is the responsibility of the director to provide the necessary facilities for putting on the demonstration. Most of the facilities will be available, and the director should arrange for the use of these through the proper channels.

Provision of Lighting Effects

Proper lighting will enhance the effect of certain activities. The director should arrange for either a student or a faculty member to handle the lights. This is an important assignment if the demonstration includes activities which need lighting effects. The person assigned to this position should have had some experience with spotlights and lighting equipment. The installation of the equipment should be done by an electrician.

Selection of Activities

The success of the demonstration depends upon the activities shown; therefore, their selection is of utmost importance. The activities will reflect the curriculum as it is being taught and portray this curriculum to the audience. While the selection of the activities should be a cooperative venture the final selection should be in harmony with the objectives and should be the responsibility of the director.

Cooperation of Committees and Personnel

There must be complete harmony among the committee personnel. The director should act as a liaison between the different groups. There will be numerous occasions when two or more committees will need to work closely together. This will also be true among different departments as they are all working on the demonstration.

Delegation of Authority

The director should delegate authority and responsibility early. In order that misunderstandings may be reduced to a minimum, he should clearly indicate the chairman of each committee. The director who permits two different members of a committee to believe that each has complete authority over the committee members is asking for trouble. Lack of clear delegation of responsibility will provide an excuse for some one to avoid a portion of the unpleasant or arduous tasks while other conscientious members will do more than their share. The director should point out to the chairman that he is held accountable for the proper functioning of his phase of the program and that he has the authority to act on all matters concerning that committee.

Establishment of Policies

The director should take the initiative and be responsible for the establishment of policies which are to be used as guide lines for the administration of the demonstration. He should assume the responsibility for the establishment of policies which are based on facts and all decisions should be the result of these policies.

The director should be careful of criticism of any committee or individual, for he should keep in mind that most of the help, committee-wise, will be from members other than those in his department. He should make every effort to make everyone feel that he is a significant part of the demonstration and that his help is necessary in order to make the demonstration a success. The director's suggestions should be given in a courteous, dignified manner.

Meeting the Objectives

It is the responsibility of the director to see to it that provision is made for the meeting of the objectives of the demonstration. Opportunities should be provided for the students to assume responsibility and share leadership roles. Staff members should also be given recognition for a job well done. (Credit and recognition are synonymous here.)

Selection of Activities

The director should be fundamentally responsible for the type of activities that are presented in the demonstration. He should see to it that every student has the chance to participate in some form or other. It is his responsibility to make the demonstration an all-school affair in which each student has an opportunity to be a part. He must see to it that provisions are made for the protection of all participants in regard to personal rights as well as injuries.

News Coverage

The director should work closely with the publicity committee to assure the complete news coverage of the demonstration. The committee should see that the parents are well informed regarding the demonstration previous to the time of its presentation, and that complete coverage is given after the event.

Work with Administration

It is the responsibility of the director to work in close harmony with the school administration in order that the stated aims and objectives of the demonstration will be in accord with the established goals of the school's overall program and education in general. There can be no justification for the demonstration if the objectives set up for it do not coincide with those of education.

Cooperation with Other Departments

The director should be most cooperative with other departments within the school. In a program of this magnitude, it will be necessary to share facilities as well as personnel, and, by so doing, the department will build faculty good will—a very important asset in any school. Complete harmony is essential if the demonstration is to be successful.

Decision-Making

The director should act as coordinator of all committees. He is the trouble-shooter—the person who makes the final decision. He becomes the hub around which the committees revolve. He is held fully responsible for the success of the demonstration. Yet, while he is in charge, he should attempt to be a member of every committee at group meetings rather than someone "bossing" it. In so doing, he will create an *"esprit de corps"* so necessary in any group undertaking.

Establishing Good Morale

The director is responsible for establishing and maintaining good morale, which is a necessary accompaniment to good personnel administration. Morale is not easy to define, yet its absence is easy to detect. It may be defined as one's willingness to subordinate his personality to the good of a larger group. This is necessary in any organization, if the venture is to succeed. The director, in seeking to obtain and keep good morale, should utilize the abilities of all for the welfare of the whole organization. Evidences of good morale which the director should look for are:

1. Quality and quantity of output.
2. Getting the job done as soon as possible.
3. The self-discipline of each person.
4. Suggestions from workers in an attempt to better the demonstration.
5. Cooperation.

Good morale does not just happen. The director should provide incentives, some of which may include:

1. Encouraging constructive ideas from everyone.
2. Establishing a feeling of security within the working group.
3. Expressing appreciation openly, both verbally and in writing.
4. Rewarding good work by praise.

The director should realize that good morale is a significant "building force" in any group action.

It is the responsibility of the director to work in close harmony with each committee whenever possible. He can help build morale within the group by meeting with them to discuss policies and procedures under which they may function. He may be able to help develop a unity of purpose and create a feeling of group enthusiasm toward the task at hand.

Final Responsibility

In summary, the director is fully responsible for the production of the demonstration. He should, along with other members of his physical education staff, coordinate the entire production. He will be held personally responsible for every detail from the beginning until the end of the demonstration. Everyone will look to him for leadership, information, and inspiration. He will be the "take-charge guy," and he must do this with finesse and diplomacy so that things will run smoothly and successfully.

Evaluation of the Demonstration

The director and planning committee should evaluate the demonstration as soon after it has been presented as possible. Each activity should be evaluated separately as well as the placement of it in the program. The activities and all the details will be fresh in their minds and any corrections necessary will be more easily made directly after the performance. The director should call a committee meeting with the goal of improving next year's demonstration.

THE SUPERVISOR

The demonstration supervisor assumes the role of a liaison between the director and staff personnel. He serves in the capacity of a special adviser to the director. He is the "trouble-shooter" and, although many of his exact duties may be pinpointed, he must be ready at all times to step into the breach and assume the responsibility of performing tasks whenever and wherever needed.

Placement of Events

The proper placement of events in the program is necessary to assure continuity and to give proper perspective to each activity. The same type of activities should not be placed in sequence on the program. The spectacular events should follow the less spectacular ones so that the contrast will be more noticeable and therefore will tend to "show off" each activity more advantageously.

Discussion of Chairman Duties

The supervisor should discuss the duties and responsibilities with each chairman. He should meet with the chairman of each committee and discuss with him the central theme of the demonstration and go over the responsibilities of each committee.

Scheduling of Practice Rehearsals

The supervisor should determine whether a dress rehearsal is to be held. His decision will be determined to a large extent by school policies, time available, and other factors.

If a dress rehearsal is held with all groups present, it must be planned and organized well in advance. One of the main purposes of the rehearsal is to find out how much time is needed for each and every activity so that the events are completed within the allotted time schedule. Adjustments should be made if necessary. Ample time for change of costume and equipment should be allowed in scheduling the dress rehearsal. The supervisor should plan the rehearsal time so that it is broken down into a schedule which will give each participating group a fair share of available time. He should work closely with each group so that, if there is difficulty and some groups need more help and more time, it can be arranged. Different groups may find it necessary to rehearse at different times and all schedules should be flexible enough so that they may be changed as needed. A working schedule should be made by the supervisor and placed in the hands of each group. If any are changed, it must be done only through the supervisor.

Procurement of Supplies

The supervisor should aid the maintenance chairman in obtaining the necessary supplies and equipment for the demonstration. More than likely the custodian from other departments and areas will be needed to obtain equipment from there. Some equipment will need to be constructed, such as platforms and curtains, and here again the committee will need to work closely with the custodian. An itemized list of all materials should be kept, and this list should be given to all committee chairmen with those items checked for which they are to be held responsible. This list helps in the return of all equipment and supplies.

Preparing of Uniforms

Usually most of the uniforms needed for the demonstration will be those which are used in the regularly scheduled physical education classes. However, there may be special costumes needed for special activities. The supervisor should work closely with those students who are in activities that require special costumes. He should make sure that the costume is appropriate and bears a reasonable relationship to the person it represents. For example, the clown costume should explain the character to the audience yet should be made so that the wearer will have complete freedom to carry out the movements necessary for the act.

Some costumes may have to be rented, and the supervisor should be responsible for ordering and returning them. The supervisor should see to it that all participants are in clean uniforms at all times.

Timing of the Demonstration

One of the criticisms of any school function is that it usually lasts too long. People become tired of the long delays between activities, or there are so many activities that everyone goes home worn out, vowing never to attend another such function. This can be avoided by having the supervisor work closely with the announcer and the music chairman to assure the proper timing in presenting the activities. This means, of course, the complete cooperation of the music department. Arrangements and provisions should be made with the administration for the band to rehearse with the participants.

Supervision of Student Help

Usually the chairman of student help will be a member of the physical education department because of the nature of jobs the students will be asked to do. The supervisor should communicate often with the chairman of the student help committee, because there will be numerous jobs that will develop during the rehearsals and during the demonstration. This committee should be closely supervised.

The first meeting should be used for the formulation of committees for specific duties. Leaders for various groups should be selected and information disseminated after the committees have been formed. Duties of each committee should be discussed at this time with instructions to meet with the chairman at various intervals.

Supervision of Clean-up

Students should not be expected to do the janitorial work, yet cleaning up after the rehearsals and after the demonstration is a must. All equipment should be put away in the correct places and all borrowed materials returned. The floor should be swept and everything left as it was found. The supervisor should work in close harmony with the clean-up committee.

Coordination of Committees

In a demonstration of this kind, where there are many participants and a number of committees doing many duties, there is bound to be an overlapping of responsibilities and assignments, resulting many times in a clash of personalities. The supervisor, in cooperation with the director, works to prevent this if possible and to create as much harmony within the working groups as possible.

Performance of Participants

The supervisor should inform all instructors in charge of activities to impress upon the participants the importance of doing their best at all times in order to show the activities to best advantage. If the activities have been taken from the regular curriculum, this should not be difficult.

Making of Costumes

The providing of any necessary costumes is the responsibility of the supervisor. He should work closely with the instructors of physical education and the art and home economics departments. It might be possible to rent certain costumes, and if this is true the supervisor should take the initiative in ordering them. The supervisor should plan far enough in advance so that there will be no last-minute problems in obtaining the costumes.

Student Participation

The supervisor is responsible to see that every student has an opportunity to participate, even though it is a small part. He also should guard against allowing one individual to appear in several activities. If students are unable, for some reason, to appear in the activity, arrangements should be made for him to help in some other area.

Provision of Supplies

The demonstration will not require many supplies other than those which are available within the different departments of the school. The supervisor should have each committee chairman and each instructor list any supplies needed and he should procure them.

THE ANNOUNCER

Qualifications and Performance

Since the position of an announcer is very important to the presentation, it is essential that the individual performing this task have a good clear voice, have command of the English language, and be well acquainted with program work. He should be able to establish close contact with the spectators and make the program interesting to them. Spectators attending a presentation should go away feeling that they have enjoyed the program and understood what was occurring. A member of the speech department such as the debate coach or another qualified faculty member could do this job adequately or a talented speech student.

The announcer should consult with the director and have all the needed information relative to what he is going to say. This should be written down so that there will be no repetition, no hesitation; all the pertinent facts should be given. These facts should be organized and planned ahead of time in such a way that they follow a definite pattern and are in perfect sequence with the entire program. Writing down the information will clarify his thinking and lead to an effective announcement of what is to transpire. He does not have the opportunity to arrange the program, so he must do the best he can to create a unified presentation, fitting everything together harmoniously with smooth transitions.

The announcer should speak in a full voice. He should speak clearly, keep his mind on what he is saying, and speak directly to his audience. The old saying that "You stammer in speech because you falter in thought" is an adage worth remembering. A firm and pleasing voice will command the attention of the audience. Know what to say and then say it. Don't clutter up the talk with ah's, uh's, but's, and well's. A few well-chosen words are better than a great many. Remember that a story is a good one only if it drives home a point. The announcer should always speak slowly and distinctly. He should not run his words together. Every word is important in his remarks and should be clearly conveyed to each member of the audience. He should talk to an audience as if he were talking to one person.

The qualities that go into the making of a good announcer are a pleasing personality, charm, naturalness, sincerity, conviction, enthusiasm, spontaneity, accuracy, culture, and salesmanship. Add to these a fine voice with an excellent vocabulary, and you will have an ideal announcer.

The quality of any program will depend, in part, upon the qualifications of the announcer and how well he can achieve rapport with spectators as he coordinates the various factors that are in the program.

The Announcer's Skills

Announcing can be learned. It is a highly specialized speech activity, but the student having the proper qualifications and a desire to improve can learn announcing just as readily as he can any other speech activity. Announcing is nothing more than an attempt to communicate information—to make something known. There is complete communication only when the announcer succeeds in four fundamental responsibilities: First, he must gain the attention of the listener; second, he must get the listener interested in his message and hold that interest despite distractions; third, he must evoke the listener's comprehension; and fourth, he must interest the listener in the forthcoming activity.

The announcer's skills are:

1. Communication of ideas
2. Communication of emotion
3. Projection of personality
   a. Naturalness
   b. Vitality
   c. Friendliness
   d. Adaptability
   e. Appearance
4. Pronunciation
5. Voice control
   a. Pitch
   b. Volume
   c. Rate
   d. Quality

Microphone Technique

The announcer who speaks into the microphone in such a manner that his speech faults are minimized and its excellences magnified is said to have "mike technique." To acquire this technique the announcer should acquaint himself with the different types of microphones currently in use and know the speech input characteristics and peculiarities of each. He should know the rated response to the pitch range, the directional features, and the sensitivity of each microphone commonly used.

In addition to acquiring technical knowledge about microphones, the announcer should work for personal knowledge. He should know the response of each microphone to his own voice and be aware of the heightening of some voice peculiarities by certain ones. He should know at what distance to stand before the microphone for the best voice reception. He should know how to make use of the live and dead sides of the microphone for effects and for most complete interpretation.

Script handling is merely a mechanical detail, but it can cause so much turmoil that a few instructions seem necessary. The superior announcer holds his script in one hand and when nearing the bottom of the page slides the first page down with the other hand until the top of the second page is visible. It is thus possible for him to read from one page to another without stopping to turn them, and he can then dispose of the pages he has read.

Public Address Equipment

The success of the entire program is contingent upon how well the audience can hear the speaker. Thus it becomes necessary to have a public address system of the proper capacity, properly installed, and thoroughly tested before the program.

Setting up a system which will give optimum performance becomes a rather technical problem because the acoustical qualities in most gymnasiums are not too good. The shape and cubic foot area of the room compound the problem.

Most present-day gymnasiums have a permanently installed system which should only need to be tested out prior to the program. Many schools have assigned one faculty member the responsibility for public address systems used in the school. Then one needs merely to notify this individual well in advance of the program so that he has time to set up and test the necessary equipment. This faculty member very often has students trained as a "sound crew" who operate the equipment during the performance.

Where there is no permanently installed system, it would be strongly recommended that professional technical assistance be sought, either from commercial sources or staff members such as the electronics or physics teacher.

Where no professional help is available, it is suggested that the amplifier be a minimum of 50 watts with separate speaker controls to permit individual adjustment of each speaker. There should be at least four 20-watt driver speakers, of the re-entrant horn type, centrally located. The microphone should be of good quality, low-impedance type, having an on-off switch.

The following check list would be helpful in installing and testing the equipment prior to the program:

1. Check phasing of microphone.
2. Check phasing of loudspeaker.

3. Check placement and directivity of loudspeakers for the following points:
   a. Uniform loudness and tone quality over area covered
   b. Minimum feedback
   c. Minimum reverberation
   d. Minimum echo
4. Adjust output levels of loudspeaker for uniform loudness throughout installation area.
5. Check for naturalness and intelligibility of sound reproduction. (Adjust base and treble controls.)
6. Check for proper sensitivity of pickup, distance of pickup from anticipated sound source, and uniformity of pickup coverage without producing feedback when outlet level is high.

Organization of the Material to Be Presented

The presentation should be well organized. All participants should have a program of the events to maintain coordinated effort and provide smooth-functioning units. The announcer will then be able to call attention to each event, in sequence, relating a brief definition and explanation of the demonstrations. This will keep spectators informed, achieve harmony, and prepare participants for the next event.

It is the responsibility of the announcer to see that each aspect of the program fits into its proper time relationship. To make the best possible use of time, the announcer should work with practice demonstrations on the timing of music with the various acts. The length of a piece of music should coincide with the length of the act. There should also be a means of filling a time period if necessary. This might call for the preparation of a special act to be used if it is required. Much of the success or failure of demonstration presentations depends upon timing. The announcer holds the key to achieving a smooth-flowing and coordinated program.

As with many things, the harmonious functioning of the presentation depends on practice. The announcer and the participants should be prepared and then go over the material repeatedly.

CHAPTER IV

The Importance, Selection, and Assignments of Planning Committees

INTRODUCTION

Considering the number of students who may be served by a properly organized and administered physical education demonstration, one must conclude that demonstrations are a necessary part of any excellent physical education curriculum. It is up to the planning committee to organize and carry out this philosophy in their school.

The committee should realize that the teachers and the school have as a responsibility the proper direction of all students. This directing can be done by channeling student energies into wholesome experiences which may help form desirable lifetime traits. The characters of boys and girls are so pliable that they are very open to influences of direction; students are eager to explore, to try new experiences, and to learn. For these reasons, the planning committee should plan a demonstration that is based on their needs for recognition and on their total interests.

A physical education demonstration can also make many contributions such as development of social relationships, better health, recreational skills, and attitudes which are conducive to finer sportsmanship and fair play.

There are several factors which are considered necessary to insure the development of a successful physical education demonstration, and these factors include:

1. Support and encouragement of the program by the entire faculty and the administration.
2. Provision by all physical education teachers and the athletic director of maximum support and leadership.
3. A varied type of program to meet all the needs with adequate facilities and activities to permit the greatest number of students to share in the benefits of the demonstration.
4. Adequate publicity prior to the program to create and maintain a high level of interest.
5. Some form of homogeneous selection of students to aid in obtaining unity; e.g., home rooms, clubs, and other school groups.

PHILOSOPHY AND OBJECTIVES OF
THE PLANNING COMMITTEE

The committee in planning a program should establish a basic philosophy and should list specific objectives prior to actual organization. These objectives are listed as follows:

1. To provide the opportunity for boys and girls to compete and to gain recognition.
2. To provide a varied program of events, and to include those events which are interesting and entertaining as well as educational to the audience.
3. To provide wholesome fun experiences which are conducive to the establishment of desirable traits.
4. To provide the opportunity for public recognition of the physical education department.
5. To allow all students who are interested to participate.
6. To coordinate and try to enlist as many other departments of the school in the program as possible, such as the band, shop classes, dramatics class, art class, etc.

PLANNING THE PROGRAM

Success breeds success. Start small, make it good—and build. To initiate a new program, choose activities which have great appeal to a large percentage of the student body. This activity should be so well planned and organized that those participating will find great enjoyment. Once one activity is "sold" in this manner, all new activities can be initiated more expediently. Eventually, with constant effort by the director and the committee, it will snowball into a full, year-round inclusive program.

ORGANIZATION OF THE PLANNING COMMITTEE

The initial work on any production is to divide the staff, class leaders, and students into various committees. People placed on these committees should be those who have indicated a keen interest in the program and are willing to work diligently. The director should appoint an assistant and a planning committee, as this will save him the burdensome task of making all the decisions. To avoid further confusion it is suggested that the planning committee chairman give each of the other committee chairmen selected a copy of the tentative program with a detailed list of instructions to be followed. The successful program depends upon each committee's fulfilling its obligations on time. A series of time deadlines for each committee should be worked out in order to keep things moving at a prescribed rate of speed. Care should be taken that duties of one committee will not overlap the duties of another. Sometimes certain duties must be followed in sequence and one task must be finished before another can be started. The planning committee will need to coordinate the work of all the committees and perhaps work out a check list so that when each committee is ready to begin its work, it will not be delayed because of the negligence of other committees in the performance of their duties. It will take perfect coordination of all the committees to get the job done.

Care should be taken that all members of each committee are interested in being placed on a particular committee. In contacting the person to serve on the committee, it should be made certain that everyone understands his duties and is willing to accept them.

The systematic organization of the committees and the selection of efficient personnel to man these committees are important elements in the administration of the demonstration. The success of the demonstration will depend to a large extent on how well the committees function. They will furnish the key to the proper administration of the program. It must represent the best there is in thought and planning and should provide for those elements which will facilitate its operation. Administration is the means by which the demonstration is created and its growth and success are in direct proportion to the right kind of administration: care and thought in reaching the objectives.

The purposes of the demonstration should be reflected and should therefore be the guide lines by which every committee functions. There should be no values except those which are stated from the beginning and these must be understood by every member of every committee.

The committees should be formulated in a democratic fashion and the members should be made well aware of the purposes of the demonstration and how it is to be administered. The successful administration of the demonstration rests on the shoulders of the various committees; consequently, their importance must not be overlooked.

COMMITTEE APPOINTMENTS

The appointment of committee chairmen and committee members is very important, for the success of the demonstration is directly proportional to the ability and concern of the committees, especially the chairmen. The chairman of each committee should be contacted and his permission obtained before he is appointed. He should understand that this appointment involves a great deal of work, but also some recognition. If the school is large, a number of committee chairmen may be members of the physical education department. However, some of the committees will require other faculty members to be chairmen, as the duties of the committee will involve different departments. For instance, the chairman of the music committee would be a member of the music faculty. He would pick his own committee in order to work closely with each member. He would naturally pick students and faculty from his department.

QUALIFICATIONS OF THE COMMITTEE CHAIRMAN

The most important member of the committee is the chairman and he should be appointed by the director rather than elected by the group. This appointment should be based first of all on his knowledge of the task at hand. Some other attributes might be whether he will or can present those facts which are based on his experience and knowledge to the group for their consideration. He should also be the type of person who will ask the committee members for their suggestions and make them feel that they are a well-knit group working for a common goal. He should have the ability to steer the discussion along channels of mutual agreement so that a decision which is agreeable to all may be reached. He should have the ability to coordinate and pull together the different ideas that have been presented in such a way that no one will be offended—yet the outcome will be a group decision.

A good chairman will take an active part in committee undertakings. He will get the meetings started on time, will push the committee through its work, coordinate the thinking of the group, and reach difinite conclusions. He must be a person of integrity, initiative, and "know-how"—one who has the ability to lead and contribute. He must be able to keep the committee members on the task at hand and not let them wander in their discussions. A strong chairman will speak often and is not afraid to say what he feels he should say. (See Figs. 4-1 and 4-2.)

ASSIGNMENT OF SPECIFIC DUTIES

The assignment of specific duties to each committee is the responsibility of the director. This should be done after the first meeting of all the chairmen, during the first week of the two weeks to be devoted to the organization of the demonstration. After the duties have been assigned, the chairman should select his committee. He should meet with the director of the demonstration and carefully go over the specific duties of his committee. The chairman should then meet with his committee and the director and again go over the duties. Suggestions may be made and questions answered at this meeting. Any questions or problems of the committee may then be carried from the chairman to the director personally and worked out between them. The chairman should be in close contact with every member of his committee and should be able to meet with them at short notice. Each chairman should have in his possession a list of the duties assigned to his committee. This list may be added to or subtracted from, as the situation dictates. He may make assignments as he sees fit, depending upon the ability of the committee members. The chairman should work through the director whenever possible; however, if the problem involves another committee, he may bypass

PHYSICAL EDUCATION DEMONSTRATION

AGENDA

February __, ____

General Committee Meeting #1

I.   The purpose, aims, and objectives of the demonstration

General Chairman: Mr. William Brown
                    Director of Physical Education

II. The general organization of the program, physical layout,
     time allotment and related activities

Demonstration Supervisor: Mr. Fred White

III. Discussion of duties of the Committee Chairmen

1. Distribution of mimeographed material relative to the
    duties of the chairmen

2. A brief question and answer period relative to the
    duties of the chairmen

3. Setting of the dates for individual meetings between
    the director and each committee chairman

4. A discussion of the general procedure regarding the
    chain of command for the relaying of information and
    the general overall plan of communication

5. A discussion of information relative to the general
    make-up of the committees

General Chairman: Mr. William Brown
                    Director of Physical Education

IV. Director's Summary

1. Suggestions to all personnel

2. Questions regarding areas needing further study, etc.

3. Announcement of the date and time of the next meeting

General Chairman: Mr. William Brown
                    Director of Physical Education

Fig. 4-1

PHYSICAL EDUCATION DEMONSTRATION

AGENDA

March __, ____

General Committee Meeting #2

A. General Comments

    1. Importance of finalizing plans
    2. Scheduling of practice sessions
    3. Scheduling of rehearsals
    4. Scheduling of final dress rehearsal

    General Chairman: Mr. William Brown
                   Director of Physical Education

B. Reports of Committee Chairmen

    1. Each chairman will discuss the duties and respon-
        sibilities of his committee so that there will be
        no overlapping of duties and complete harmony will
        exist between the committees.

    2. Question and answer period so that any misunder-
        standings which might exist within the committees
        relative to any part of the demonstration may be
        straightened out.

C. Special Instructions

    1. Specific order of events
    2. Correlation of all reports
    3. Discussion and notation of conflicts
    4. Discussion of any problems pertaining to any phase
        of the demonstration

    General Chairman: Mr. William Brown
                   Director of Physical Education

D. Director's Summary

    1. General review of preparation
    2. Question and answer period
    3. Suggestions and criticisms

    General Chairman: Mr. William Brown
                   Director of Physical Education

Fig. 4-2

the director to save time. Any major problem, however, should be handled through the director.

The success of the demonstration administratively depends to a great extent upon the work of the committees. The smoothness with which the demonstration is run off will be in direct proportion to the efficiency of the committees. (See Fig. 4-3.)

February ___, ____

To: All Personnel Concerned

From: Mr. John Jones, Director of Physical Education

Subject: Committee Appointments for Physical Education Demonstration
           April 6, _____.

Director . . . .   John Jones . . . . .   Physical Ed. Dept.

Demonstration Supervisor   Fred Smith . . . . .   Physical Ed. Dept.

Announcer . . . . Dean Brown . . . . .   Speech Dept.

Student Personnel . . . . Eric White . . . . .   Physical Ed. Dept.

Publicity . . . . Jack Johnson . . . .   English Dept.
                                                  Art Dept.
                                                  Home Ec. Dept.
                                                  Ind. Arts Dept.

Maintenance . . . . Bill Howard . . . .   Custodian

Equipment and Supplies .   Howard Dill . . . .   Physical Ed. Dept.

Music . . . . Floyd Fellows   Music Dept.

First Aid . . . . Sue Black . . . . .   Nurse

Programs . . . .   Frank Brown . . . .   Ind. Arts Dept.

Parking and Police . . .   Mike Whitson . . . .   Chief of Police

Concessions . . . . Roger Miller . . . .   Varsity Club

Facilities . . . .   Duane Alexander . .   Physical Ed. Dept.

Hospitality . . . . Bill Rodney . . . .   Physical Ed. Dept.

Planning . . . .   Dwight Reading . . .   Physical Ed. Dept.

Tickets . . . . Joe Freend . . . . .   Business Dept.

Ushering . . . .   Fred Jones . . . . .   Social Science Dept.

The first meeting of the committee chairmen will be held Monday, February 26, 19___ at 3:30 P. M. in the faculty lounge.

Fig. 4-3

POLICIES

It is important in the administration of any demonstration, if it is to function smoothly and efficiently, that the planning committee establish guiding policies or rules as a basis upon which all committees should operate. All committee members should be made aware, through published material which is given to them, of the rules and regulations upon which the entire school operates. Any decisions made by the planning committee or any of the other committees must be made with these in mind. Policies will differ in local situations and may, in many cases, deviate from the generally accepted ones thought to be applicable to most situations. The policies must be modified to meet local conditions, but must coincide with those under which other departments and the entire school system are governed.

It is imperative that decisions relative to the operation of the demonstration be carried out through the regular chain-of-command for all school functions. Where certain policies or normal procedures do not fit the situation, an all-out effort should be made to modify them so that they will fit into the general pattern of school procedures. If this is not possible, then a temporary policy should be offered to the school governing body for acceptance before any action is taken. It should be kept in mind that the general public will be viewing the demonstration, and every effort should be made to promote good public relations and create a good impression. Any policies or rules which might appear on the surface to be objectionable should be abandoned for the moment in favor of some which will be more suitable to the situation. Arrangements must be made for meetings to be held at regular intervals whereby the aims, purposes, objectives and policies may be worked out to the satisfaction of everyone concerned.

It is important, therefore, that a great deal of thought be placed on the selection of the committee members and especially the chairman. If the committee is to function effectively, it must have the following attributes:

1. A strong chairman who is acceptable to the majority of the committee members. It is not necessary for him to be able to win a popularity contest, but he should have a likable personality and not have an antagonistic attitude or "rub people the wrong way."

2. A free hand to make decisions without too much interference from superiors. Every committee tends to feel that the decisions they have agreed upon after careful study and deliberation will be accepted in good faith as the proper solution to the problem. Intelligent people do not like to feel that they are serving a useless function, that all their efforts, their time, and their energy have been expended in vain. Therefore, they should have authority to carry out their assignment.

3. An opportunity to obtain all the information that is needed for the proper functioning of the committee. It is most important that all information needed to make decisions should be made available to the committee. Provisions should be made for a feedback on the results of committee decisions. A knowledge of how these decisions are being received by others is necessary in order to facilitate further the work of other committees.

4. An opportunity to reward the efforts of those individuals on the committee who have done a good job. There is always a place for a good word or a pat on the back; however, group awards will do more for overall morale than singling out certain individuals.

5. A chance to evaluate the results of the work of the committee. It is the duty of the director to work closely with each committee and make periodic checks to see if the job is being done.

CHAPTER V

Duties of Committees

Committees are necessary in demonstration planning. Each committee should have specific tasks to perform and should be under the direct supervision of the director, who works closely with them at all times. The number of committees will be determined by the director and will depend upon the type of demonstration, the number of people involved, the desires of the director, and the use of other departments. The duties of each committee will be determined by the director and will be dependent to some extent on the abilities of the personnel as well as the desires of the director. The duties may be of a general nature, with the chairman taking a great deal of responsibility, or they may be very detailed and circumscribed, in which case the committee will know exactly what is to be done, but will have little initiative in the planning, and will be deprived of making any original contribution to the demonstration. On the other hand, if the duties are detailed, it will afford less chance of errors which might result from slipshod thinking, planning, and execution of duties.

The chairman assumes the major share of the work and responsibility of the committee. Because of the very nature of the duties which will be performed by the committees and because of the overlapping of these duties, it will be necessary for the committees to work very closely together for maximum efficiency. Complete harmony must prevail at all times within each committee and between all the committees. Their functions should be clearly defined so that each may know its sphere of responsibility and will not entrench on the duties of some other committee.

It should be clearly understood by the members that the committee was formed to perform a definite function and not for effect—an unfortunate occurrence which sometimes takes place.

The success of the committee depends upon the chairman. He should have skill at impartial presiding. Rare is the man who has talent for setting forth his own ideas and at the same time encouraging others to do the same. Nevertheless, he should try to preside impartially. A chairman should be the servant of the committee, not the master—or even the wise man of it.

The director should spell out the limits of the power, duty, and responsibility of the committee before it is organized. There should be an understanding of these duties among the other committees. This will eliminate much of the confusion among committees' relationships.

The first and foremost item in setting out a committee's duties and responsibilities is to determine whether it shall simply pass information upward or serve the broader function of passing on recommendations for action. The committee should not be run just as an advisory body to decision-making individuals.

Limiting the committee in power and in scope limits it in its decision-making. The committee therefore cannot adequately offer advice unless it has responsibility.

The general duties fall into three distinct categories, namely:

1. To furnish group judgment where a problem overlaps into another element of the demonstration.

2. To study and analyze the problems, then recommend action to the director who must eventually make the decision.

3. To carry out the specific duties as outlined by the director and supervisor.

It should be remembered by the reader that all the duties of the committees that are discussed here need not be used in every situation. They are discussed here with the idea that many of them can be used and it is up to the individuals presenting the demonstration to select those which are apropos. There are some that overlap and those duties are to be given to the committee which is able to do them more effectively in a particular situation.

MAINTENANCE COMMITTEE

The maintenance committee should realize that its duties and responsibilities bear an important relationship to the success of the demonstration. The director should instruct the committee members as to the following:

1. An understanding of the school's policies regarding the adaptation of school facilities to the educational program.
2. Explanation of all duties and responsibilities. Each member should be given a carefully prepared outline of the duties to be performed, besides other information pertinent to the assignments.
3. A firsthand demonstration of all the duties required with an opportunity to practice these duties.
4. A full explanation of the time the members will be required to be on duty.
5. An acquaintance with all supplies, materials, cleaning and operating tools, equipment, storage, and other facilities, with an opportunity to ask questions.
6. An orientation period long enough to thoroughly acquaint each member with the duties he is expected to perform.

Lines of Communication

Definite lines of communication should be established between the maintenance committee and other committees, as well as all school personnel, since this committee, in performing its duties, will of necessity come in contact with all phases of the school program and all types of school personnel. The lines of communication, already established within the school system from the board of education and the superintendent and the principal through the director of physical education, should be adhered to as closely as possible.

Duties and Responsibilities

The maintenance committee's responsibilities and duties are innumerable and never-ending. These duties may differ, depending upon school policy. Many of these duties are custodial in nature. The committee merely sees to it that they are done.

1. Cleaning of the school building in general and the gymnasium in particular.
2. Care of walks, halls, and areas related to the demonstration.
3. Reporting of all needed repairs.
4. Security of the school building, including doors, windows, stair treads, and panic bolts against fire and the weather.
5. Elimination of all hazards likely to cause injury.
6. Maintenance of proper temperature and ventilation within the gymnasium.
7. Checking of all lights, and prevention of any damage or destruction whenever possible.
8. Helping with the conduct of pupils.
9. Maintaining a courteous manner at all times.
10. Delivery of supplies.
11. Performance of routine building inspection.
12. Inspecting all equipment for needed repairs.
13. Placement of all needed equipment.

Safety

State and local building codes provide for adequate safety standards in all school buildings. Older buildings, however, do not usually meet the standards required in the newer buildings. A critical analysis should be made of all possible hazards in and around the building. This might include inspecting heating and ventilation systems, checking fire escapes, seeing that doors have panic bolts and are unchained, checking the condition of stair treads, anticipating hazardous weather conditions, removing obstructions when necessary, repairing all equipment used in the demonstration, and inspecting all electrical equipment involving possible fire hazards.

Safety is the business of everyone connected with the demonstration, and everyone must assume responsibility for it. Nothing will put a damper on a function of this type more quickly than an accident of any kind. Therefore, everything possible should be done to avoid any mishap.

Maintenance by Clean-up Committee

There should be a clean-up committee comprised of students that work through the demonstration chairman. The chairman of this committee must have his duties outlined and assigned well in advance of the demonstration. He will appoint sub-committees to take down chairs, sweep the gym floor, clean the locker rooms, clean the lobby, remove all posters and decorations, and return all apparatus and equipment to its proper place.

The duty of special clean-up will be the responsibility of the chairman. These duties will be more specific than the regular janitorial duties and will include such things as removing signs, posters, banners, decorations, or any special markings used in the demonstrations. Removing any additional chairs or bleachers following the demonstration, as well as a general cleaning of the area at the conclusion of the evening activities, will also be included. Whoever is delegated the authority for being in charge of the special clean-up group must first of all remember that, however the clean-up is to be handled, the people he selects must be capable, responsible individuals willing to work. This is no job for lackadaisical or irresponsible personnel, since in most cases the facilities used for the demonstration will also be needed for the following day's school activities and will have to be put in order immediately after the demonstration.

Usually sufficient personnel can be selected from students in physical education classes who are willing to accept the added responsibility and work. This would probably be the most economical way to handle the situation.

All the equipment needed for the special clean-up should be secured ahead of time, such as brooms, mops, disposal containers, chair carts, etc., and should be at the immediate disposal of the group as soon as the demonstration area is cleared following the activities.

It will also be the duty of the individual in charge to brief the clean-up group on each person's job, or he may separate the workers into four or five groups with one person in charge of each of the areas to be cleaned.

Maintenance by Custodians

The custodian should play an integral part in the overall planning of the demonstration. He can be of assistance by giving advice in the planning and preparing of the facilities used during the demonstration and helping in many other areas.

It will be his duty to arrive well in advance of the starting time of the demonstration in order to open the building and check on proper heating and ventilation. He should remain on duty and be of assistance to committees that have maintenance duties. After the demonstration he should see that the building is in order, the lights are out, and the building is securely locked.

In most schools it is the policy of the school or organization to pay the custodian for his services. This should be taken care of by the demonstration chairman after the conclusion of the demonstration.

Importance of Custodian

The custodian is one of the most important members of the school personnel. All committee members will find it necessary to seek his services and help at one time or another.

Fire Protection

Fire protection is important, especially when a large number of people are involved. The custodian should check all fire regulations and see that all exit doors leading to the street or to the fire escapes are equipped with panic bolts. He should see if all fire exits are indicated by illuminated signs. The electric fire alarm should be checked to be sure that it is in good working order. The custodian should cooperate with the fire marshall in every respect.

Cleaning of Rest Rooms

The custodian must be sure to check on all rest rooms before the demonstration to see if they are unlocked and clean. The corridors of the school and the lobby of the gymnasium should be made presentable.

Gymnasium Temperature

The problem of temperature in the gymnasium is important, and the custodian should be aware of this and regulate the temperature according to the need.

Gymnasium Lighting

The lighting of the gymnasium usually will be the responsibility of the custodian, although this duty may be delegated to a responsible student.

Cleaning of Floors and Mats

The floors, windows, and all equipment, especially the mats, should be cleaned before the demonstration.

TICKET TAKERS, TICKET SELLERS, AND TICKET COMMITTEE

The method used in selecting ticket takers will depend on the policy of the school system. Larger schools may have a ticket manager who takes charge of handling the tickets to all school activities. Faculty members may be assigned this responsibility as a part of their extra duty, or they may be paid for this service. As with the supervisory duties, this should be assigned on a rotation basis.

Students are often willing to assume this responsibility. They may be members of the Student Council, Athletic Association, Varsity Club, or they may be business majors in the school program.

The chairman of the ticket committee should make sure that ticket takers are provided with tables and chairs, change, tickets, and report forms. He may designate an area where these items may be obtained or have them delivered to the proper location, and the person in charge should see that they are returned or indicate a location where they should be delivered after the demonstration.

DEPOSIT ENVELOPE

Amount..Date..

Source..

Credit to..account.

Anyone Depositing Money
Should Fill Out This Form
Deposited by.. .

FORM 124—METROPOLITAN SUPPLY CO., CEDAR RAPIDS, IA.

Fig. 5-1

As in any other well-organized business, there should be standard forms to be used for the deposit of money and for payment orders. All income should be deposited with a central treasurer, who will credit the department with the correct amount. (See Figs. 5-1, 5-2, 5-3, 5-4, 5-5, and 5-6.)

CEDAR FALLS TOWNSHIP HIGH SCHOOL

Ticket Sellers Report Form

Date _____

COLOR	NAME OF ACTIVITY
Last Ticket No.	— Football
First Ticket No.	— Basketball
Tickets Sold	— Baseball
Price	— Track
Amount	— Tennis
Total Sales _ _ _ _ _ _ _ _ _ _ _	— Golf
Sig. Ticket Seller	— Wrestling
	— Play
Other Income	— Dance
From For	— Demonstration
	— _____

Total Income _____

Plus Change _____

Deposit _____

Deposit Receipt No.

Fig. 5-2

CEDAR FALLS TOWNSHIP HIGH SCHOOL

CEDAR FALLS, ILLINOIS

Ticket Sales Form

Date of Activity _____

           Total Number of Adult Tickets Sold   _____

           Total Number of Student Tickets Sold   _____

     _____ Adult Tickets Sold @ $1.00   _____

     _____ Student Tickets Sold @ .50   _____

           AMOUNT OF MONEY ENCLOSED   _____

Signature of ticket seller _____

Note: Please return this blank with money and unsold tickets
       to ticket office on or before _____ P. M., _____.

Fig. 5-3

FINANCIAL REPORT FORM

Activity _____ Date _____
DISBURSEMENTS:
    Custodial: Hours   Amount   TOTAL

                 _____

                 _____   _____

    Advertising: _____   _____

                 _____   _____

    Tickets: _____   _____
    Programs: _____   _____
    Ticket Takers: _____

                 _____   _____

    Public Address System: _____   _____

    Ticket Sellers: _____

                 _____   _____

    Miscellaneous:

                 _____

                 _____   _____

                     TOTAL DISBURSEMENTS   _____
RECEIPTS:

                 _____

                 _____

                     TOTAL RECEIPTS   _____

Fig. 5-4

TICKET TAX REPORT FORM

Type of Ticket	Number Sold	Price	Net Amount	City Tax Rate	Total City Tax	State Tax Rate	Total State Tax	Total Amount

Attendance

Paid Admissions
  1. Reserved _____
  2. General _____
  3. Student _____

Gross Receipts
  Gate Receipts _____
  Programs
  Student Tickets _____

Student Paid Admissions
  1. Activity Tickets _____

  2. Complimentary _____

Total Attendance _____

Total Receipts _____

Fig. 5-5

Account of Extra-Curricular Activities
PAYMENT ORDER

Please issue check to...

for...Dollars   ($................)

for..

charge to.. Date...............................
                          (ORGANIZATION)

TREAS'. NOTATION	
Date................................	....
Check No...........................	Approved...
	Sponsor or Manager

Metropolitan Supply Co., Cedar Rapids, Ia. No. 123

Fig. 5-6

Printing

Tickets should be distinctive, but not necessarily expensive. (See Fig. 5-7.) Some schools may have the equipment to make their own tickets if a printing course is offered. If tickets are to be purchased

PHYSICAL PANORAMA

Sponsored by D.H.S. Letterman's Club

Presented by
D.H.S. Physical Education Dept.

Saturday, March 27, 1965

7:30 p.m.   Lancaster Gym

PRICE 50c

Fig. 5-7

from a ticket manufacturer, it would probably be cheaper to do this by bids. If only general admission tickets are sold, then common roll tickets could be used or tickets could even be made on mimeograph paper and run off in the business machines class at little or no expense.

Cost

The cost of tickets will depend primarily on how the tickets are made. If the tickets are printed by the school printing class, they can probably be made for little or nothing, depending upon the type of paper used to print the tickets and the regulations of the school concerning the distribution of this paper. If the tickets are printed by a ticket manufacturer, the cost will be determined by the type of ticket, the number of tickets, the number of colors used, whether a detachable stub is necessary, whether all tickets are to be reserved, and the amount of printing needed on the tickets. Prices for 2,000 reserved seats may cost as high as $100.00 a set.

Passes or Complimentary Tickets

If complimentary tickets are to be prepared and distributed, it should be done early. A definite policy should be established regarding complimentary tickets. The school council or administration usually can remove considerable pressure for complimentary tickets by adopting a list of persons entitled to them and then adhering strictly to this list. In most cases, those who make themselves nuisances in seeking complimentary tickets are not entitled to them.

Handling

A definite method of charging tickets to student salesmen may be used. If this plan is adopted, business methods in handling this and all financial matters pertaining to tickets must be followed. This point is of particular importance because, in some instances, state admissions tax reports must be prepared. If a previous agreement has been made, other schools and places of business should have an available supply of tickets for advance sale. Keep duplicate records of all ticket releases and sales.

PROGRAM COMMITTEE

The program committee should meet after the type of program and time of the program have been decided upon.

Type of Printed Program

The program committee should first discuss which kind of printed program is suitable. The choice will probably be one of three types:

1. A professional program done by a local printer. The following plan should then be followed.
   a. Put the program up for bids.
   b. Secure advertising to help pay for the program.
   c. Gather and arrange all material to be included in the program.
   d. Make sure all material reaches the printer on time.
   e. Arrange to have the programs delivered to the school or to have them picked up.
2. A program done by the school print shop. The following plan should then be followed.
   a. All the above steps should be carried out.
   b. Close cooperation with the department head should be obtained, as students will be doing the work and need more time to make up the program.
3. An inexpensive program done on the duplicating machine. Secure permission from the principal to use the machine and materials.

Advertising and Costs

If a professional program is desired it will be necessary to solicit advertising and determine the charges for space. A list of potential advertisers should be made. Sources are advertisers in past programs (or if no previous programs have been attempted those sponsoring ads in football and basketball programs are good possibilities) and local service groups.

Organization and Delivery of Material

The organization and delivery of material will mean close cooperation with the head of the program committee. He should help compile a list of events and names of participants. This can then be prepared, checked thoroughly, and sent out on time.

Number Needed

There are three determining factors influencing the number of programs needed. These are the number used at previous programs, the seating capacity of the gym together with the number of nights the show will be held, and the advance ticket sale.

Attractive Cover and Theme

The theme of the program will help determine the program cover. Cooperation and aid will usually be given by the school art department—or by the printer, if it is a professional program.

Paying Bills

It will be necessary for one member of the committee to collect all bills and submit them to the committee which in turn will approve them and send them to the proper authority for payment. Prompt attention to financial matters will be of the utmost importance. A financial secretary for the entire program would be a great aid to all who must obtain materials.

Obtaining Help in Program Arrangement

The committee should work under the supervision of an adult. This could be done by students in physical education classes who are excused because of injuries and are not participating for a day or two. If there is no sponsoring organization, it might be possible to get the Lettermen's Club or the GAA to help with folding and arranging programs.

Distribution and Collection

The committee will distribute the programs. There should be a central supply to draw upon and ample help at each entrance. If the programs are sold, an adult should be in charge of change and central supply to aid the students distributing the programs. (See Fig. 5-8.)

PROGRAM SALES REPORT

_____ Invitational Tournament   Date_____

	Name	Change Received	Returned	Sold	Amount
1.					
2.					
3.					
4.					
5.					
6.					
7.					
8.					
9.					
10.					
	Totals				

Programs Received   _____

Complimentary Copies   _____

Number Sold   _____

Number Returned   _____

_____
              Athletic Director

_____

Fig. 5-8

Designing

The front page of the program should be discussed with the head of the art department. One or more classes could be given the assignment of designing a cover which would be fitting to the event. Recognition should be given, inside the program cover, to the student, the instructor, and the art department.

Interior

The interior of the program gives the order of events, the names of the participants, and the various times of each performance; and it must be arranged, typed, mimeographed or stenciled, and rolled off. The cooperation of the business department should be obtained. The instructor may assign each phase of the work and this work, in return, gives the students experience which is beneficial to them and to the school.

Cost

The cost of printing the program can be held to a minimum by the use of inter-school departments and the use of school supplies. There may or may not be a charge for the program to the spectators, but a small donation may be accepted in case no charge is made. (See Figs. 5-9, 5-10, 5-11, and 5-12.)

Thanks to Helpers

A special thank you in appreciation of all aid in arranging the program should be given immediately, either through a page in the rear of the program or a direct letter to each. This will assure close cooperation in the future when planning other programs.

FIRST-AID COMMITTEE

The chairman of this committee should be concerned with the safety and welfare of both participants and spectators. There should, therefore, be provisions made to take immediate care of anyone who is in need of first aid.

Usually the school has definite procedures to follow in case of any accident or illness on the part of a pupil or school personnel. These procedures should be followed as closely as possible and with as few changes as possible to fit the situation.

The committee should be charged with the responsibility of mimeographing these procedures and giving them to those individuals

HARVARD COMMUNITY   UNIT DISTRICT

JUNIOR HIGH SCHOOL

Physical Education

Demonstration

JUNIOR HIGH GYMNASIUM

TUESDAY, MAY 11, 1965
7:30 p.m.

V. DAVID FREDERICK, Principal
CAROL McCLAIN, Girls Physical Education
GENE GRAY, Boys Physical Education

Fig. 5-9

PROGRAM

ANNOUNCERS: RANDY KOSMAN AND MELINDA BEETSTRA

1. **CHEERLEADERS - Girls**
   Cheerleading helps develop poise, leadership and sportsmanship, in addition to the increased coordination and strength gained by doing cheering motions.

2. **CALISTHENICS - Boys**
   LEADERS: Craig Baird, Dennis McEnaney and Dan O'Neil
   Calisthenics are used as a means of developing the muscles, and for preparing for more strenuous activity.

3. **RELAY RACES - Boys**
   LEADERS: Kelly Camp and Ken Bell
   While providing for good competition relay races also aid in the improvement of skills.

4. **BASKETBALL SKILLS - Girls**
   LEADER: Kristy Rice
   Endurance, coordination and the ability to think are some of the characteristics of a good basketball player.

5. **SQUARE DANCE - Boys and Girls**
   LEADERS: Pam Pagles, Dick Crone and Roland Hayes
   A fine and enjoyable social activity emphasizing rhythm and coordination.

6. **TUMBLING - Girls**
   Strength, flexibility, balance, and pure enjoyment can be derived through active participation in this sports area.

7. **TUMBLING - Boys**
   LEADERS: Nick Leschuck and Arnold Ratzlaff
   Tumbling provides for daring while offering an opportunity for individual initiative and achievement.

Fig. 5-10

78

DEMONSTRATIONS IN PHYSICAL EDUCATION

8. **PYRAMIDS - Boys**
LEADERS: Kurt Ulmer, Tom Millard and Rick Dopke
Working on pyramids enables the boys to work together to achieve a common goal while developing
improved timing.

9. **WRESTLING - Boys**
LEADER: Kelly Camp
Wrestling is a sport designed for boys enjoying
individual competition and is conducive for participation by a boy of any size.

10. **JUMP ROPE - Girls**
LEADER: Carla Johnson
Children can certainly think of many ways to make
a simple exercise look very difficult.

11. **PHYSICAL FITNESS RUN and HIGH JUMP - Boys**
LEADERS: Greg Amelianovich and Ken Bell
The physical fitness run is used as a conditioning
device in which the boys are competing with one
another. The high jump is a part of the decathlon
upon which the boys are now working.

12. **RHYTHMS - Girls**
The students chose the music, made up their own
movements and presented their composition to the
classes. These are a few of the many good rhythms
composed.

13. **MASS ACTIVITY - Boys**
LEADERS: Ken Bell and Nick Leschuck
The boys are playing crab soccer, a combative activity calling for the use of the muscles of the
shoulders and arms.

14. **RELAY RACES - Girls**
LEADER: Barb Moore
What can arouse more spirit than competition while
having fun!

15. **CHEERLEADERS - Girls**

Fig. 5-11

SIXTH GRADE

Gary Alt	Wayne Gratz	Marilyn Bauman	Carla Johnson
Earl Andrews	Don Greenlee	Gayle Bell	Karen Johnson
Craig Baird	Steve Hagstrom	Karen Busch	Nancy Lenhart
Roy Barnes	Mark Hayes	Mitzi Casteel	Janet McClelland
Dan Barrett	Roy Jeffers	Kay Crone	Pam McCormick
Ed Bentley	Tony Jones	Debby Czech	Kathy Millard
Henry Blazer	Doug Kirchoff	Debbie Davis	Alice Nelson
Dan Blazier	Dan Lentz	Marsha Davis	Rita Oost
Ken Burton	Mike Lundin	Mary Dickson	Lorna Ozman
Frank Butts	Dennis Lyle	Kathy Firn	Becky Palmer
Craig Camp	John McConnell	Ciri Garbrecht	Debbie Richardson
Mike Church	Jeff MacDonald	Elaine Gratz	Susan Roberts
John Conley	Mike McCullough	Debbie Hage	Gayle Saunders
Phil Dickerson	Larry Meade	Debbie Hagstrom	Shirley Schuetz
Terry Donner	Mark Peterson	Susan Hellenga	Janice Seaver
Keith Eickstaedt	Mike Rowe	Pat Herriott	Kathy Stoxen
Mark Ferris	Ken Slavin	Nancy Hettinga	Cheryl Trebes
Greg Fiegal	Mike Van Lue	Lynne Hoernig	Linda Way
Ken Frenk		Janet Horton	Barbara Weter
		Chris Iftner	Sharon Yerke
		Kitty Jasper	Leanne Yuenger
		Alice Johnson	Gaye Zimmerman

SEVENTH GRADE

Rick Adams	Mike Hackman	Midge Anderson	Judy Kyle
Johnnye Bankson	Jay Hagstrom	Linda Andrew	Marge Lacy
Mike Bannwolf	Roland Hayes	Judy Antonsen	Marsha Lehman
Steve Bell	Steve Johnson	Linda Aubrecht	Pam McComb
Tom Bentley	Rick Lester	Myrna Barrows	Mary Jo McCullough
Charles Burton	Joe Lewis	Linda Boller	Nancy Menzies
Dennis Case	Steve Martin	Sue Conley	Michele Noe
Larry Church	Dennis McEnaney	Marcie Coulter	Connie Oost
Randy Davidson	Jim Mulvenna	Janet Dail	Nan Pope
Henry Davis	Gene Munger	Sandy Gerrish	Nola Sciacca
Jim Elder	Robert Munger	Vickie Gile	Gayle Shaffer
Bill Fisher	Kent Robinson	Janet Koenig	Cindy Smith
David Griesemer	David Rogers	Carol Koltz	Rozanne Sward
		Roberta Korslin	Karen Venable

EIGHTH GRADE

Greg Amelianovich	Randy Kosman	Charlene Anderson	Pam Martin
Terrye Bankson	Nick Leschuck	Kristy Anderson	Ollie Miller
Dexter Barrows	David Martin	Lydia Bauman	Alice Mius
Gene Bauman	Tom Millard	Melinda Beetstra	Jean Moede
Ken Bell	Dan O'Neil	Paula Behrens	Barb Moore
Kelly Camp	Dick Perkins	Dixie Berryhill	Judy Nelson
Dick Crone	John Perrin	Tina Borgeson	Pam Pagles
Steve Crone	Dennis Powell	Pat Carbonetti	Juanita Reyes
Walter Dahle	Arnold Ratzlaff	Connie Davidson	Kristy Rice
Marshall Davis	Ray Schoon	Nancy Davidson	Paula Schultz
Rick Dopke	Cliff Sherman	Robyn Dennis	Pat Schutt
Al Fiegal	Ed Smith	Sue Dickson	Gail Seagren
Bob Goad	Rod Sytsma	Linda Earl	Sherry Starr
John Groff	John Tharp	Sheryl Englebrecht	Karen Sternberg
Russ Hollister	Kurt Ulmer	Barb Fisher	Sandy Tharp
Steve Iftner	Richard Vance	Sue Gratz	Helen Trites
Don Jones	Ron Wallace	Diane Guttschow	Debbie Weir
John Jones	Ken Wolf	Alice Kistler	Susan Wells
Bob Kerschke		Barb Klingenberg	Chris Wittmus
		Stephanie Lewerenz	Melody Zimmermann
		Karen Lundin	

Fig. 5-12

engaged in the program of first aid along with all material pertaining to the school's first-aid program. This material might be listed under the following headings:

1. General statement regarding school accidents.
2. Steps to be followed in case of an accident.
3. Steps in reporting an accident.

```
                        NAPERVILLE PUBLIC SCHOOLS
                            ACCIDENT REPORT

(Fill out in duplicate.  Send white copy to Superintendent's office and file
other copy.)

Name_____    School _____

            Pupil                    Custodian

            Teacher                  Other (specify)

Address_____

Name of Parent (if pupil)_____

Date _____ Time_____ Place_____

Witnesses_____
_____

Describe what happened_____
_____
_____
_____

What action taken?_____
_____
_____
_____

First aid administered? _____  By whom?_____
                                    Name and address
Was parent notified? Yes___No___  of Doctor_____

Was report blank for Workmen's Compensation completed? (Employees Only)_____

If student, do not fail to file claim with insurance company as soon as
doctor's statement can be secured.

Recommendation to prevent future accident of this kind.  (Use back of sheet)


_____        _____
        Date                                 Principal
```

Fig. 5-13

Accident report forms should be made available to the first-aid chairman. Instructions should be given as to how these forms are to be made out. (See Fig. 5-13.)

Emergency Treatment Room

This special room during the regular school day may also serve the purpose of being an office, lounge, concession room, lecture room, or any other room that meets certain minimal standards. The size and equipment for this area will vary some according to the size of the school, the available space, and the budget. There are certain minimum standards for such a facility which would be desirable for every such demonstration. Although it does not naturally follow that the provision of these basic requirements will automatically produce a good first-aid program, it would be difficult to establish a good program without them.

The following facilities not only should provide for any emergencies, but should also be conducive to parental appeal and approval. The first-aid room should be immediately adjacent to the demonstration area and should contain an adjoining bathroom equipped with a sink, hot and cold water, soap, toilet, mirror, and towels. The general consideration of the layout should provide good ventilation, adequate heating, and sufficient lighting. Air conditioning is advisable but not mandatory. The items of necessity should include a cot, pillows, sheets, blankets, training table, desk and chairs, phone, waste cans, stretcher, refrigerator or ice container, and medicine cabinet or table. Smaller equipment of equal importance includes splints, crutches, walking cane, ice bags, hot water bottle, paper cups and dispenser, flashlights, tourniquet, and thermometer.

Nurse and Physician

The first matter to be considered should be that of providing a nurse for the demonstration. In larger schools where a school nurse is available, it would be advisable to engage her services. In smaller schools where a full-time nurse is not on duty, the services of the local doctor's nurse should be obtained if possible. A physician should be present on the night of the demonstration. However, a nurse must be on duty if a doctor is not available. It should be remembered that first aid is the first temporary treatment given to an injured person in an emergency. It should be given only by an experienced and trained person. Second aid should be given by a doctor. The actual purpose of first aid is to offer temporary and immediate care to the victim of an accident or sudden illness until the services of a physician can be obtained.

If a doctor is not readily available, provisions should be made to have a phone installed in the first-aid room with the phone number of a local doctor easily accessible. Arrangements should be made with the doctor so that he is alerted.

First-Aid Helpers

A faculty sponsor should be in charge of the first-aid helpers, if possible, but the actual work is carried on by the student helpers. There should be a director of first aid in charge of the station. The qualifications necessary to hold this position are successful completion of an American Red Cross First Aid Course, and at least one year of experience. The director of first aid is appointed by the faculty sponsor. During all demonstrations there should be two attendants present. The junior attendant should have also successfully completed the requirements of an American Red Cross First Aid Course or one year of experience. After the junior attendant has successfully completed one year, he automatically becomes a senior attendant. If no students with the above qualifications can be found in the school, a call for students with previous first-aid experience in the Boy Scouts or some other organization along this line should be made.

The student first-aid helpers' responsibilities are these: A record of all services should be kept, the main purpose of which is to protect the school, should any charges be made against the first-aid helpers; only those services listed in the *American Red Cross Manual* should be rendered—no internal treatments should be given; should the immediate services of a physician be needed, either the student is taken to a neighborhood physician, or a physician is called to the school. In the first-aid station there should be posted a list of physicians and the time each is available.

In concluding it might be said that student first-aid helpers through this experience get a chance to develop leadership, a cooperative spirit, and an appreciation of the value of first aid.

Emergency Equipment and Transportation

Emergency equipment which may be needed at a demonstration should include an oxygen tank. This could no doubt be obtained from the local fire department. Although it will probably not be used, it is a good idea to have one available and ready for use. An ambulance should also be on hand at any demonstration involving a large number of participants. All participants involved in the demonstration should be informed ahead of time as to where they should go to receive first-aid treatment in case of minor injuries such as floor burns, blisters, minor cuts and abrasions, headaches, etc.

First-Aid Supplies

In addition to the first-aid room, a kit should be available near the area of the demonstration. The kit should be neat in appearance and well organized in content. It should also be available to both spectators and participants, but at the discretion of a qualified school official. The first-aid kit should include the following:

Sterile dressings:	4″ x 4″ and 3″ x 3″ gauze pads
	adaptable-type roll bandages (1-,2-,3-inch)
	cotton and cotton balls
	band-aids in various sizes
Nonsterile items:	bandages and wraps
	elastic-reinforced 5-yard bandages (2-,3-,4-inch widths)
	ankle wrap
	arm sling and safety pins
Adhesive tape:	regular
	elastic
Pads:	felt
	foam rubber
Solutions:	alcohol (70%)
	tape remover
	eye wash
	tincture of benzoin, spray container
	aromatic spirits of ammonia
	mild antiseptic
Equipment:	tongue depressors and applicators
	scissors, surgical and bandage
	eye dropper or eye cup
	razor and blades
	tweezers
	nail clippers
	oral screw
	needles

CONCESSION COMMITTEE

Organization—Handling Concessions

Concessions at the demonstration can be profitable if handled in an efficient manner. The arrangements will vary from school to school and will often depend on the size of the school. In large schools, where there may be a sizable attendance at a certain event, the cash may become too difficult for school organizations to handle, and this service is often transferred to a commercial group that is better able to cope with the large volume of business. Under this system, the school may derive a percentage of the sales. In other situations, organizations from within the school—the athletic association, the student council, the senior class, or some other such group —may handle this money-raising activity.

Extent of Enterprise

The extent of the enterprise will be determined by the anticipated attendance and the possible market. In some cases there will be a great variety of items available for purchase; in others, the variety may be quite limited. The advisability of offering a considerable choice will usually be determined by previous experience.

Supervision

As with any phase of a school activity, these concessions should be supervised. If the authority to sponsor such an activity is delegated to a particular school group, an advisor of this group should be responsible.

Sellers

An adequate number of sellers should be selected to work at the concessions stand. Too many sellers will only be in the way and will slow down the operation. On the other hand, not enough sellers will cause much confusion and smaller profits.

Records

Students who function as sellers should complete standard forms indicating the cost of items purchased, the items sold, items returned, and the total sales. This will prove to be a valuable record in determining future purchases.

Sources for Purchasing Items

Most items needed for the operation of a concession stand may be obtained through any wholesale company. If more than one source of supply is available, it would be wise to compare prices and service before buying.

Price of Items

Almost all items to be sold have a standard retail price. The cost of the items purchased should determine the retail price. It is best to keep prices low and make a fair profit than to have prices high and limit the number of sales.

Change and Change Boxes

To try to operate a concession stand with a limited amount of change is a serious error. If most of the items will be selling for a dime it is well to keep a good supply of nickels on hand for change. If the stand is rather large, and there are several sellers, an extra change box or two may help to speed sales.

Signs

Signs indicating the items that are available and the prices of each should be placed where customers can see clearly. Signs will aid in helping customers to make their selection and help to speed sales.

Containers

An ample supply of trash containers should be placed within close proximity to the stand. This will help to facilitate clean-up.

USHERING COMMITTEE

The ushering can be handled in various ways. It is best, however, to have an adult in charge if students are to be used. Faculty members can be used, but students do a very commendable job. The ushers assist the public in finding seats and help to enforce laws and rules which have been set up by the administration.

Organization

The chairman of the committee should be responsible for the organization of the ushering crew. It is most important to select reliable personnel to serve as ushers because these individuals will have direct contact with the general public. These ushers should be given special instructions in how to greet and serve the public. There should be enough ushers to insure smooth operation and each usher should know his duties well for his area of work. These people should be selected on the basis of their personality and courteous manner.

Responsibility

The ushers should be responsible for enforcing the rules and regulations of the building as well as directing people to their seats. They should control the entrance of late comers so that the audience is not distracted from the program. They also should control the traffic of small children going in and out of the gymnasium.

They should be ready and willing to help out in an emergency, should they be called upon to do so. They should always bear in mind that they are the direct contact between the public and the administration of the school.

Head Usher

A student may be appointed as a head usher. He should be stationed just inside the door of the main entrance and direct the spectators to the proper sections of the building. He should know where these sections are as well as know the exact duties of all the other ushers. All ushers should come directly to him for any needed information, and he, in turn, should seek needed advice from the chairman of the committee. The latter should be stationed in the immediate vicinity and be readily available. The head usher is responsible for all seating arrangements and all decisions regarding seating.

Ushers

The ushers should be students. Because of their duties, they are most directly and most continuously in contact with the spectators. The head usher should assign one or two of the ushers to each aisle of the building. One should be stationed at the front of the aisle and one at the rear. This will allow for little movement on the part of the front usher as the spectators come to him. The ushers should enforce the rules and regulations in regard to safety, smoking, etc. During the performance they must see to it that the spectators are not disturbed by movements of people up and down the aisle or by loud talking.

Dress

The ushers should be distinguishable from other helpers. They may be dressed in white shirts or letter sweaters for the boys. All should wear arm bands. The girls may be dressed in white with GAA insignia or arm bands.

CHANGE OF SCENERY AND EQUIPMENT COMMITTEE

The changing of scenery and moving of equipment between acts is an extremely important part of the demonstration. This must be done as quickly and as efficiently as possible for a successful demonstration. The chairman of this committee is the director's right-hand man. He synchronizes all behind-the-scene activities and has authority over all the crews. He knows how, where, and when each piece of equipment will be used.

A crew of 12 students will usually be required in the changing of the scenery and moving of the equipment. It is advisable to divide the crew into three or four sections, each assigned to handle the equipment or scenery on some particular part of the building floor.

The Demonstration Crew

This group should be assigned to the moving of all heavy equipment. They must work in coordination with the property and lighting crew if the demonstration is to be successful.

The Property Crew

The property crew should assemble all equipment and scenery needed for the demonstration under the direction of the chairman and the director of the demonstration. It is responsible for having all equipment and scenery present for the demonstration crew to move on and off the floor.

The Lighting Crew

The lighting crew must be divided into two sections for specific purposes. The floor crew has charge of all lighting instruments mounted on the building floor. Examples are tower spots, horizon strips, and table or floor lamps. Usually this crew will consist of six members. The beam crew has charge of instruments mounted in the beams over the building floor or along the balcony front if there is one. Usually this crew will consist of three or four members.

Changing of Scenery Check List

1. Check to see if all equipment and scenery are present.
2. Check lights for desired effects.
3. Check to see if all participants are present 30 minutes before starting time.
4. As they come to the floor area have them check their names on the demonstration list; after this they are not allowed to leave the area until they have performed.
5. After spectators are seated, all crew chiefs and crews must take their assigned positions for the opening.
6. Make sure house lights are off when spots or other lighting is in use.
7. The business manager must check to see that all personnel under him are present and on duty at the appropriate time.

Practically all of the equipment and supplies needed in the demonstration should be furnished by the school. The care of this equipment is important and is the responsibility of the committee and its chairman.

Type and Amount of Equipment

The equipment chairman in cooperation with the director should determine the type and amount of equipment and supplies necessary for the demonstration. He should prepare a check list of all necessary equipment from the following areas:

1. Operational equipment
2. Audio-visual equipment
3. Safety equipment

Securing of Equipment

The designated chairman must secure all equipment. If permission for use of the equipment is necessary, he must secure permission through the proper channels. The chairman must arrange for transportation and temporary storage of equipment if necessary. The preceding equipment should be classified under:

1. Equipment and supplies on hand
2. Equipment and supplies to be borrowed
3. Equipment and supplies to rent
4. Cost of equipment and supplies if it is necessary to rent or purchase it

Equipment Crew

The equipment chairman cooperates with the student personnel chairman in the selection of an equipment crew. In agreement with the demonstration supervisor, the director selects a uniform or dress for those crew members who will be seen during the demonstration. The director should hold one or more meetings to clearly define the duties and responsibilities of each crew member. These would pertain to such duties as the following:

1. Boys in charge of heavy equipment
2. Boys in charge of lighter or smaller equipment
3. Boys in charge of scenery
4. Boy in charge of lighting

Positioning of Equipment

The equipment chairman should cooperate with the demonstration supervisor to determine the position of each piece of equipment prior to the performance so that it can be moved into position with the minimum of effort and time.

Designation of Equipment to Be Used

The equipment chairman should also arrange with the demonstration supervisor the designation of the equipment and supplies used during the actual performance.

Safety Precautions

Proper and safe use of equipment must be demanded once it is secured. Safety rules and regulations must be followed and all equipment should receive a safety check after once moved into position. All equipment to be used in the demonstration should be placed in an area where it will be readily accessible. A check list for all equipment should be prepared and given to the custodian so that no mistakes are made the night of the demonstration. Delays may be avoided by using some forethought and being prepared ahead of time. Every instructor should be aware of the dangers peculiar to certain activities because of variation in the abilities and physical development of the participants. Good administration will eliminate chances of injury due to faulty equipment.

For the safety of the participants, the gymnasium floor should be treated before the demonstration so that it will not be slippery. The floor markings for special areas should be painted with washable paint. Lighting should be thoroughly checked so that everything will be in readiness on the night of the demonstration. Shower, locker and rest rooms, hallways, and storage areas should be closed off and locked wherever possible. All rooms where the participants will be stationed should be inspected and all material which is being used by other classes should be removed. A check should be made on the heating and ventilating system to be sure it is in good working order.

Safety Check

The equipment chairman should supervise a thorough safety check of all equipment and supplies prior to the dress rehearsal and prior to the actual performance. He should supervise all equipment adjustments and repairs. The care, upkeep, and storage of all equipment and supplies are his responsibility.

Moving of Equipment

At the dress rehearsal the chairman should coordinate all moving on and off of equipment and supplies with each event or demonstration. This should provide for a minimum of lost time and interference with performers during the actual presentation.

Return of Equipment

The responsibilities of the equipment chairman should include the return of all equipment and supplies. If any equipment is damaged or lost it should be repaired or replaced.

A report to the demonstration director should be made following the performance in regard to the following:

1. Cost for any repair or replacement of equipment.
2. Recommendations for improvement of the program for future demonstrations.
3. Effectiveness and cooperation of the student crew.

PUBLICITY COMMITTEE

The publicity committee should do everything possible to make sure that the overall publicity given the demonstration will be favorable and enhance the program. This is its primary function. Although the committee should assume this responsibility, every one connected with the program must share in making the demonstration a success.

Working Arrangement Guide Lines

There are several policies which may be used as guide lines by the committee in establishing a working arrangement for publicizing a demonstration:

1. The committee needs to work in close harmony with the regular school publicity program.
2. The committee should be well informed as to the policies and procedures of the school as well as those set up for the demonstration. These policies must be agreeable to all committee members.

3. The committee should agree on the type of facts that are to be stressed in publicizing the demonstration.

4. The committee should single out the media of publicity which will help the most in the particular situation.

5. The publicity committee should assume the full responsibility for using all public relations media, including newspaper stories, radio and television interviews, films, slides and pictorial materials, public addresses, student newspapers, etc. It should be the policy of the committee to treat all public relations media the same in regard to the release of news at the same time.

6. The chairman of the committee should be either the person who handles all of the school's publicity or someone appointed by the chairman who will act in this capacity. His job would be to make the news regarding the demonstration available to the press, radio, and every other news media. He should be available to talk personally to the representatives of the press and be fully responsible for the channeling of all news to the correct destination. He should proofread all material so that there will not be any mistakes.

7. The committee should meet with the school principal and explain to him the policies under which the committee will function.

8. All news media personnel should be invited to cover the event.

9. Whenever possible, photographs should be furnished the newspaper. Permission should be given for pictures to be taken during both the rehearsal and the demonstration.

10. The money needed for the demonstration should be appropriated from the general fund. All money received from gate receipts should be placed in the general fund.

The Role of the Newspaper and Radio

There will be many problems that will come up during the course of planning for the demonstration which will result in policies being made for each particular situation.

There are many facets of public relations, all of which will be important in publicizing the demonstration. The newspaper and the radio will take precedence. Therefore, one of the prime tasks of the committee will be to prepare and schedule press releases to the newspapers.

Most families within a community subscribe to the local newspaper, and, since all pay taxes, the mention of a school function will usually catch the reader's eye. Information of this type can be conveyed to the public in various portions of the newspaper so as to attract attention to a wide variety of readers. For example, the various areas in which this information may appear are the news column, sports page, school news, community news, or advertisement section in the form of a purchased ad.

This committee should compose and release articles, with pictures if possible, so that maximum effects may be achieved. In most communities the local newspaper will welcome news from the public schools. Usually, simply typing the article and giving it to the newspaper is enough to have the article printed. But a few simple rules must be followed in organizing the story to save the editor time and hold the interest of the public. The article should be as brief as possible and the information must be complete and accurate. Also, details should be arranged in order of importance so that if the story is condensed before publication, the essential items will appear.

When writing the article, this committee should remember that it is of paramount importance that English be clear and correct. Names should be used whenever possible and must be correctly spelled.

It is the responsibility of the committee to present the story to the newspaper pretty much as they would like to have it written. The chairman should ask the editor how he wants the story written. If pictures are to be furnished, they should be good ones and show the activities to advantage. The newspaper photographer may be good at taking a picture, but he may take the wrong activity at the wrong time. What the newspaper thinks is interesting to the public may not be important in the opinion of the physical education department.

All editors must face deadlines. This means that a story brought in close to the deadline has less chance of being published in the next issue, and there is a good chance that it will be cut, with a great deal of the interesting and important details eliminated.

Each school system should have at least one person responsible for dealing with the press, and this person should be chairman of the publicity committee. He would, therefore, become acquainted with newspaper, radio, and television personnel, and with public officials in the community. All information about the demonstration should be channeled through the committee, with the chairman responsible for all personal contacts with news agencies. This does not mean that the chairman will be responsible for answering all the questions himself, but he will work closely with those people engaged in publicity to find the answers. This will cut down the number of people the press will need to contact to get the story. The committee will need to check with school officials concerning policies which govern the release of school news. The chairman, if he is connected with the school news service, can be of assistance in this respect.

CHAPTER VI

Methods of Publicizing the Demonstration

The publicity given the demonstration will do much to determine its success. The success, to some extent, of course, is measured in terms of how many people are informed of the type of physical education carried on in the school. The publicity campaign should be begun well in advance of the demonstration and what it entails. It should always be borne in mind, however, that publicity which is in any way connected with the schools should conform to certain practices which have already been established. Definite procedures should be used in soliciting and retaining the confidence and support of the public. There are many avenues available for use in publicity and only those which are best for a particular situation should be used.

What methods are best in bringing a demonstration before the attention of interested people? Newspaper stories, advertisements, posters, windshield stickers, circulars, direct mail, programs, school papers, bulletin boards, letters, yearbooks, speeches, official reports, motion and still pictures, movie theaters, special campaigns, photographs, radio programs, handbills, leaflets, cards, folders, letterheads and envelopes, booklets, blotters, banners, window displays, tags, seals, etc. are some that may be used. Only a few of these will be discussed here. Other phases may be used as the situation dictates.

Schools have been engaged in publicity in one form or another for a long time. Publicity takes many forms and extends over many areas in order to reach the majority of people. These people are entitled to know what is being accomplished with the tax money that is being spent for educational purposes. How this is done will depend upon the facilities available and the established administrative procedures. The determining factor in deciding what media to use in publicizing the demonstration should be to use the best one available for the specific purpose, depending upon to whom the information is to be presented. Other factors could include expense involved, time, and ease of preparation.

The methods presented here are adaptable to most situations and are appropriate for a physical education demonstration. The selection of the best media is the responsibility of the publicity committee.

USE OF PARADES

Clubs, such as Lettermen's, varsity, and physical education clubs, offer one opportunity for publicizing the demonstration. These clubs, or certain members of them, probably have a great deal of influence on the students and the community. They could be used in various ways, including parades, sign carrying, and talks by varsity club members.

Usually the members of these clubs are well known to the students and the townspeople, consequently anything that these individuals support will be thought of as a worth-while venture by everyone. These people are the leaders and others will follow. Getting the right people behind the project will do much to assure its success.

Parades could take place within the school and in the community, depending upon the size of the parade. Permission would need to be obtained from the proper officials; namely, the school authorities and community police. If conducted at school a specific time should be set aside for it so that classes are not disrupted. The homeroom period is probably a good time. Usually a clown or pep band leads a parade of this type, followed by others in costumes which will be used in the demonstration. Signs indicating what the parade is about should be carried by certain members in the parade, such as "Come to the PE demonstration on March _____;" "Support the Gym Show on March _____;" "Everybody is going to the PE demonstration on March _____."

A short speech may be made by a member of the varsity or physical education club, after the parade has passed through each homeroom. This speech should solicit everyone's help and support and should urge students to bring their parents to the demonstration.

The same type of parade may be carried out in the downtown section of the community. The full cooperation of the police should be obtained. The parade may be very small or it may be one involving a great deal of work. Suggestions for and illustrations of the parades and speeches follow.

Outdoor Parades

After the parade has assembled, the marching band plays an introduction and the school song. Riding a horse directly behind the band, the grand master announces, "The Central High School presents a parade to thrill and excite you. Watch closely as dancers, tumblers, gymnasts, and many others perform some of their tricks which you can see in their entirety at Central High School, Friday night, May 25."

A blare of trumpets is heard and with cymbals crashing, the parade begins. (Band plays "I Love a Parade.")

First comes a float with seven gymnasts building human pyramids. Next in line come two boys carrying a banner reading, "Come to the Central High Frolics." Behind the banner is a group of boys performing different formations from a marching drill position. A float follows with a model of Mount Olympus and at the top are two boys dressed like ancient Greek wrestlers performing different holds. Next are twenty girls performing rhythmic movements. A float follows with a boy dressed in leopard skin performing feats of strength with a mock bar bell.

During this period the band is playing several appropriate selections.

A group of boys appear, performing various drills with a basketball. A mixture of boy and girl tumblers follows, doing flips and leaps. Pretty girls adorn the floats dressed in ancient Greek costumes with sashes saying "Health Fitness." On the sides of all the floats are signs advertising the demonstration. At the end of the parade march the members of the various classes in their gym suits. The parade ends with five boys carrying a huge banner saying, "Central Physical Education Demonstration, Friday Night, May 25, 8:30, Admission Free."

* * *

The demonstration to be publicized is entitled "Physical Fitness Through Sports." It will consist of 14 units.

First Unit: Two boys carrying a large sign saying: "Physical Fitness Through Sports—to be presented at C. A. Hills Gymnasium, Wednesday, May 5, at 8:00 p.m., Admission Free." The boys are dressed in phyical education uniforms.

Second Unit: The high school band in full uniform. It will play marches and school fight songs.

Third Unit: A group of students wearing football uniforms and carrying a sign saying "Fall—Football."

Fourth Unit: A group of students wearing track uniforms and carrying a sign saying "Fall—Cross Country."

Fifth Unit: A group of students wearing soccer uniforms and carrying a sign saying "Fall—Soccer."

Sixth Unit: A group of students wearing basketball uniforms and carrying a sign saying "Winter—Basketball."

Seventh Unit: A group of students wearing wrestling tights and carrying a sign saying "Winter—Wrestling."

Eighth Unit: A group of students wearing swimming trunks and carrying a sign saying "Winter—Swimming."

Ninth Unit: A group of students wearing basketball uniforms and carrying a sign saying "Winter—Volleyball."

Tenth Unit: A group of students wearing tennis uniforms and carrying a sign saying "Spring—Tennis."

Eleventh Unit: A group of students carrying golf clubs and a sign saying "Spring—Golf."

Twelfth Unit: A group of students wearing track uniforms and carrying a sign saying "Spring—Track."

Thirteenth Unit: A group of students wearing baseball uniforms and carrying a sign saying "Spring—Baseball."

Fourteenth Unit: Two boys carrying a sign saying "Attend the physical fitness demonstration at C. A. Hills Gymnasium, Wednesday, May 5, at 8:00 p.m."

* * *

Still another parade could include the following:

1. Baton twirlers.
2. High school band or pep band.
3. Two physical education students (male)—dressed in their gym suits and carrying a banner publicizing the demonstration. (See Fig. 6-1.)

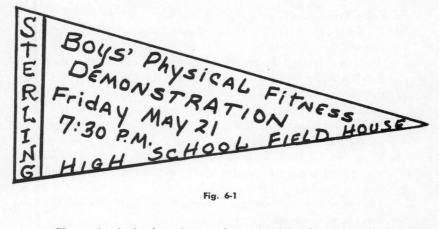

Fig. 6-1

4. Sixty physical education students (male)—dressed in their gym suits and marching in six rows, ten deep.
5. One comedy float depicting boys in poor physical condition.
6. One comedy float depicting boys in good physical condition.
7. Two floats with the leader of each physical fitness test area with a sign indicating the test and the leader's record. Signs:
   a. Push-ups—number in one minute.
   b. Sit-ups—number in two minutes.
   c. 20-ft. rope climb—time.
   d. Zone run—time.
   e. Standing broad jump—distance.
   f. Three consecutive jumps—distance.
   g. Pull-ups—number.
   h. 300-yard-run—time.
8. One car with school adminstrators: principal, athletic director, director of physical education, etc.
9. One car with staff members of the physical education department.
10. Two physical education students—in their gym suits and carrying banner publicizing the demonstration. (Banner similar to the one in No. 3 above.)

* * *

Still another parade could include the following:

1. Police squad car.
2. Fire truck.

3. Convertibles carrying the physical education staff.
4. 3′ x 6′ sign advertising the demonstration, carried by three boys.
5. Six boys dressed in sweat suits skipping rope in unison.
6. Six boys and six girls dressed in jeans, plaid shirts, and cowboy hats. Once each block a square dance routine is carried out.
7. Six boys and six girls carrying signs and advertising the demonstration.
8. Four boys dressed as clowns to represent football, basketball, and baseball players, and a trackman. They go through routines representing their sport.
9. Four boys and four girls dressed as tumblers doing cartwheels, walking on their hands, etc.
10. Six boys and six girls carrying signs advertising the demonstration.
11. Eight boys dressed in uniform and carrying equipment to represent different sports.
12. Four boys dressed as clowns doing tumbling stunts, exercises, etc.
13. Six girls in modern dance outfits doing different modern dances.
14. 3′ x 6′ sign carried by three boys advertising the demonstration.

* * *

Another such parade could be led by banner-carrying students, with the banner stretching across the span of the street indicating what is being publicized, such as: DEERFIELD HIGH SCHOOL PROUDLY PRESENTS ITS 5TH ANNUAL PHYSICAL EDUCATION SHOW. Following this group could be an R.O.T.C. marching unit, followed by a marching band. This could precede an open convertible carrying the principal and the physical education director. Next in line of march could be the cheerleaders and pompon girls, followed by a large marching section of placard-carrying students. The placards should be simple; they should give the data of the show, the names of places where tickets are available, and other features. Another group could comprise the various athletic teams in uniform and a station wagon sound car giving all the details about the demonstration group to the spectators. This group could be followed by boys' and girls' physical education marching units and gymnasts doing cartwheels, flip-flops, etc. The parade could be concluded by the marching of the remainder of the student body and another wide banner reminding spectators when and where the demonstration is to be held.

USE OF SCHOOL ASSEMBLIES

School assemblies may be used for publicizing a demonstration. The purpose here, of course, is to inform the students and create interest among them so that they will look forward to the demonstration and carry the word home to their parents. The assembly program serves a purpose in that it gets the students thinking and talking about the demonstration and their particular part in it. These assembly programs may be in the form of talks by instructors and students as to the value of such a demonstration and the benefits derived from it. It could be in the form of a play or a skit. If a play or skit is used, care should be taken that it is not too serious. It would meet with greater approval if it had some humor connected with it, without being allowed to get out of hand. The assembly program may very well be one or two of the activities which will be a part of the demonstration. It need not take up the entire assembly time but should be put on often, especially during the weeks just before the demonstration is to be presented.

The talk given by either the instructors or students should not be too long and should give information relative to the demonstration such as the purpose, objectives, etc., rather than the administrative details of the demonstration. The talk should inform the students as to the benefits derived from the demonstration and its importance to the physical education department and to the health and welfare of every boy and girl in school. Students should be told that the success of the demonstration is dependent upon them and that its success will help other departments and help make a better school.

The play or skit can be both entertaining and informative. The dramatics department may be called upon to help out in putting on the play. The play need not be one which is directly associated with the demonstration itself. It can be a play or skit which will inform the students of the coming demonstration and its purpose. If it pertains directly to the demonstration, it could be a take-off on one of the activities, showing a practice session or perhaps students planning and preparing for the opening night.

Assembly Skits

1. Presentation of the colors
2. Jims and Jills with spins and spills—freshmen boys and girls
   a. Forward rolls the length of the mat
   b. Backward rolls the length of the mat
   c. Barrel roll the length of the mat
   d. Cartwheels (girls only)
   e. Headstands, rolling down to the mat
   f. Shoulderstand (one pair), falling forward as if to land on face and doing a forward roll
3. A dance of yore—The Rye Waltz—junior and senior boys and girls
4. Seniors show their vim and vigor—rope jumping exercises
   a. Double hop
   b. Single hop
   c. Right foot only
   d. Left foot only
   e. Isometrics with ropes
5. Movement to music—modern dance—six senior girls
   a. The seasons—tune of "Moon River"
6. Sophomore boys' pyramids
7. Wrestling matches
   a. Tag team match using fake holds, etc.
   b. Regular wrestling match
8. Fun and frolic with "The Square Dance Club"
   a. "Turkey in the Straw"
   b. "Dig for the Clam"
9. Interclass tug of war
10. Invitation for all to attend the physical education demonstration show

* * *

Place of skit: Field House

Length of time: 10 minutes

Personnel: 14 male students (2 dressed as instructors, 6 dressed in required gym suits, 6 dressed in sloppy T-shirts and shorts).

Act I: Introduction of an instructor and of 6 young men who have never participated in a physical fitness program. The boys who are dressed sloppily come in and line up poorly. A short exercise routine is given (push-ups, leg lifts, squat thrusts and sit-ups). The boys suffer through the routine using some comedy action. The boys are marched off looking much the worse for wear.

Act II: Introduction of an instructor and of 6 young men who have been involved in a physical fitness program. The boys are dressed neatly and their movements are sharp. The identical short exercise routine is given to these boys. The boys perform with precision and skill in each exercise. The boys march off in step, looking as fresh as when they came.

The brief skit will be followed by a short speech by either a physical education instructor or a student. NOTE: This speech can also be given to an assembly without the skit by changing the introductory remarks.

SPEECH OUTLINE: (3- to 5- minute speech)

I. Introduction: You people have witnessed a comedy skit pertaining to the importance of a physical fitness program. Natturally the extremes were emphasized in this skit, but the fact still remains that physical fitness should be an important concern to each of you students.
   A. General criticism of the youth of today as being physically unfit.
   B. Emphasis on the President's fitness program.
   C. Physical fitness and job opportunities.
   D. Physical fitness and enjoyment of leisure time activities.
   E. Physical fitness and high school
      1. School work
      2. Popularity
      3. Extracurricular activities

II. Conclusion: The physical education department would like to cordially invite all of you students to attend, free of charge, a Physical Fitness demonstration Friday, April 23, at 7:30 p.m. in the Field House. The participants in this program are students from our high school.

This skit is conducted as a radio interview program. It is a comedy, yet gets the message across to the students.

Reporter: Hello. This is your inquiring reporter, Scoop Shovel, on the corner of Hollywood and Vine Streets, where I will interview some famous movie stars and ask them the question, "If you could do anything that you wanted this Saturday night, what would you do?" Here comes a star now. It's that famous Shakespearean actor, Skodney Siltski. Skodney—(*reporter proceeds to ask question*).

Skodney: Why, my good fellow, without a doubt, I would go to the Pasadena High School demonstration on gymnastics, being held Saturday night, December 7, 19—at—8:00 p.m. The members of the senior boys' physical education class will show what they have learned in their gymnastics unit. By Jove! That should be a jolly good show. I shall enjoy that even more than performing my fabulous death scene in "Richard XXVIII."

Reporter: Thank you, Mr. Siltski, and here comes that fabulous entertainer, Sammy Swinger. Sammy, I have a question to ask that is of great interest to our listening audience— (*proceeds to ask question*).

Sammy: I am always interested in picking up new ideas, being one of the world's greatest entertainers. I have come halfway across the world to see the demonstration being put on by the Pasadena High School students Saturday night, December 7, at 8:00 p.m. No one should miss this colossal performance. I hope I can get a ticket.

Reporter: Thank you, Sammy. Now, ladies and gentlemen, I have standing beside me that famous comedian, Zed Selton. Zed, I have a question I would like to ask you—(*proceeds to ask question*).

Zed: Saturday night promises to be one of the most important and exciting times of my life. I have heard from some of the most famous comedians about the clown acts to be presented by the members of the Pasadena High School physical education classes in their annual demonstration. I am waiting with bated breath and extreme anticipation for this colossal event.

Reporter: There—you see; even such a famous comedian as Zed Selton will be in attendance at the annual physical education demonstration to be held at the Pasadena High School gymnasium at 8:00 p.m., Saturday, December 7. This performance will be the highlight of the entertainment season. We have one more celebrity who is with us and I want to ask her a question. She is the famous dancing star, Miss Diamond Square. Miss Square, I would like to ask you a question—(*proceeds to ask the question*).

Miss Square:
Oh, I would go to the physical education demonstration being held at the Pasadena High School gymnasium, Saturday, December 7, at 8:00 p.m. and see the dancing which is going to be presented. I am especially interested in the square dancing and the beautiful costumes the dancers will be wearing.

Reporter: Thank you. It's all very obvious that there is something special going on at the Pasadena High School gymnasium on Saturday, December 7, at 8:00 p.m. Everyone seems to be going to see the demonstration, including yours truly. If all these famous people are going to be there, it must be worth-while. See you all at the Pasadena High School gymnasium on Saturday, December 7, at 8:00 p.m. This is your inquiring reporter, Scoop Shovel, returning you to our studios.

Assembly Speeches by Students

Fellow students, I appear before you today to invite you to publicize the physical fitness demonstration to be held in the Greenville High School gymnasium Wednesday, April 21, at 8:00 p.m.

This demonstration is intended to show our parents and the remainder of the community what we are doing in physical education to improve our fitness. We are constantly being bombarded with radio, TV, and newspaper propaganda to the effect that we teenagers are a soft generation. This is our opportunity to show the older generation what we are doing and how hard we are working.

A demonstration of this type can help sell taxpayers on the desirability of building additional facilities for physical education and athletics. If they understand what is being done here, they will be more willing to spend money to support our school's program.

Many of you will be participating in this physical fitness demonstration. I urge all of you, as well as those who are not participating, to have your families and friends attend. Admission is free.

The demonstration will consist of mass calisthenics, push-ups, sit-ups, chinning, dips, rope jumping, and rope climbing. There will be a speech, "Fitness in the World Crisis," by Dr. David Johnson of the University of Illinois Physical Education Department. His speech will deal with the importance of physical fitness in today's world. Superintendent Peterson will serve as master of ceremonies for the program.

I urge you all to attend and ask you to get your parents and friends to attend. This is our chance to let the public know what is being done in physical education in Greenville High School.

* * *

My fellow students: The physical education staff of Greenville High School has asked me to speak to you regarding the coming physical education demonstration. This program will be presented on Friday, March 26, at 7:30 p.m. The benefits derived from a show of this kind are not unlike those gained from all physical education activities.

Physical education is not only a time for fun, but also a time for learning new skills, sportsmanship, and the way to keep physically fit.

It is the purpose of the demonstration to show the general public many areas of physical education, one of which will be tumbling stunts. These stunts teach balance, coordination, and agility. The skills learned in tumbling enable one to have better posture and to move more freely and easily in everyday living.

Another part of the demonstration will be wrestling exhibitions. The benefits derived from wrestling are many. This vigorous activity requires strength, endurance, balance, and agility. These factors aid immeasurably in keeping us physically fit and helping build strong bodies.

There will be some examples of various rope-jumping exercises. The benefits derived from rope jumping are similar to those mentioned in other physical education activities. It is probably one of the best single exercises that one can do to keep good muscle tone.

It is hoped that by my brief description of the events to be presented in our show, the importance of physical education in our everyday living both today and in the future will be better understood.

Your parents and friends are cordially invited to attend the demonstration and see many of the daily activities that take place in our physcial education classes.

* * *

Good morning, fellow students. It is my pleasure this morning to remind you of the coming physical education demonstration on Friday, April 29, at 8:00 p.m. in the gymnasium. As a participant in this demonstration, I would like to urge you to ask parents and friends to attend. I am sure it will be worth their time. The purpose of this demonstration is to show your parents and friends what we are accomplishing in physical education. In this way we hope that they will develop an interest in physical education. We will demonstrate the actual activities of our classroom work. This is not a specially prepared show, but is an actual demonstration of class work. We will show not only the accomplished performers in physical education, but also all levels of performers. Everyone who is participating in physical education will have a chance to show their skills. Some of the activities shown will be extremely difficult and others will lend humor to the show. I hope your parents and friends will all attend. There will be something that will be of interest to everyone. And remember, best of all, it is free.

Assembly Speeches by Instructors to Students

Members of the student body of Rochelle Township High School, it is my privilege to appear before you this afternoon to speak briefly about a subject of great importance to all of us. That subject is physical fitness. As students of this high school, you are well aware of the importance the physical education staff attaches to physical fitness. We believe that fitness is essential if each of us is to lead as complete and full a life as possible.

An individual is able to carry on strenuous activity for longer periods of time if he is in good physical condition. An increase in fitness brings better physical appearance, more skill in athletic activities, and release from tensions. The person who is physically fit has more vitality and energy.

The health of a person is greatly affected by his fitness level. Heart disease is our nation's number one killer. Exercise appears to be one of the methods of combating ailments in the circulatory system. There is a positive relationship between the body's resistance to disease and its fitness level.

Our nation is only as strong as its youth. The Communist countries are emphasizing sports and physical fitness activities. They know that an active, vigorous, healthy group of young people will make it more nearly possible for them to achieve their desired role of world domination. Our nation must answer the challenge of the Communist world by being physically strong enough to fight the Communist menace. In case of war, the fitness of a country's people will be an important factor.

You young people are well aware of what is being done at this high school to develop your fitness. The purpose of the physical fitness demonstration to be held Wednesday, April 21, is to acquaint your parents and the rest of the public with what is being done and what needs to be done about physical fitness in our schools. The public needs to know about this program so that they will support it with their tax dollars and so that they will think about the need for improving their own fitness level.

The physical fitness demonstration will be held Wednesday, April 21, at 8:00 p.m. in the gymnasium. Many of you, as members of the physical education classes, will participate. Activities that will be demonstrated include mass calisthenics, push-ups, sit-ups, dips, rope jumping, rope climbing, and chinning. Dr. David Johnson from the University of Illinois Physical Education Department will speak on the topic, "Fitness in the World Crisis." Admission is free. We hope that each of you will encourage your parents and anyone else you know to attend.

* * *

I am happy to have this opportunity to advertise our physical education demonstration and to inform you regarding the functions and objectives of our physcial education program.

We are having a demonstration on Friday, March 26, at 7:30 p.m. in the high school gym. We invite your parents and friends to see tumbling stunts, modern and square dancing, wrestling matches, and rope-jumping exercises. Most of the students in the physical education classes will take part in the activities.

I have been asked to comment on the functions and objectives of physical education in the schools. The general function of physical education in the schools is to assist in providing a place for normal growth and natural development of each student. Strength, vigor, vitality, and neuromuscular coordination must be part of the development of the physical capacities of youth. I think the objectives of physical education can best be put in the following categories:

1. Physical objectives:
   a. The health of the youth.
   b. The development of skill.
   c. Physical growth and development.
2. Social objectives:
   a. Accent on freedom of the individual.
   b. Less formal relationships which are conducive to social development.
3. Emotional objectives:
   a. Need for recreational activities for relaxation.
   b. Control of emotions through competition.
4. Recreational objectives:
   a. Individuals' present and future needs.
   b. Activities with carry-over value.
5. Intellectual objectives:
   a. Sufficient knowledge of healthful living.
   b. Knowledge of fundamentals, rules, strategy of sports.
   c. Medium for efficient and effective intellectual development, not only in physical education, but in academic fields.

A physical education class is a time for fun, but it is also a time for learning. As you improve your old skills and add new ones, you will want to learn more about the fine points of games you play. This knowledge will take you out of the beginners' class, but it takes work and practice. It is important for you to know the rules of the games. The traditional courtesies and conventions which belong to each activity are important, too. Knowing these things will put you at ease when you meet other people at play outside of school.

Another important phase of physical education is keeping fit. You need a strong and healthy body to enjoy strenuous activities. You can learn to move more freely and easily so that you will stand straighter, look better, and be able to work and play without unnecessary strain. In physical education classes you are given physical fitness tests so that you can see how you compare with national averages on the same tests.

Finally, physical education classes give you an opportunity to discover your abilities. You develop confidence in your own ability to learn and enjoy new activities and are ready to try new sports or new dance steps which appeal to you. Since you learn to recognize and appreciate good performance in many activities, you should get pleasure out of watching top-flight performers for the rest of your life.

It is hoped that these remarks help you understand more fully the purposes of physical education. The demonstration that is being presented by the physical education department is another means of accomplishing some of the aforementioned objectives.

USE OF THE NEWSPAPER

The newspaper is the number one means of informing the public of a coming demonstration. This can be done through the local or the school newspaper. This information can be conveyed through the sports news, the community news column, the school news, or any other informative column.

The story or article must be brief. The information must be accurate and it must contain all the facts. The first sentence of the paragraph is the one that catches the public eye; therefore, it should answer the questions: Who? What? Where? and if possible, Why? and How? Short clear sentences should be used. Write news, not literature. The use of names other than those connected with the physical education department or the administration should be avoided in order that favoritism not be shown. This is sometimes unavoidable, as credit must be given where it is due.

The articles for the various sections of the newspaper must be written differently. For instance, the sports news article will slant toward the athletic side of the demonstration, while the school news will attempt to portray the demonstration as a regularly-scheduled school activity participated in by almost everyone. The community news column will portray the demonstration as a community activity sponsored by the high school for the enjoyment of every citizen. It will publicize the demonstration as it would a school play or a school operetta.

The school newspaper will take for granted that the students already know about the demonstration because the majority of them are taking part in it; therefore, the information given will be more or less routine.

The newspaper has always been a powerful advertising force, and it should not be overlooked as the best means of making the demonstration a success. Every courtesy should be extended to the reporters, and every attempt should be made to cooperate with them, even to the extent of writing the news items to ease their load.

Examples of good publicity releases for the various types of gym demonstrations are illustrated here.

Local Newspaper

SPORTS NEWS

The Morris Community High School boys' and girls' physical education show will be presented on March 26, at 7:30, in the MCHS
gym. The purpose of this demonstration, besides providing an evening's entertainment, is to give our students the opportunity to show
what they have accomplished in neuromuscular coordination, physical strength, body vigor, and the social graces.

During the year you have seen our teams competing in inter-schol-
astic athletics. Members of these teams have learned sportsmanship
and cooperation in a truly American style of competition. In our
intramural program all boys and girls have an opportunity to learn
and enjoy these and many other worth-while activities.

Friday will show you some of the activities that are carried on
during our daily physical education classes. We hope they give our
students alert and open minds, well developed bodies, a spirit of
fair play, and well adjusted personalities.

The MCHS physical education staff extends an invitation to the
public to attend this show free of charge.

* * *

Basketball passing drills will be featured at the annual gym
demonstration by the boys' physical education department of Kaneville High School on Friday, February 27, at 7:00 p.m. Coach Tom
Jones will explain the various drills as they are performed by the
boys of the physical education classes. Groups of five students each
will perform drills which attempt to develop peripheral vision, quick
hands, and good timing.

* * *

Physical fitness demonstrations of the boys' physical education classes will be held Thursday, February 25, at 7:30 p.m. in the high school
gymnasium.

The public is invited to attend this demonstration, which will
be indicative of the training being given in regular physical education
classes at Rochelle Township High School.

The physical education staff feels it is essential that students
attain and appreciate the highest level of physical development possible.

Is the physical education in the lower grades helping to build better teams through an efficient and well rounded program? Find out Wednesday night at the University School at 8 o'clock in the North Gym! The fifth and sixth graders will demonstrate tumbling and trampoline acts and foreign dance steps. In addition, a brief explanation of the purpose and objectives of the program will be discussed by the physical education instructors. If *you* support the athletic program and are concerned about it, come to the University School at 8:00 o'clock.

* * *

A physical fitness demonstration will be presented Friday, March 15, at 7:00 p.m., in the Sterling High School Field House. Participating in this program will be the outstanding high school boys in each of the physical fitness test areas.

The public is invited to share in recognizing the accomplishments of these boys and to increase its own knowledge and understanding of the local high school physical education program.

School Newspaper

SCHOOL NEWS

The Morris Community High School boys' and girls' physical education departments have announced the date for the physical education show. It will be held on Friday, March 26, beginning at 7:30 p.m. in the MCHS gym. The purpose of this entertaining and informative program is to give the students an opportunity to display some of the skills learned in their physical activities this year.

During the year you have seen our teams competing in interscholastic athletics. Our boys and girls have also been participating in a wide range of intramural activities. It is hoped that the demonstrations in our show will acquaint the public with our daily physical education program.

The physical education staff extends an invitation to the students and the general public to attend this show free of charge.

* * *

Rochelle students are invited to attend the third annual tumbling demonstration to be held Tuesday, March 30, at 8:00 p.m. in the high school gymnasium. Boys from the nine classes will participate in the program, which will culminate in the physical education department's tumbling unit.

Principal Jack Johnson will act as master of ceremonies for the event. Physical education students will participate in activities such as forward rolls, backward rolls, handsprings, cartwheels, shoulder rolls, dive and roll over mats, monkey roll, elephant walk, and pyramid building.

COMMUNITY NEWS

The Morris Community High School boys' and girls' physical education department announced today its coming physical education show. It will be presented March 26, at 7:30 p.m. in the MCHS gym.

This evening entertainment will give our students an opportunity to show what they have accomplished in their many physical activities this year.

The MCHS physical education staff extends a warm welcome to the public to attend and enjoy these demonstrations. There will be no admission charge.

* * *

Kaneville High School boys' physical education department will present its annual gym demonstration this coming Friday, February 27, 19____ at 7:00 p.m. at Swanson Gymnasium, Kaneville, Illinois. Basketball passing drills will be performed in groups of five by students of the physical education classes. Coach Tom Jones, commentator, will describe and explain the purpose of each drill.

* * *

A physical fitness demonstration open to the general public and entitled "Health and Fitness in the World Crisis" will be presented by members of the physical education classes at Rochelle Township High School Wednesday, March 3, at 8:00 p.m. in the C. A. Hills Gymnasium. The program, sponsored by the boys' physical education department, will demonstrate the role the department is assuming in promoting health and fitness in today's youth to enable them to meet the challenge of the world crisis.

Leroy R. Peterson, the superintendent of schools, will serve as master of ceremonies for the program, and Howard B. Anderson, the president of the school board, will give the opening address. Boys from each of the nine physical education classes at the high school will demonstrate mass calisthenics, rope jumping, and a series of fitness tests consisting of chinning, dips on the parallel bars, push-ups, sit-ups, and rope climbing.

USE OF THE RADIO

A medium used frequently as a means of publicity is radio. The radio may be utilized with the local station's sports programs, by tapes, interviews, spot announcements, and local newscasts. Many stations will allow a certain amount of time free of charge for community and school events. The short spot announcements may be worked in at various times during the day about one week before the demonstration. The announcement should be in the form of a short statement telling of the demonstration, giving the date, time, etc., with the invitation to the public to attend.

If the information on the demonstration is to be given during the regular sportscast, it should contain more detailed information and should be broadcast as an announcement coming from the school officials and treated as a regular event put on by the school as part of the physical education and sports program.

The demonstration itself may be broadcast very easily by radio and this would do a great deal to publicize the demonstration for the next year. If this is done, members of the physical education staff could be utilized to explain and describe the activities as they are being demonstrated. By using staff members or, possibly, the director of physical education to broadcast the demonstration, it will be possible to give first-hand information to the listening public about the school physical education program. This will take a great deal of preparation but will be well worth the effort.

The interview is a very interesting type of radio publicity and, of course, may be done "live" or by tape. It usually involves one or more persons to be interviewed and consists of a series of questions and answers. The questions should be planned ahead of time to a certain extent, or at least a few questions should be made available so that the interview does not lag and so that the right information may be given to the listening public. Students, as well as staff members, may be used. An interview may be completely planned ahead of time so that all the correct information may be given. This will avoid any mistakes which might be brought out in an unrehearsed, impromptu interview.

Examples and descriptions of radio interviews, local newscasts, spot announcements and taped records are presented here. These may be changed to fit local situations, for they are used only as examples.

Radio Interviews

Announcer:

The Central City high school physical education class will present a demonstration at the high school field house on Friday, February 3, at 7:30 p.m. Let's everyone attend and see the tremendous job being done in the physical education program of our high school.

* * *

Announcer:

Ladies and gentlemen, tonight we have the great pleasure of having for our guest, Mr. James Doe, head of the physical education department at Central City High School. Jim is here to tell us about the upcoming physical education demonstration being put on by the high school. Tell me, Jim, who are involved in the demonstration.

Jim:

The boys and girls of the high school physical education classes. This will include all students from all skill levels.

Announcer:

What types of activities will be demonstrated?

Jim:

We will present an overall picture of what is being taught in our high school physical education program. There will be calisthenics, dancing, tumbling, gymnastics, and apparatus skills demonstrated. We will present a program that will show how the student progresses from the very elementary skills to those more advanced.

Announcer:

When and where is this demonstration going to be held, Jim?

Jim:

The demonstration will be held on Friday night, February 3,

at the high school gymnasium which is located on 5th and Main. It will start at 7:30 p.m. and the public is invited to be our guests. You will see how the needs of the students are being met by all forms of physical activity designed to fulfill the requirements of each individual. In this way each will benefit according to his needs and to the objectives of a modern program in physical education.

Announcer:

Thank you very much, Jim, for taking the time to come over here and tell our listeners all about your demonstration.

Jim:

It was a pleasure.

Announcer:

Remember, ladies and gentlemen—February 3, at the high school field house at 7:30 p.m. Come out and see what a good job the high school physical education teachers are doing for the youth of our city. Get first-hand information about the physical education program and how it affects your boy or girl and others like them. Find out what the words "physical education" mean in our modern-day living. Here is the opportunity you have been waiting for. Support your school. Show the youngsters and teachers that you are interested in their program.

* * *

Mike Shea:

Tonight, radio station WRMI-FM welcomes to its studios Mr. William R. Ferguson, Director of Athletics and Physical Education at Morris Community High School. Mr. Ferguson will reveal some of the plans for the gym show to be presented at M.C.H.S. Welcome to our studios, Bob.

Mr. Ferguson:

Thank you, Mike. It is always a pleasure to talk to you regarding our athletic and physical education program at M.C.H.S.

Mike Shea:

Would you like to tell our radio audience the date, time, and place of your upcoming physical education show?

Mr. Ferguson:

I would be happy to, Mike. The gym show will be held in the M.C.H.S. gymnasium on Friday, March 26, starting at 7:30 p.m.

Mike Shea:

In an event of this kind, how many students will be participating?

Mr. Ferguson:

Unlike an interscholastic contest where only a relatively few
actually participate, we hope to utilize almost every boy and
girl in the physical education classes. Naturally some of our
events will call for large numbers participating at the same time.

Mike Shea:

Speaking of the events, can you give our audience a few
examples of the type of activities they can expect to see in
the gym show?

Mr. Ferguson:

Surely. We will have tumbling, stunts, modern and square
dances, wrestling matches, mass games, and rope-jumping exercises, to name a few.

Mike Shea:

This sounds like a very enjoyable evening for everyone. We
certainly want to thank you, Mr. Ferguson, for taking the
time to come out to our studio. Would you want to remind
our audience once more of the date, time, and place of the gym
show?

Mr. Ferguson:

Thank you, Mike, for the opportunity of discussing our gym
show with you and the radio audience. The show will be held
on Friday, March 26, at 7:30 p.m. in the M.C.H.S. gym.
Admission will be free of charge.

* * *

Announcer:

We have with us today Mr. John Smith, head of the boys'
physical education department at Rochelle Township High
School. Mr. Smith, I understand that your department has
planned something special for the public.

Mr. Smith:

That's right. We are presenting a physical education demonstration.

Announcer:

What is the purpose of this program?

Mr. Smith:

Our department is trying to show the public what can be

done through physical education to prepare our students to meet the problems they will face in our world. We believe that physical education can help a great deal to develop the physical, emotional, and social traits of an individual. This demonstration will also point out what we are doing in terms of a physical fitness program. This, however, is only one part of our total program.

Announcer:

Who are participating in the demonstration?

Mr. Smith:

All students in the physical education classes will participate.

Announcer:

What activities will the public see?

Mr. Smith:

The boys will demonstrate mass calisthenics, rope jumping, dips, chinning, push-ups, sit-ups, and many other physical education activities.

Announcer:

When and where will this demonstration be held?

Mr. Smith:

On Wednesday, March 7, at 8:00 p.m. in the C. A. Hills Gymnasium at the high school.

Announcer:

What will be the admission charge?

Mr. Smith:

Admission will be free to everyone. We hope that a large number of people will give support to this program.

Announcer:

Thank you very much, Mr. Smith.

Local Newscasts

Tomorrow night M.C.H.S. physical education students will present their gym show. The public is welcome to attend free of charge. The show will begin promptly at 7:30 in the high school gym.

The students will demonstrate tumbling stunts, modern and square dancing, wrestling matches, and rope-jumping activities.

The instructors and students have been working hard on this show and you will find it very entertaining and educational.

* * *

The boys and girls of Central City High School will present a demonstration of activities which are learned in their physical education classes. This demonstration will be presented on Friday, February 3, at 7:30 p.m. at the Central City Field House. The public is cordially invited to view the demonstration.

* * *

Rochelle Township High School's C. A. Hills Gymnasium will be the scene of a physical education demonstration Wednesday, March 7, at 8:00 p.m. The purpose of the demonstration is to inform the public of the role physical education is playing in preparing our youth to meet the world crisis. Members of the boys' physical education classes at the high school will participate. Activities to be included in the demonstration are mass calisthenics, rope jumping, rope climbing, chinning, dips, push-ups, and sit-ups. The public will be admitted free.

* * *

Mr. Ferguson of the Morris Community High School physical education department announced today that a demonstration show will be held on Friday, March 26, starting at 7:30 p.m. The show will be in the MCHS gym and the public is cordially invited to attend. Mr. Ferguson reports that most of the boys and girls taking physical education will have some part in the show.

There will be a wide variety of activities for everyone to enjoy. Tumbling stunts, modern and square dances, wrestling matches, and rope jumping are a few of the events scheduled for the night's festivities.

Don't forget, mark the night of March 26 on your calendar and plan to attend the gala demonstration show presented by the MCHS physical education staff.

Spot Announcements

The public is cordially invited to attend, free of charge, the physical education demonstration show to be held on Friday, March 26, at 7:30 p.m. in the MCHS gym. The show is sponsored by the physical education department and will consist of tumbling stunts, modern and square dances, wrestling matches, and rope-jumping exercises.

Keep the date of March 26 in mind and plan to attend the gym show in the MCHS gymnasium.

* * *

The Central City High School physical education classes will present a demonstration of activities learned in their high school physical education classes. The event will take place on Friday night, February 3, at 7:30 in the high school field house. The demonstration is open to the public.

* * *

Are you concerned about your nation's future? Here is an opportunity to see what your high school physical education department is doing to meet the challenge of today's world. Attend the physical education demonstration at the Rochelle Township High School gymnasium Wednesday, March 7, at 8:00 p.m.

Tape Announcements

The physical education staff at Morris Community High School reminds you of its forthcoming gym show to be held Friday, March 26, at 7:30 p.m. in the high school gym. Most of the boys and girls in the physical education classes will have an active part in the demonstration.

Tumbling stunts, modern and square dances, wrestling matches, and rope climbing exercises are a few of the events of the night's program.

The public is cordially invited to attend, free of charge, the MCHS gym show on Friday, March 26, starting at 7:30 p.m.

* * *

This is Jack White of KBCS, Rochelle. I am speaking to you from C. A. Hills Gymnasium at Rochelle Township High School. Tomorrow night, Wednesday, March 7, at 8:00 p.m. this gymnasium will be a beehive of activity. It will be the scene of a physical fitness demonstration to be presented by the members of the physical education classes at the high school. The public is invited to attend the demonstration of mass calisthenics, rope jumping, rope climbing, chinning, push-ups, and sit-ups. This program is designed to demonstrate the importance of physical education in today's world. This is Jack White returning you to our studios.

USE OF NEWSLETTERS, BULLETINS, AND LETTERS TO PARENTS

Media used frequently for publicity are in the form of newsletters, P.T.A. bulletins, and the like. They provide an easy and

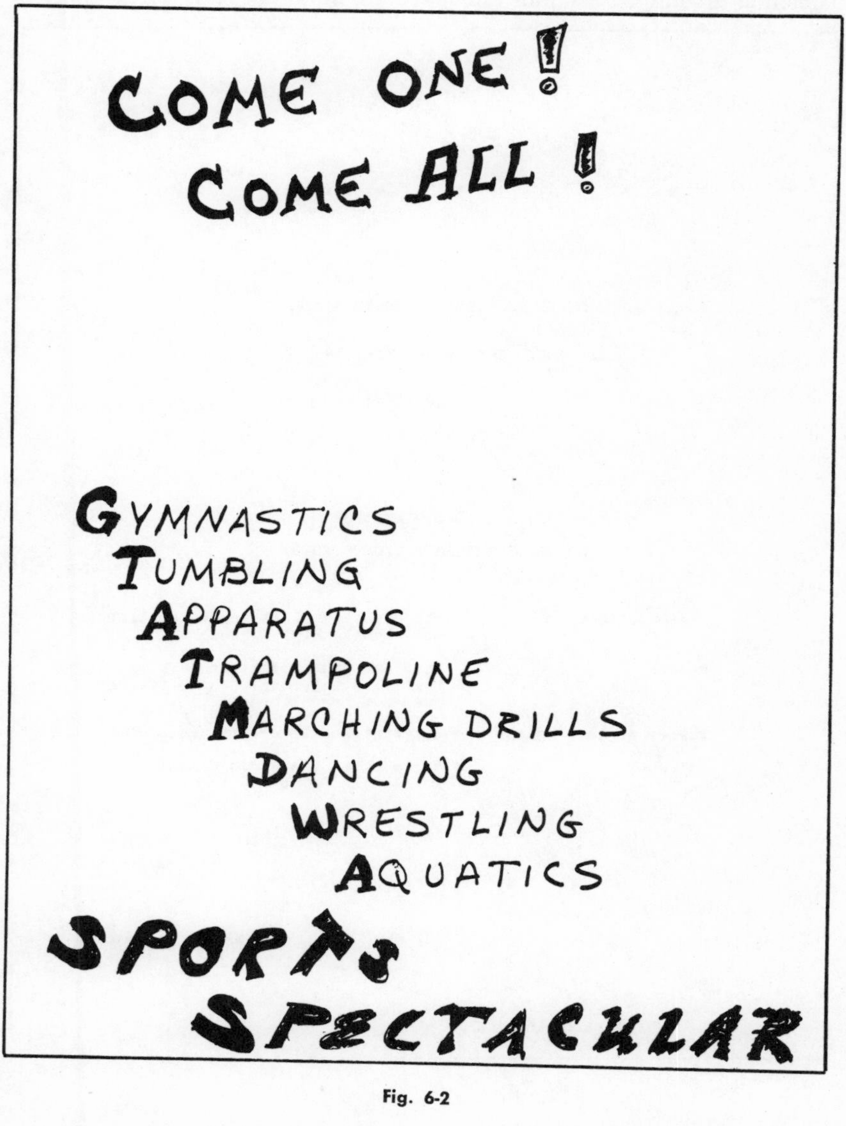

COME ONE!
COME ALL!

GYMNASTICS
TUMBLING
APPARATUS
TRAMPOLINE
MARCHING DRILLS
DANCING
WRESTLING
AQUATICS
SPORTS
SPECTACULAR

Fig. 6-2

efficient way to inform the public of a physical education demonstration. Examples of these media would be letters to the parents of the students, bulletins placed in all classrooms, and newsletters sent to community groups, leaders, and others. There are various kinds of letters and bulletins, the nature of which will be determined by the particular group for whom they are to be used. The letter to the

ANNOUNCING

A

PHYSICAL FITNESS DEMONSTRATION

WEDNESDAY, APRIL 7TH, 19__

at

8:00 P. M.

in

C. A. HILLS GYMNASIUM

ROCHELLE TOWNSHIP HIGH SCHOOL

Presented by:	The boys' physical education classes at Rochelle High School
Events:	Mass calisthenics, rope jumping, rope climbing, dips, chinning, push-ups, and sit-ups
Master of Ceremonies:	Superintendent Leroy R. Peterson
Address:	"Fitness in the World Crisis" by Dr. Gerald Smith

ADMISSION FREE

Fig. 6-3

parents should explain to them the purpose of the demonstration and present the program of events, an invitation to attend, and other pertinent information. The letter should be short and to the point but should give the parents the feeling that their presence is desired, that they will be most welcome, and that the success of the demonstration will be enhanced by a large attendance of parents.

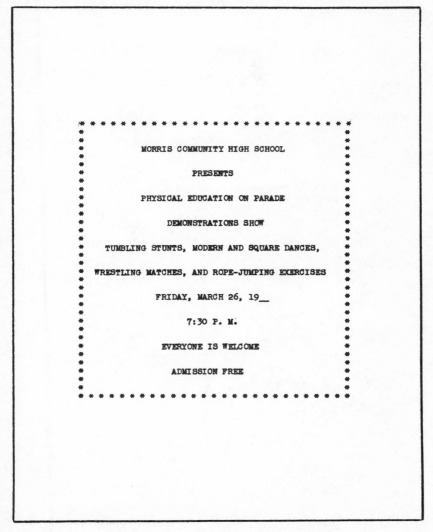

Fig. 6-4

A bulletin will contribute a great deal to the publicizing of the demonstration. The bulletin can be in the form of a short statement to the effect that the demonstration is being held. This can be read in class or in the assembly, or posted on the bulletin board in halls and classrooms. (See Figs. 6-2 through 6-5.)

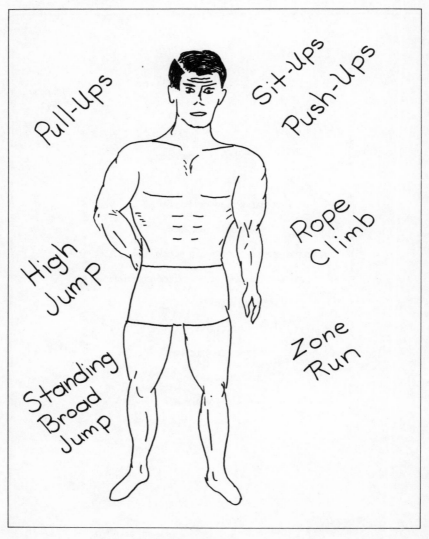

Fig. 6-5

CITY OF PORTLAND, MAINE

PORTLAND HIGH SCHOOL

OFFICE OF THE PRINCIPAL

February 19, 19__

Lions Club
Portland, Maine

Dear Lions:

The Portland High School boys' physical education department
will present a demonstration in the gymnasium, Wednesday, April 7,
at 8 p.m.

Superintendent Leroy R. Peterson will serve as Master of
Ceremonies. The address, "Fitness in the World Crisis," will be
presented by Dr. Gerald Smith.

The demonstration is intended to show a phase of the role
physical education is playing in meeting the challenge before
today's youth. Members of the physical education classes will
perform activities included in the program.

Admission is free, and all of those who are interested are
invited to attend.

Sincerely,

Boys' Physical Education Staff
Portland High School

Fig. 6-6

The newsletter should contain all necessary information regarding the demonstration. It should not be too lengthy, yet it should
contain the purpose, date, place, time, admissions procedure, and information relative to the program content. The letter should contain
an invitation to attend the demonstration, with an appeal for the

support of the program as a community activity—one which will benefit the youth of the community. It should contain a statement to the effect that the demonstration will provide an enjoyable and interesting evening.

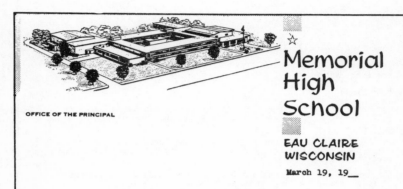

OFFICE OF THE PRINCIPAL

☆
Memorial
High
School

EAU CLAIRE
WISCONSIN
March 19, 19__

Kiwanis Club
Eau Claire, Wisconsin

Dear Kiwanians:

    The physical education staff of Eau Claire High School is presenting a demonstration show on Friday, March 26, at 7:30 p.m. We would appreciate your cooperation in advertising this event to your organization.

    Most of the boys and girls taking physical education will have a part in the show. Tumbling stunts, modern and square dances, wrestling matches and rope—jumping exercises are a few of the activities included on the program.

    Thanking you in advance for anything you and your organization might do to promote this show, we hope to see a number of your members and their families present. The students and faculty of Eau Claire High School will be grateful for your support.

              Sincerely,

              William R. Ferguson
              High School
              Eau Claire, Wisconsin

Fig. 6-7

The newsletter should be sent to all civic groups and clubs which are active in the community with the request that it be read and, if possible, discussed with the club members. The letter should contain

Department of
Physical Education and Athletics

ANDERSON HIGH SCHOOL, ANDERSON, INDIANA

April 1, 19__

To: All members of _____ _____

From: _____ Director of Physical Education
         Anderson High School

Subject: Physical Education Demonstration

  The Physical Education Department of Anderson High School cordially invites you to attend the Physical Education Demonstration to be conducted in the Field House at 7:30 P. M. on Friday, April 9, _____.

  It is hoped that this demonstration will present you with an increased understanding of how the Physical Education Department is contributing to the total development of the youth of this community.

  The program will involve all the students in all the physical education classes. The activities will include only those taught in the regular physical education classes.

  This demonstration is offered free of charge. We sincerely hope you will find it possible to attend this demonstration and give these deserving boys recognition. You will also learn more about our Physical Education program.

       Sincerely,

       C. E. Newton
       Director of Physical Education

Fig. 6-8

all necessary information to enable each club member to understand fully all about the demonstration.

(Sample letters are shown in Figs. 6-6 through 6-12.)

Fayetteville High School Athletic Association
Fayetteville, North Carolina

March 19, 19__

Dear Parent:

This letter is to inform you of the coming Physical Education Demonstration, sponsored by the Physical Education Department of Fayetteville High School. The program will be held on March 26, 19__, at 7:30 p.m. in the high school gymnasium.

Highlighting the evening's activities will be tumbling stunts, modern and square dances, wrestling matches and rope-jumping exercises.

It is very likely that your child will be a participant; therefore, the physical education staff of Fayetteville High School extends this cordial invitation to you to attend.

We hope to see you at our show on Friday, March 26. There will be no admission charge.

Sincerely,

William R. Tucker
High School
Fayetteville, North Carolina

Bulldogs

Fig. 6-9

BOZEMAN SENIOR HIGH SCHOOL
ATHLETIC DEPARTMENT
BOZEMAN, MONTANA

1211 West Main
Phone 586-6111

April 1, 19__

Dear _____:

    The Physical Education Department of Bozeman Senior
High School cordially invites you to attend the Physical
Education Demonstration to be conducted in the Field House
at 7:30 P. M. on Friday, April 19, 19__.

    It is hoped that this demonstration will present you
with an expanded understanding of how the Physical Education
Department is contributing to the total development of the
youth of this community.

    The program will involve all students who are enrolled
in the physical education classes.

    This demonstration is offered free of charge. We
sincerely hope you will find it possible to attend this
demonstration and give these deserving boys recognition.
You will also learn more about our Physical Education
Department.

        Sincerely yours,

        _____
        Director of Physical Education
        Bozeman Senior High School

Fig. 6-10

WASHINGTON SENIOR HIGH SCHOOL

CEDAR RAPIDS, IOWA 52403

ATHLETIC
DEPARTMENT

March 19, 19__

Dear Parent:

The Physical Education Department of Washington Senior
High School would like to take this opportunity to personally
invite you to the Physical Education Demonstration being
presented at the high school field house on Friday, February 6,
at 7:30 p.m.

This demonstration is being presented so that you,
as parents, may become better acquainted with the physical
education program of your high school. As parents we know
that you are vitally interested in what your child is
doing in school. Through this demonstration we hope to
show you what the Physical Education Department is doing
to further your child's development.

The demonstration will consist of activities in which
the students actually participate while they are in
physical education classes. Each child will be given an
opportunity to demonstrate his skills in a particular
activity.

I am hoping that you will attend and spend an
enjoyable evening with us.

Sincerely yours,

Department of Physical Education
Washington Senior High School
Cedar Rapids, Iowa

Fig. 6-11

NATRONA COUNTY HIGH SCHOOL

CASPER, WYOMING
—
DEPARTMENT OF PHYSICAL EDUCATION
AND ATHLETICS

March 19, 19__

Dear Parent:

This year, as in the past, Natrona County High School will present its annual Physical Education Show. Every student at Natrona County High School has played an active part in the planning, organization, administration and performance of this year's show. It promises to be most interesting and educational.

Through our conferences, sample academic work is presented for your examination. There is not much opportunity for you to know your child's motor ability. We strongly urge you to attend one of the performances, Thursday, May 20, through Sunday, May 23. There will be double performances on Saturday, May 22, and Sunday, May 23. The show starts at 7:30 P. M. Thursday and Friday, and at 2:30 P. M. and 7:30 P. M. on Saturday and Sunday.

Enclosed are two tickets to the show. If you desire more tickets, they are available at the physical education office.

Let's all support our students and children by attending this fine show.

Most sincerely,

John T. Ronson
Principal

Enc.:   2 tickets

Fig. 6-12

USE OF FOLLOW-UP ARTICLES
AND LETTERS

One medium that is often overlooked and one that is a good advertisement for any future demonstration is the follow-up article. An article of this sort provides a description of the demonstration, the size of the crowd, and the overall success of the demonstration. This article usually is published in the community and the school newspapers. The article should be written in such a manner that it gives a complete description of the demonstration in terms of its relationship to the overall objectives of the school curriculum. The success

GEORGE HIDINGER
athletic director

JEFFERSON HIGH SCHOOL
ATHLETIC DEPARTMENT
Cedar Rapids, Iowa

TELEPHONE 365-4661

March 25, 19___

To All Staff Personnel:

Our Physical Education Demonstration last Friday was a great success. Your cooperation and help with the planning definitely made this performance one of the highlight programs of the school year.

I would like to take this opportunity to thank all of you. With your helpful suggestions in the future, we can continue to make such demonstrations meaningful to the general public.

Sincerely,

Edward Hope
Physical Education

"THE J-HAWKS"

Fig. 6-13

of the demonstration should be brought out as determined by the enthusiasm and response of the audience to the activities as they were presented. This article will do a great deal to enhance the success of any future demonstrations, because of the fact that it was well received by the spectators and was enjoyed by the participants. If possible the number of spectators should be mentioned.

JAMES V. MOON, SUPERINTENDENT   RALPH E. WRIGHT, PRINCIPAL

John Marshall Senior High School

DEPARTMENT OF ATHLETICS
Rochester, Minnesota

E. W. SILVERNAGLE, DIRECTOR

                                              W. R. McKIBBEN, ASS'T. DIRECTOR

March 11, 19__

Mr. John Doe
John Marshall Senior High School
Rochester, Minnesota

Dear Mr. Doe:

The Physical Education Department of John Marshall Senior High School wishes to take this opportunity to express its appreciation for your services and help in making the annual gymnasium demonstration an outstanding success.

This kind of cooperation strengthens the bond between the community and the school and also makes the public aware of the physical education program at the high school.

If at any time we can be of assistance to you, please feel free to contact us. Again, we thank you for your time and services. It was really appreciated.

Sincerely yours,

Peter J. Klos
Athletic Director

Fig. 6-14

Letters should be sent to the faculty members and school personnel who helped in various ways with the demonstration. The letters should be written in appreciation of what was done by those individuals who helped and should include words of thanks to them. This gesture is not only in good taste, but sets the stage for another

---

MUSKOGEE CITY SCHOOLS

MUSKOGEE, OKLAHOMA 74401

DEPARTMENT OF ATHLETICS & PHYSICAL FITNESS

ALPH STANPHILL, DIRECTOR

March 25, 19__

Dear

       Just a note of thanks for a job well done in helping with our physical education show last Friday. It is always gratifying to know that one can enlist the aid of interested people from the community to lend a hand in the various and sundry details of this type of demonstration.

       The Physical Education Department of Muskogee High School really appreciates your efforts. We hope that you will be available next year when we again put on our physical education show.

       Thank you again.

                    Sincerely,

                    Robert Mobeck
                    Director of Athletics and
                      Physical Education
                    Muskogee High School
                    Muskogee, Oklahoma

Fig. 6-15

year when these same individuals may be asked again to donate their services. It also creates a great deal of good will, as everyone appreciates a written expression of thanks. This will take time, but it is time well spent and will produce the desired results in the long run. The nonfaculty helpers such as the custodians, school nurse,

MINOT SENIOR HIGH SCHOOL
215 FIRST STREET S. E.
MINOT, NORTH DAKOTA
TE 8-6194

Administration:

Norman D. Howe
Acting Principal

William H. Edwards
Acting Assistant Principal

"MINOT MAGICIANS"
PHY. ED DEPT.

March 25, 19__

Dear Mr. Feller:

It is with sincere appreciation that I take this opportunity to thank you on behalf of the Physical Education Department for your tireless effort in helping to make our recent Physical Education Demonstration a success. Without your cooperation, the demonstration could not have been nearly as successful as it was.

It is indeed gratifying to know that we do have citizens like yourself who take an interest in their community and its children.

Thanking you again, I remain

Most sincerely,

John J. Sullivan
Director of Physical Education

JJS:ab

Fig. 6-16

and maintenance personnel will be especially appreciative of any recognition. Their services can prove to be invaluable, and therefore a special effort should be made to solicit their good will. The letter will help to do this. (See Figs. 6-13 through 6-17.)

CHEYENNE PUBLIC SCHOOLS

C. R. INGILS, SUPERINTENDENT
ASSISTANT SUPERINTENDENTS
A. DARREL BECKMAN,
PERSONNEL AND ADMINISTRATIVE
LOYD D. CRANE, INSTRUCTION
J. O. REED, BUSINESS AND PLANT

District Administration   •   School District No. 1   •   Cheyenne, Wyoming, 82002   •   Telephone 632-0591

March 25, 19__

Dear Participant:

The physical education staff of Cheyenne High School would like to take this opportunity to express our sincere thanks and appreciation and that of the administration for the part you played in making our physical fitness demonstration of March 10 so successful.

We know that you are well aware of the benefits to be derived from participation in physical education, and it is through the efforts of people such as you that we are able to present a true picture of the physical education program to the public. The public needs to be made aware of the benefits derived from an organized program of physical education so that they will support such a program wholeheartedly.

Again, let us express our thanks for your help in making our exhibition a tremendous success.

Sincerely,

Physical Education Staff
Cheyenne High School

Fig. 6-17

Community Newspaper Follow-up Article

Physical Education Demonstration Termed a Success—The physical education demonstration held last night in the MCHS gym was attended by a large crowd. The audience, estimated at 1500, enjoyed the demonstrations put on by the boys' and girls' physical education classes.

The modern dance routines and the square dances seemed to be especially appreciated, while the rope-jumping exercises and wrestling matches were also well applauded.

The physical education staff termed the show a great success and plans are already underway for a bigger and better show next year. The department wishes to publicly express its appreciation for all those who helped in any way in the production of the physical education show.

School Newspaper Follow-up Articles

The physical education demonstration show held on March 26 was attended by a large and appreciative audience. The show was termed a success by the physical education staff, and plans are underway for next year's presentation.

The modern dance routines and the square dances, as well as the rope-jumping exercises and wrestling matches, were especially applauded. However, the entire show seemed to be enjoyed by the audience.

The physical education staff would like to thank all those students, members of the faculty, and employees who helped immeasurably to make the production a success. In an endeavor of this kind, there are numerous details and it takes the cooperation of many people to make it a success. Mr. John Jones, director of physical education, and his entire staff are to be commended on this excellent presentation of what is being taught in the physical education classes at Greenville High School.

Donald Black, acting as master of ceremonies, did an outstanding job and his interpretations and explanation of the activities as they were being presented helped the audience understand and appreciate them.

* * *

An enthusiastic crowd of parents and students came to the demonstration, Wednesday, February 25, at the University School to watch their children and classmates perform. The demonstration started at 8:00 p.m. in the North Gymnasium of the University School. The boys started the program with a series of calisthenics; then the girls joined the boys in demonstrating some of the basic tumbling stunts that they have learned in the physical education classes. During and between the different sections of the program, Mr. Farley, director of physical education, explained to the parents the basic parts of the physical education program at the University School and the main objectives of each program. The boys and girls concluded the program with a variety of dance steps, both domestic and foreign. The demonstration was a *big* success and warrants congratulations to all those who took part in organizing and presenting the program.

* * *

Rochelle Township High School's gymnasium was the scene of a physical education demonstration Wednesday, March 10, at 8:00 p.m. A crowd of 800 enthusiastically witnessed the exhibition. Superintendent Leroy Peterson served as master of ceremonies, and school board president, Stanley Ohlson, delivered the opening address, emphasizing the need for physical education at the high school level.

The fitness demonstration included mass calisthenics, rope jumping, chinning, dips on the parallel bars, push-ups, sit-ups, and rope climbing. All members of the physical education classes at the high school participated in the highly successful demonstration.

A great deal of effort went into this demonstration and those individuals responsible for its success are to be complimented, not necessarily because it provided good entertainment for the many parents and friends of the participants, but for the real reason for presenting the demonstration—that of informing the general public and enabling it to obtain a better understanding of physical education.

Those people attending the demonstration saw first-hand the activities which are being offered in the physical education program and how they are being taught to the boys and girls.

The aims and objectives of the demonstration, as well as those of the entire program, were fully explained by Mr. John Jones, director of physical education, before the demonstration began. He brought out the interesting fact that the purpose of the demonstration was the same as that for any other school function and compared with those set up for the entire school curriculum, because the demonstration educates the student the same as does any other agency within the school.

Mr. Jones emphasized the fact that the activities presented were those which are being taught in the regular classes.

The parents were able to see not only the end results of the teaching of certain physical skills but also the actual teaching situation. He pointed out that learning comes only through the activity of the learner. The skill is acquired by the student through his own efforts.

Everyone left the gymnasium with a clearer picture of what physical education is and what it is doing for the boys and girls of Greenville.

The entire school is to be congratulated for this fine demonstration. Almost everyone had a part in its success as other departments contributed a great deal.

USE OF SERVICE CLUBS

Service clubs such as Kiwanis, Rotary, and Lions may be asked to sell tickets and help publicize the demonstration. They must, however, understand and be made aware of the program if they are expected to cooperate. Many service clubs have projects of their own which consume a great deal of the time and energy of the members; therefore, some may look upon the request for help as uncalled-for and, consequently, an imposition. On the other hand, if the members are properly informed of the purpose of and values derived from the demonstration, they are usually more than willing to assume a share in the work of putting it on. Publicity to the effect that the service club is behind the venture will help tremendously in the promotion of the demonstration.

There are several ways in which the service clubs may be informed of the demonstration, one of which is a short skit which will clearly point out to the members what it is all about. Another is a short talk given by a student or instructor, in which he fully describes the purpose and composition of the demonstration along with the necessary details.

The skit should be one which will both entertain and instruct the members of the club about the demonstration. It can be amusing or serious; but in either case it should not be boring, as this will do more harm than good. It should be a good example of what may be expected in the demonstration. The skit, if given without the talk, should include all the necessary information regarding content, date, time, and purpose, along with admission procedures. The skit, of course, is more entertaining and is just as effective as the talk, providing it gives the listeners the needed information.

The following skits are examples of those which might be used to advertise the demonstration.

Skits to Present to Service Clubs

The following skit might be presented to a local service club to serve as publicity for a physical education demonstration to be given at Rochelle Township High School, Wednesday, March 3.

Characters:

Three male commuters: George, Tom, and Harry

Scene:

A commuter train carrying the men to work. The time is 7:30 a.m. George is reading from a newspaper and discussing its contents with Tom, his seat mate. A third man, Harry, is seated directly across the aisle from them. He is pretending to read his paper, but he is, in reality, eavesdropping.

The scene opens with George speaking first.

George:

These papers are full of stories about teen-age murders, robberies, sex crimes, riots, drinking, and every other illegal activity you can think of.

Tom:

I know it. I don't know what's wrong with this younger generation.

George:

I'll tell you what's wrong with them. They have too much free time on their hands.

Tom:

They don't have respect for law and order, either. Respect for authority is disappearing.

George:

Yeh! It doesn't seem like these kids can get along with other people, either.

Tom:

Not only that, but they have no direction. They don't have any ambition, desire to excel, loyalty, or intestinal fortitude.

George:

And you talk about weak! Why when I was a kid we worked hard. I was always in good physical condition. I had to walk two miles to school every day. These kids just hop in their cars and drive. This must be the weakest generation in history.

Tom:

That's right! Did you read about all of those boys that have been rejected by selective service because they are physically unfit?

George:

Something should be done about it.

Tom:

That's what I say. They always say it's the parents' responsibility, but I say the schools have the best opportunity to help.

George:

I agree! Why don't they do something?

Tom:

I don't know!

Harry:

Pardon me, fellows, but I couldn't help overhearing your conversation. I've a son who attends Rochelle Township High School, and from what he tells me they are trying to do something about these problems.

Tom:

How?

Harry:

Well, in many ways, but the way I hear it, it's in physical education class and athletics that they are really doing something.

George:

Well, if they are, it must be different from my high school physical education program. All our teacher ever did was roll a ball out on the floor and go back to his office and smoke.

Harry:

It's different today. They have organized instruction in touch football, volleyball, dodge ball, softball, dancing, tumbling, track and field, and other sports, and what's best in my mind is the physical fitness program they have there. They have those kids doing exercises, running, jumping ropes, taking fitness tests, climbing ropes, and running relays. My son has really improved his physical condition in the two years he has been in the program. He also learned something about respect for authority and living according to the rules, and, brother, you talk about intestinal fortitude and a will to win!

Tom:

Boy, that sounds great! I'd sure like to get a look at that program in action.

George:

Me, too!

Harry:

Well, you've got a real good chance.

George:

How?

Harry:

They're having a big physical fitness demonstration at the high school Wednesday, March 3, at 8:00 p.m. I understand that there will be a demonstration of the activities that make up the physical education program, and they are also going to have a demonstration of some of the sports activities that they are participating in.

Tom:

Say, I think I might take my wife and go to that.

George:

Let's go together. If they're really doing that much good there, I want to see it.

Tom:

When did you say that is?

Harry:

Wednesday, March 3, at 8:00 p.m. at the Rochelle Township High School.

George:

Good! We'll see you there. This is our stop. Come on Tom, let's get moving. We'll be late for work as usual.

* * *

Scene:

Two teen-age boys meet on the street. Their names are Bill and Jim.

Bill:

Hi, Jim! How's it going?

Jim:

Okay, I guess.

Bill:

It's been quite awhile since we've done anything together, hasn't it?

Jim:

Yeah, two weeks at least.

Bill:

Why don't we go out on a double date Wednesday night?

Jim:

Sounds like a swell idea, but we'll have to make it some other time.

Bill:

Why?

Jim:

I'm going to be in a physical education demonstration at the high school gymnasium Wednesday night.

Bill:

A physical education demonstration? What's that?

Jim:

Guys out of each of the physical education classes are going to demonstrate some activities taught in our physical education program.

Bill:

What are you doing?

Jim:

We're all going to do calisthenics, jump rope, climb ropes, and do chinning, dips, push-ups, and sit-ups. There will be a speech by Dr. Johnson on the importance of physical education, too.

Bill:

Who's going to be there to watch?

Jim:

Anybody can come who wants to. There isn't any admission fee and the public is invited.

Bill:

What time will it be over?

Jim:

It starts at 8:00 p.m. and I imagine it will be over by about 9:30 p.m.

Bill:

Maybe I'll come to the demonstration and we can get together for a coke afterward.

Jim:

Okay! Why don't you meet me at the gym doors after the demonstration is over?

A Skit to Present
to a Civic Group

Setting:

A carnival sideshow, with various weights placed strategically around the stage.

Cast of Characters:

Barker; Beefo, the strongman; skinny young lad; crowd.

Position:

Barker—to the right of stage on podium; Beefo—behind curtain; skinny young lad—mixed in crowd.

Announcer:

The Auburn High School Iron Knights present a skit entitled "Beefo Gets Ground UP."

Barker:

And now, introducing that giant of muscular magnitude, the great Beefo, who will challenge anyone from the audience to duplicate his astounding feats of strength.

Crowd:

Yea! Yea! Yahoo!!

(The great Beefo enters, dressed in a lionskin and flowing cape. A large handlebar moustache adorns his upper lip. He proceeds to lift a huge square weight, weighing 500 pounds, with two hands. He is grunting and groaning.)

Crowd:

Yea! Yea!

Barker:

And now, the fabulous Beefo will challenge anyone in the crowd to give him a feat of strength to perform which he cannot do but the challenger can. The prize is $500!

Skinny Young Lad *(raising his hand, meek-voiced)*: Lift 1000 pounds by two fingers.

Beefo *(moving up to 1000 pound bar bell)*: Grrr! All right, you turkey neck! Grrrr! *(He grasps the bar by two fingers. Straining and grunting, he cannot move the weight.)*

Crowd:

Hiss, hiss, boo!!

Barker:

If the great Beefo cannot accomplish this feat, it is impossible.

Skinny Young Lad (*meekly*):

I beg to differ, sir. I shall perform the feat. (*Stepping up to the stage, he concentrates fully, and, bending over towards the bar, suddenly stands erect. Between his two fingers is a piece of paper with "1000 pounds" written on it.*)

Crowd:

Yea! Yea! Yahoo!!

Beefo:

Grrr!

Barker:

The joke's on us. You win the $500.

Announcer:

If you would like to see a demonstration of weight-lifting, using bonafide weights, come to the Auburn High School Gym on Friday night, August 22, at 8:00 p.m., and see the Iron Knights demonstrate their weightlifting skills.

"The New Student," a Short Skit

Setting:

The beginning of fifth-hour class. One of the physical education instructors approaches a new student.

Coach:

Hello, son. My name is Mr. Finn. What's yours?

Student:

Joe Davis.

Coach:

Is this your first day in high school here?

Student:

Yes, sir.

Coach:

Well, Joe, we are going to put on a physical education demonstration; would you be interested in participating?

Student:

What are you going to be demonstrating?

Coach:

We will have some tumbling, wrestling, gymnastics, relay races, rope skipping, and basketball and boxing techniques.

Student:

Are you going to have any rifle shooting or fencing?

Coach:

No, they are much too dangerous.

Student:

Those things you mention are for girls.

Coach (*pointing in the direction of a group of boys*):

Boys, will you show our new student, Joe Davis, some of the things we are going to do in the demonstration? It will give him an idea of what we work on in class. Bob, will you do a handstand?

Bob:

Yes, sir. (*He gets into position and starts doing the exercise.*)

Coach:

Mike, will you do an iron cross on the still rings? Sam, you do a back flip with a one and a half twist on the trampoline. Ralph, you might demonstrate the four basic basketball passes. Clyde, you can demonstrate the timing necessary to beat the speed bag. Floyd, how about skipping the rope backwards with a cross-over on every other skip? Ray, will you and Kent go over on the mats and do a duck-under for Joe?

Ray:

Yes, sir.

Coach (*turning to the new student*):

Can you do any of these things?

Student (*observing the situation and the demonstration in action*):

No, I don't think so.

Coach:

Then you can't be classified as a girl.

Student:

No, I guess not. Are these exercises very hard to learn?

Coach:

Not too hard. Why don't we start working on them so you will be ready for the demonstration?

Student (*looking into the instructor's face and starting to smile*):

OK. How long do we have to practice?

Coach:

About two weeks. The demonstration is Friday, March 19, at 6:30 p.m., here in the gymnasium.

Speeches by Varsity Club Members

Members of the Rochelle Lion's Club, I wish to thank you for this opportunity to appear before you. As a high school student and athlete, I am particularly interested in the subject which I will discuss—physical fitness and what our high school is doing about it.

Rochelle Township High School believes in a strong physical fitness program through physical education. This belief is shared by members of the board of education, the administration, the faculty, and the student body. These groups know the importance that physical fitness plays in enabling each student to reach his fullest potential. Education includes teaching and learning in all phases of life, not just in terms of the so-called academic disciplines.

Knowledge gained from books is of little value to the person who lacks the physical health to make use of that knowledge.

A physical education program which develops fitness and teaches the individual how to maintain fitness is essential to the well-being of the individual.

Mental, physical, social, and emotional health and well-being are affected by the amount of regular vigorous exercise an individual receives. A high level of physical health generally bears a positive relationship to good mental, social, and emotional health.

In the light of the previously mentioned facts, the physical education program at Rochelle Township High School has included a good deal of physical fitness work. The boys' physical education department has prepared a program to show the public what it is doing in this area.

This program will be presented Wednesday, May 4, at 8:00 p.m. in the C. A. Hills Gymnasium. Members of the nine physical education classes will present a program of mass calisthenics, push-ups, sit-ups, rope jumping, rope climbing, dips on the parallel bars, and chinning. Superintendent Leroy R. Peterson will serve as master of ceremonies for the event. Dr. Jack Johnson of the University of Illinois physical education staff will give an address entitled "Fitness in the World Crisis." Admission to the demonstration is free, and the public is invited to attend.

I urge each of you to take this opportunity to see what our high school is doing in this important area of physical fitness.

I am glad for the opportunity to appear before you to explain why we are planning a demonstration on May 4.

* * *

It is a pleasure for me to represent Morris Community High School and to tell you a little about our physical education demonstration show to be presented on Friday, March 26.

This show will demonstrate to you some of the activities that the boys and girls participate in during their daily classes. These events help develop the strong, healthy body that is needed to enjoy strenuous exercise. Physical education classes are not only a time for fun, but also a time for learning new skills, sportsmanship, and how to keep physically fit.

For instance, during the demonstration you will see tumbling stunts. These stunts teach us balance, coordination, and agility. The skills learned in tumbling enable us to have better posture and move about more freely and easily in everyday living.

Another part of the show will present wrestling exhibitions. The wrestling matches you will see are much different from those you have seen on television. This vigorous sport requires strength, endurance, balance, and agility. Wrestling is a fine sport for developing physical fitness and strong bodies.

Probably one of the best single exercises to keep good muscle tone is rope jumping. In our show we will have a group of boys demonstrating different exercises that can be done with ropes.

Another event in the show will be modern and square dancing which teach the student rhythm and social grace. In addition to learning these dances, the boys and girls also learn good manners.

The benefits derived from our physical education classes are many. We learn new skills and improve old ones, and this makes us want to learn more about the fine points of the games we play. This also points out the importance of keeping physically fit for a healthier and happier life. We develop confidence in our own ability to learn and enjoy new activities and are ready to try new sports or new dance steps which appeal to us. It also increases our pleasure in watching top-flight performers.

We would appreciate anything your organization can do to promote our demonstration show. Remember, the events will be on Friday, March 26, in the Morris Community High School gym.

* * *

Good evening, gentlemen. It is a great pleasure to be invited to speak to you this evening. The purpose of my visit with you is to describe the physical education demonstration that the high school physical education classes are soon going to put on. As a participant, I am quite familiar with the good job that the physical education program is doing for the students of the high school. A great many people feel that all physical education is to the students is play time. I will agree that I look forward to it as a relaxation, but I assure you that it is not just play.

Many people do not realize that there are many skills that can be learned, but that in order to learn them the student must have someone to teach him the proper way. In our physical education classes we learn many activities and skills that will be useful for leisure-time activities now and when we are out of school. Besides being enjoyable, physical activity makes us healthier and better prepares us to meet the demands of our classroom work.

The demonstration will consist of a display of all activities in which we participate. It is not a special show that we have prepared to be put on just for the public, but it is actually a look into our classroom. The less capable students will perform in addition to the very able students. We want every student to have the opportunity to show what he can do. Also, we want every one of you to be there to see every student perform. We are sure that you will all enjoy yourselves. Remember the day—Friday, February 6, at 7:30 p.m. The place is the field house. We hope to see you there!

* * *

This talk might be given to a service club in order to secure cooperation in publicizing the demonstration. After being introduced by the president of the service club, the president of the Varsity Club addresses the group:

Thank you, Mr. President. Gentlemen: As in the past, Deerfield High School will again present its annual Physical Education Show. Your organization has been so effective in publicizing our show that we have had to turn people away for lack of seats at the performances. This year, we have arranged to have the show two extra days and instead of the usual single performances, we shall have double performances on Saturday.

It is the hope of the student body that with the proceeds from the demonstration we will be able to install new electric scoreboards in the gym and on the football field. In addition, we hope to install collapsible bleachers at the north wall of the gym. This will add 800 seats, which will certainly come in handy when we host the regional playoffs for the State Basketball Tournament next year. If we publicize this show as successfully this year as we did last, our goal will be achieved. I certainly hope that your organization will undertake this responsibility of selling tickets again this year for the students of Deerfield High School. Your president, Mr. Jones, will inform you at a later date as to the procedure followed last year in regard to selling these tickets.

USE OF MOVIES AND PICTURES

Usually movies and pictures are taken of the demonstration. These may be used to advantage for publicity purposes the following year. The pictures may be used as a display on bulletin boards and in store windows, with an explanation that they were scenes of last year's demonstration. Pictures may be taken of rehearsals so that they may be shown the same year, but this is not practical and involves a great deal of unneeded expense. The pictures of last year's demonstration may be made up into a complete window display in a downtown area or a bulletin board display at school publicizing the coming demonstration.

The motion pictures of the previous year's demonstration may be shown at P.T.A. meetings, service clubs and other functions, not only to promote the demonstration for the present year, but also to sell the physical education program to the general public. The films may be shown to other community groups, clinics, and conventions, if the films are good ones. The old proverb that "a picture is worth a thousand words" certainly will hold true here and will do much to promote and publicize the demonstration without a great deal of extra work after the initial picture taking. The taking of the movies is not a difficult task and can be done by the camera club or any individuals who are interested in photography. It will be money well spent, as these movies may be used throughout the year at various functions where this type of program is appropriate.

The pictures that are taken may be used by the community and school newspapers and the school yearbook. They may be sold for a nominal fee to interested individuals or auctioned off to the highest bidder along with yearbook pictures, as is the custom in many schools at the end of each school year.

The demonstration usually will last over an hour so that a time element in taking the pictures is involved. The director should discuss the taking of the movies with the operator, so that only the essential activities and main events are taken as is the case in athletic events. It is not necessary to show the moving of equipment in between acts. The director may assign someone who is familiar with the demonstration to work with the operator during the demonstration, or at least during one of the rehearsals.

USE OF POSTERS

Posters strategically placed are another means of publicizing the demonstration. Posters may be placed on school and community bulletin boards, in the windows of local stores, and in the school at points that all students pass.

The posters should be colorful in order to draw attention and clever in order to draw comments. Complete information as to what, when, and where should be included on the poster, as well as any other information regarding price of admission, participants, etc. The art department may help in the making of these posters, but the ideas and information must come from the physical education department. (See Fig. 6-18.)

The placing of these posters is important. A great deal of work may go into making them, but they will lose their effectiveness if they are not placed where the general public can see them. The posters should be displayed prominently in conspicuous places.

Teams may be selected to place the posters. Each team member should be told how to approach a business man and sell him on the idea of displaying a poster. The purpose of the posters and the benefits of good will derived by the displayer should be emphasized. The posters should be placed by the student if possible, because if this is not done immediately, there is always the chance that they will be placed to one side and not displayed at all. Usually store owners will be happy to cooperate, as an attractive poster will not detract from any window display he may have. Posters may be placed on counters or hung on walls in restaurants, service stations, and stores. The posters should not depict anything that will cause the displayer any embarrassment or cast any reflections on anyone or anything.

The posters shown at school may be a different type because most of the students will be aware of the demonstration and the date it is to be given. Permission must be obtained from the school principal for the display.

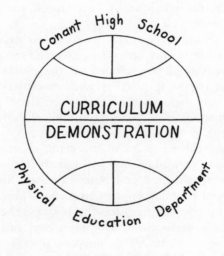

All   Responsible   Citizens
Are   Attending
The

Conant High School

CURRICULUM
DEMONSTRATION

Physical Education Department

Tuesday Evening - October 17th
8:30 -10:00 P.M.
In The Main Gymnasium

Fig. 6-18

CHAPTER VII

The Use of Other Departments
in the Demonstration

Every effort should be made by the physical education department to use other departments within the school to help with the demonstration. This will bring about a feeling of cooperation within the entire school; and with proper recognition, each department will be willing to contribute as much as possible to the success of the demonstration. The demonstration should reflect the work of the entire school program. It should always be the desire of the department to cooperate with other departments insofar as possible, as this will create a feeling of good will with the entire faculty.

The physical education department also needs the help of the other departments in the ways discussed below. Diplomacy should be exercised in every way possible by the entire physical education staff to obtain this much-needed help.

Cooperation must be a two-way street. If the physical education department is constantly asking the help of others, but is not willing to help others in return, bad feelings can result. Subsequent demonstrations could, therefore, become very difficult to produce through lack of help from other departments. It is important to keep the physical education department in proper perspective so that it does not become detrimental to the educational experiences of the student body. It should be an addition to the total learning situation.

There are many departments within the school system that are able to help with the demonstration. Several of these will be discussed, although there may be others not mentioned here that can contribute if called upon.

USE OF THE MUSIC DEPARTMENT

The music department can and should be an integral part of a physical education demonstration. Music plays an important role in the demonstration and can be instrumental in making the demonstration a success. There are many ways in which music can be used and there must be a complete understanding between the music department and the physical education department. This is true because the music department will need to work very closely and in complete harmony with every aspect of the program. A band is the best way to provide the necessary background music to the various demonstrations. Whether or not a full band is used is relatively unimportant as long as the musicians are capable of carrying out the music of the central theme.

Central Theme

To weave the music around a central theme for the demonstration is the first basic task for the band director. He will need to select special music for this or perhaps write some that would be appropriate. While this background music is secondary, it is important because it helps to set the mood for both the performers and the audience. This will require both time and cooperation between the director of the demonstration and the band director.

Acoustics

Acoustics will play a large part in determining the effectiveness of the band. While the band should not be conspicuous, nevertheless, it should be positioned in such a manner that the music can be heard and will aid the performers in their demonstrations and provide cues for their entrance. It would be ideal if an orchestra pit or band balcony were available for this kind of performance.

Introductory Music

In a physical education demonstration, a short introductory musical selection should be played. This music should help to establish the atmosphere of the performance. This part of the program need not be long, but should be spirited and introduce the central theme of the demonstration.

Intermission Music

At intermission time, another short musical program of several numbers can be used to display the versatility of the band. This will allow the audience to relax and yet still be entertained. Completely different types of musical selections can be used and still be appropriate for the occasion.

Special Effects

Timing and the use of special effects for the various demonstrations and techniques will be the most difficult part of the program. All music must start with the performer and end at the same time the performer completes his stunt. Fanfares and drum-rolls will enhance special performances, but it is the tempo of the music and the timing that must be worked out to perfection. This will take practice on the part of both performer and musician. In addition, the music must fit the act; i.e. the rhythm and type of music must correspond to the feat being performed. Some acts will demand a pause or complete silence in order that the performer have complete concentration for his feat.

The director of the band will probably want to practice separately until his musicians know their music. After that, however, it will be necessary to practice with the performers in order to coordinate the timing and rhythm. This is the period of time when the director will have to evaluate his musical selections and possibly cut or add to them. It cannot be mentioned too often that this phase of the program will be most tedious and time-consuming.

Coordination of the Program

While individual acts are coordinated with their musical background, it will also be necessary to coordinate the whole program. If the band has remembered the timing and procedures of the individuals, this may not take too long. However, sufficient time should be allotted to make certain that the entire program is timed and coordinated perfectly. It is most important to remember that the audience has a right to expect the best possible program from the performers and the band.

As the demonstration ends and the crowd is filing out, the band can play the complete theme or excerpts from it. This will help keep the demonstration fresh in the minds of the audience.

Cooperation of Departments

Complete cooperation between the physical education department and the music department is most important to the overall success of any demonstration of this type. There should be an acknowledgment of the significant part the band played in the success of the program.

Size and Type of Band

It shall be the responsibility of the chairman to determine the size and type of band that would be most appropriate for the type of demonstration to be presented. Determination will have to be made as to a full concert band or a smaller group such as a pep band, a clown band, a dance-type combo, or other.

Order of Events

The music director will need a detailed explanation of the events as they will occur, including the narration to be presented by the master of ceremonies. He should be completely familiar with the order of introductions, the high point of each activity, and the ending of each phase of the activity.

Type of Music

Selection of music must be made for various phases of the program. If a pre-performance concert is desired, this music should be enthusiastic and warming and create a gala atmosphere. Provision should be made for music during necessary changes of equipment or scenery. Consideration should be given to post-performance music during the exiting of the crowd.

Preparation of Music

The music director should prepare fanfares, drum-rolls, and the like and coordinate them with the introductions, climaxes, and endings. Certain activities will require special music with tempo suited to the activity.

Type of Dress

A uniform dress will have to be established compatible with the type of performance. The regular band uniform would be appropriate.

Position of Band

A decision will have to be made as to the positioning of the band for the performance. It should be such that all spectators have a clear view of the band, yet it should not be dominant, so as to detract from the performance on the floor.

Rehearsals

Rehearsals of the band should be held separately and then incorporated into individual acts during rehearsals of each act. A full dress rehearsal should be scheduled prior to public presentation of the program.

Singing

The music committee is responsible for the national anthem or any other phase of singing.

Amplification Systems

Acoustics, equipment, and working area must be considered when amplification systems are used for accompaniment. Speakers and microphones must be selected and located with care.

Stage Lighting

In demonstrations, lighting effects are mainly for the purpose of visibility and the concentration of the audience's attention on the stage. Lighting and music must be coordinated to enrich the program.

Additional Considerations

Problems of safety and properties borrowed by the band are additional considerations in stage settings.

1. *Safety*
   In planning sets which include ramps and platforms, it is well to keep in mind the weight of the individual sections and the amount of storage space backstage.
2. *Borrowed Properties*
   It is of utmost importance that borrowed properties be returned no later than the day following the performance.

Choral Music

The music committee must determine if choral music is needed. If it is, the kind or type must be determined.

Records

The director should decide which activities should be performed with records and which with live music. Although the band would play for the actual performance and practice its part in the production, the music should also be available on records; this would facilitate the various components of the production practicing at different times. Having the records would also make it easier for the demonstration to be accurately timed and programmed. In addition, if there are recordings of the music that is to be used, the musicians can learn them faster. This means that the band could be expected to help out and would still be able to work on its own musical productions at the same time.

Circus Band

A circus band or a clown band may be more appropriate for this type of demonstrative activity. Perhaps costumes of red coats with the high collar, blue trousers with stripes, etc., or clown uniforms would be more suitable than a concert type of band uniform.

Coats could be made or rented. Of course, the nucleus of good musicians would "blow up a storm," so to speak.

USE OF THE HOME ECONOMICS DEPARTMENT

Designing and Making Costumes

The home economics department can be very helpful in designing and making costumes for the different acts on the program. This department can also give information on costumes that can be made.

Some of the apparel that the home economic classes can make would be leotards which dancers might wear, flowing chiffon robes, and ballerina tutus. The department might also design and make outfits for clowns. If a take-off on television tag team matches in wrestling is part of the show, comical outfits could be made for the wrestlers to wear.

Cleaning up After the Demonstration

The home economics department may cooperate with the maintenance committee in cleaning up before and after the demonstration and may do certain clean-up jobs which the maintenance committee might not be able to do. Practical experience is a good teacher and the home economics department would benefit by participating in a physical education demonstration. Some of the many jobs which must be done in cleaning up are dusting, removing posters and streamers, and disposing of rubbish (coke cups, popcorn boxes, etc.). The home economics department can enforce the old saying "there is a place for everything and everything should be in its place."

Naturally the home economics department should work in conjunction with the supervisor of the P.E. demonstration. The clean-up group, if it is large enough, can be divided into work crews of four or five students each. Each work crew should have a student leader.

Assign Girls to Help with Coat Check

A chairman should be appointed to take charge of and be responsible for a coat-check committee. The committee should be responsible for material needed, availability of personnel, and janitorial services. The committee should see that proper arrangements for cleaning the coat-check room are made before and after the demonstration. The committee sees to it that there is a sufficient number of hangers in the coat room. Seeing that all articles of clothing are returned is the responsibility of the committee. In case of illness of a committee member, there must be someone ready to take her place.

The chairman should assign a person to be in charge of procuring necessary check stubs for the coat check. This person should be responsible for getting the type of tickets needed. If there is money involved for checking coats, this person should be responsible for counting the money, counting stubs sold, and taking the money to the chairman.

Assign Girls to Act As Hostesses

There should be a number of girls who will act as hostesses for the demonstration. Hostesses will be needed for guiding spectators through the corridors to and from the demonstration and will also be needed during the coffee hour. The chairman should appoint someone to be in charge of getting the refreshments and materials needed such as cups, coffee, sugar, cream, silverware, napkins, and coffee pots. If there is money involved, someone should be responsible for recording the amount and taking the money to the chairman.

The home economics department may serve a buffet dinner to accommodate those helping with and participating in the demonstration.

Assign Girls to Help with Decorations

The artistic touch that some girls have can be a definite aid in making the gymnasium or the stage in which the gym demonstration is to be held a place of beauty and refinement. Of course, it is out of the question to ask girls to hang high or heavy decorations, but their help in designing and decorating props and scenery can be of great value. The decorating committee should be organized with a chairman in charge and an ample number of helpers.

The chairman should have some experience in decorating, show definite artistic ability, be creative, and be able to take and delegate responsibility. She is a good chairman if she can organize her helpers, give them meaningful jobs to perform, and be able to help all her co-workers in their individual tasks. She must make sure there are enough supplies on hand to complete the project on time.

The helpers must also have some artistic ability, be creative, and be able to handle responsibilities. It would be a good idea if the girls segregate themselves from the boys when working, for this will help them accomplish their tasks more quickly. The number of girls needed on the committee depends upon the size of the project and the time they have to complete it. Too many or too few helpers will slow down the work and the result may be an incomplete decoration by show time.

USE OF THE SPEECH DEPARTMENT

Interviews

There are numerous ways in which the speech department can help in the demonstration. The department can arrange interviews with personnel that will be involved. The interviews can be done over the school public address system or at a school assembly. The questions may be worked out ahead of time so that the correct information may be given to the students. Another interview may be tape recorded and used as needed.

Panel Discussion

Panel discussions concerning the demonstration may be carried out, using the assembly or public address system.

Skits

A skit to be given at a school assembly will help publicize the program and create a great deal of interest among the students. The members of the speech department are particularly well qualified for this, and it can be used as an assignment in the speech class. Material for the skit may be obtained from the physical education department in the form of interviews and written material. Much of the written material may also be obtained from the library, another department within the school whose help should be solicited.

An actual script for a skit can be written by the language arts department and later presented in the physical education performance. Such a skit should be closely related to the demonstration and care should be taken that no derogatory lines are used.

Written Articles

Written articles concerning the skits could also be read at the community service club and civic club meetings. Articles which may be read at school assemblies or over the public address system can be prepared by the speech classes as part of assignments in looking up source material.

Debates

A debate may also be arranged by the speech class discussing the advantages and disadvantages of the demonstration.

Tape Recordings

Tape-recorded interviews may be conducted by the speech classes over the local radio station. This interview could involve both faculty and students and would be aimed at pointing out the values of the demonstration.

Instruction of Announcers

The speech department faculty can be used for instruction of student announcers. It can audition various presentations in order to coach the announcers in such things as choice of vocabulary and presentation. The speech department can also help to coordinate the speech patterns with various demonstration areas or skills (such as rhythmic activities). It can give the announcers tips on how to develop speaking ease before an audience.

USE OF THE SOCIAL SCIENCE DEPARTMENT

Historical Facts

The social science department can cooperate in various ways. One is checking on historical facts about various activities in the demonstration, such as where and when such things as folk dances, gymnastics, etc., originated. This information could provide background material for the program announcer.

Supplementary Material

Other assignments for the social studies department could be contributing supplementary material for the programs, making maps and posters for the foyer of the gymnasium, and providing photographs of actual authentic folk groups.

History of Physical Education

A history of physical education could be written by the history class and displayed in the foyer of the gym before the demonstration. This could be tied in with certain historical facts and religious beliefs.

USE OF THE ART DEPARTMENT

Displays at the Demonstration

Very often a display table at the demonstration showing equipment used will provide an interesting attraction for the audience. This type of presentation can be in the form of actual equipment and uniforms used in the demonstration, with artistic lettering and descriptions prepared by members of the art department. Another way in which the display may be arranged is to have sketches of materials used, along with explanations prepared and displayed by the art department.

Making of Posters for Publicity

Posters are vital media for publicizing the coming demonstration. Therefore, it would be wise to gain assistance in the organization and construction of the posters. The members of the art department are a convenient source to consult on this matter.

Guidance for this project could be in the form of advice in preparing the posters and possibly in the actual constructing of the posters. It may be that the art instructor will allow interested students to spend class time for designing and constructing demonstration posters, and give the student class credit. This arrangement would be a big help to the physical education department, and at the same time allow the art students to gain practical experience in this area of art work.

Signs

Posters for advertisement should be made that can be displayed on bulletin boards and in store windows. These posters should be attractive and informative. They can give the name of the demonstration, who is presenting the show, the time, place, and admission price. A list of different events on the program can be shown on some posters. The art department might make useful signs that can be placed in the gym area. These signs could be used to direct the public to rest rooms and emergency facilities. Titles can be made to designate areas of the gym. Signs can be made also to announce the acts as they are presented. If a parade is planned to advertise the demonstration, the art department can be a tremendous asset, by making signs for students to carry in the parade.

Use of Aids for Explaining Demonstrations

If certain portions of the demonstration require an explanation of the activity, the use of charts, diagrams, and sketches might possibly be of assistance. The art department can supply advice for the design and construction of these aids. Suggestions of this type might include illustrations of exercises, sketches showing certain muscles that are used, and charts and diagrams showing diet control.

Use of Special Effects

The success of the demonstration can be enhanced by using special effects and scenery. This vital aspect of the demonstration should not be overlooked. The art instructor will be able to advise and assist in the arrangement of backdrops, decorations, lettering, and special effects such as lighting.

The department should be in charge of decorating the cloth on the backdrops constructed by the wood shop. Members of the art department can paint scenes on the backdrops that would be appropriate to the act being performed. For example, a scene of a pyramid or of the Eiffel Tower may be painted on the background when tumbling stunts or pyramid acts are on the program.

Design of Program Cover

The art department should work closely with the program committee in designing the program.

USE OF THE INDUSTRIAL ARTS DEPARTMENT

Print Shop

The industrial arts department can be responsible for the printing of programs. The department should work in close harmony with the program committee.

TICKETS

The printed ticket should have data concerning the demonstration printed on the front. The ticket should show the name of the theme, date, time, place, and student price. A different color ticket should show the same information but give the adult price. If possible the ticket should be numbered, so an easy count can be made. The tickets should be printed in sufficient quantity to prevent shortage.

FLYERS OR HAND BILLS

Hand bills giving all the vital information regarding the demonstration should be printed by the print shop. This hand bill should show the name of the demonstration, who is presenting it, time, place, admission charge, and a list of the events that will be on the program. There should be enough bills printed so they could be passed out to houses, placed on cars, and put in stores downtown.

INVITATIONS

An attractive printed invitation should be sent to officers of all clubs and organizations in the community. This would be a special invitation to the officers and their membership to attend the demonstration show. The invitation should contain a brief description of the show, the time, place, and admission charged.

THANK YOU LETTERS

The print shop can also print letters to be sent to all individuals and groups that assisted in the many details of presenting a demonstration of this nature. The appreciation of the physical education staff for the efforts of individuals and the community-minded spirit of everyone should be expressed in these letters.

Photo Shop

PHOTO ENGRAVING FOR PUBLICITY

Photographs should be taken of various acts and mats made and sent to newspapers in the area. There should be enough mats made for the newspapers to have enough pictures to run several days prior to the date of the demonstration. Special efforts should be made to get pictures of large groups and many different students to show the scope of the program.

MOTION PICTURES OF THE DEMONSTRATION

A 16 mm. movie camera should be used in making the movie of the demonstration. Enough film should be available to film the entire production. The date will be marked on the film so that a film library of demonstrations can be established. This film could be shown to students, various organizations, and other interested groups. The film would also prove invaluable in studying the demonstration and making improvement in future years.

STILL PICTURES FOR THE PAPER

Still pictures of individuals and groups taking part in the demonstration should be made and sent to area newspapers. The newspapers could then choose the pictures they wanted to use to advertise events on the program. Pictures should also be made of the other persons responsible for the program. There might also be pictures of any unusual apparatus that will be used in the program.

Electrical Shop

SET UP LIGHTING

The electrical shop could be responsible for setting up special lighting effects that might be used in the demonstration. They could consist of spotlights for various performers doing their routines. A color wheel could be set up to shine colored lights on different phases of an act. This would be especially pretty where colored costumes are being used. Lighting effects might be around where only certain parts of the gym are lighted, so that the next act could be arranged unnoticed.

SET UP THE PUBLIC ADDRESS SYSTEM

The electrical shop should be responsible for wiring and setting up microphones in different locations. There should be stand-up or hand microphones according to the needs of the various acts. Care should be taken that the public address system is working, with the volume, tone, etc., properly controlled. The department should co-operate with the dramatics department in handling the public address system.

SET UP AND HANDLE SOUND EFFECTS

The electrical shop can be very useful in any special sound effects that might be needed for the demonstration. These might be carried out separately or in conjunction with the music used in the show. For example, special effects might be needed for the tumbling stunts, pyramid building, flying rings, or square dances. Some types of sound effects that could be used are sirens, auto horns, blank guns, and clapping of two pieces of wood.

Wood Shop

CONSTRUCTION OF PROPS

The wood shop can be very useful in making special backdrops for the various acts. It can build a skeleton frame covered with cloth that would be decorated by the art department. The backdrop for the country dances might be a replica of a hayloft, barn, or a country fence scene. The modern dance could have a stage set built to focus attention on a small area. Some acts might require scenes which include carts for the purpose of moving mats and apparatus readily from the scene to a designated storage area. The shop might possibly build some kind of auxiliary seating to increase the capacity of the gym.

CONSTRUCTION OF APPARATUS

The wood shop can build such apparatus as low parallel bars, teeter boards, and balance beams for the demonstration. A small raised platform might be built for the leader of the exercises in the demonstration.

Metal Shop

CONSTRUCTION OF APPARATUS

The metal shop can make weights and bars for weight lifting. They can also make such items as hand grippers, spring exercisers, and isometric bars.

Mechanical Drawing Classes

BLUEPRINT OF DEMONSTRATION AREA

The mechanical drawing classes can make blueprints of the following items: seating arrangement, including auxiliary seating and how it should be constructed; entrance and exits; routing of the crowd; places of various acts; location of lighting and sound system installations; and prints for the construction of additional concession stands and ticket booths.

BLUEPRINT FOR THE POSITION OF EQUIPMENT

The blueprint should be of the overall layout and should be a complete floor plan showing arrangements for seating the crowd, control pattern, lighting, sound effects, public address system, concession stands, location and storage of all equipment, placement of all backdrops and other staging material, ticket booths, and location of rest rooms and emergency facilities.

USE OF THE DRAMATICS DEPARTMENT

There are various ways in which the dramatics department can actively contribute to a demonstration sponsored by the physical education department. Contributions can be of a direct nature or of a more indirect type, which would include using successful techniques practiced by the dramatics department.

Some of the direct aids which can be provided by the dramatics department are narration for the demonstration, sets and props, lighting, and help with the choreography.

SETS AND PROPS

Sets and props can be used in such parts of the program as folk and square dancing or in special stunts. By providing a background or backdrop, a special effect can be given to the stunts. In using sets and props, care must be taken to keep them relatively simple and not to sacrifice the quality of the performance in order to provide backdrops. Properly used backdrops can immeasurably increase the effectiveness of a skit.

USE OF COSTUMES

Usually the effectiveness of an act, skit, or dance is enhanced through the use of costumes. The costumes owned by the dramatics department can be utilized. Dancers could be attired in costumes for performing a folk dance typical of a particular country. Skits can be made more effective by using costumes, too. Examples would be a hobo skit involving the use of tumbling skills, and a trampoline exhibition using clowns. The use of costumes may well add special emphasis to a particular part of the demonstration.

USE OF MAKE-UP

Another direct aid is in the use of make-up. In some instances the dramatics club can be placed in charge of supplying and applying the make-up. Care must be taken so that this job is done correctly.

USE OF SOUND EFFECTS

People associated with the dramatics club are generally quite familiar with the public address system and other methods of providing appropriate sound effects. Much can be added to the stunts by providing appropriate sound effects, using either a record or tape recording. A fast-moving march can be played during the part of the demonstration devoted to stunts and tumbling. Needless to say, the use of sound effects is especially important to the dance acts. The dramatics department can work in cooperation with the industrial arts department and the speech department in providing these sound effects as the industrial arts department will install the public address system and provide all physical working parts. The speech department will cooperate by writing all necessary speeches.

USE OF NARRATION

The dramatics department can be of special assistance in providing one of its outstanding performers or speakers for narration. Through effective narration, audiences will be able to understand what is happening and will enjoy the demonstration more than if no narration were provided. This can create a lasting influence on an audience, for many people will judge the demonstration on their impression of the narrator. Care should be used to select a narrator who has an adequate knowledge of the activities being performed, although several could be used if available to avoid monotony.

USE OF SKITS

In some instances the dramatics club may even provide a complete skit. Care should be taken to see that the skit is related to the physical education demonstration.

USE OF CHOREOGRAPHY

Aid in choreography can also be provided by the dramatics department. Included here is helping participants enter and exit properly and at the correct times, and aiding the physical education department in making effective use of the entire stage area, if such an area is needed.

USE OF INDIRECT AIDS

Indirect aids from the dramatics department include ideas and techniques adopted successfully by that group. The problem would be to adapt them for use in a physical education demonstration.

USE OF COMEDY

Comedy, so frequently used by dramatic clubs, can be employed in various ways. Exaggerated gestures play an important part in comedy. Skits can be presented using clowns skilled in tumbling activities. Much can be added to a demonstration in this way, because comedy appeals to all age levels. Slapstick tumbling is an excellent means of including exceptional tumblers in the demonstration.

Slapstick comedy can be used in a satire of professional wrestling as seen on television. Performers in this activity would have to be limber and possess skills in wrestling and tumbling. Such a technique could be effective if not overdone.

USE OF THE CLIMAX

Another dramatic technique, the climax, can be used to advantage. This is especially appropriate for such activities as pyramid building, dual stunts, and relay races, where some degree of tension is built up through performing the activity.

ARRANGING OF EQUIPMENT

Since dramatics personnel are acquainted with the arranging of equipment for stage productions, their help would be valuable in presenting a physical education program. This could include advice on equipment placement or the loaning of a stage crew for the program.

SEATING OF THE AUDIENCE

Advice can be obtained concerning the seating of the audience, too. In some cases the dramatic club has a group of ushers who could be used the night of the physical education show. Their advice can also be sought concerning any anticipated seating problems that might arise.

INCORPORATING IDEAS INTO THE PROGRAM

These are just a few of the techniques and procedures used by the dramatics department which can be adapted for use in a physical education demonstration. Before incorporating these methods, proper attention must be given to the program, participants, audience, and activities presented. Used in proper perspective, these techniques can provide for better and more effective physical education demonstrations which will in turn reflect directly upon the success of the required physical education program.

From the theatre department, assistance can also be obtained for swim shows and exhibitions. Lighting effects and scenery supplied by the department can be very useful in dramatizing swimming routines and acts.

CUE CARDS

Since the dramatics department will have had the most experience in the production of stage plays, it could help in making cue cards to be used during skits advertising the demonstration.

USE OF THE DRIVER EDUCATION DEPARTMENT

The Parking of Automobiles

At any public gathering where a crowd is expected, the parking of automobiles will be a major problem. Such may be the case on the evening of a physical education demonstration. Chances are that, if the demonstration is held at the school, the problem of parking has been present before and was handled by policemen and school officials.

To gain added support and interest from the school and community, the possibility of having the driver education and safety classes of the school assume a portion of this responsibility deserves consideration. This will allow more students to take part in the program as well as serve as a vital learning experience for the members of the class.

The students can be used to direct the parking of automobiles into and within the parking areas. It would be advisable for the students doing this work to wear light-colored clothing and arm bands which would make them easily recognizable. At night it would be a necessity for these students to have flashlights to aid in the directing of automobiles. Other matters which should be considered previous to the demonstration date are the preparation of signs to indicate the parking areas, and the arrangements for the loading and unloading of passengers from the automobiles in the event of inclement weather.

Crowd Control

Another problem which the driver education and safety classes can undertake is the control of the crowd going to and coming from the demonstration. Class students may be assigned to direct the people to the demonstration by giving directions and answering questions about the purchasing of tickets, the correct entrance door, etc. It is advisable that the students doing this type of work be identified by name tags or arm bands.

Also, as a class project, the driver education class may wish to designate the safest and most efficient route from the parking area to the demonstration. In doing this, they would check to see that crosswalks have been properly marked, observe any area which may be termed dangerous for pedestrians, and supply student guides to assist the crowd along the way.

Passenger Bus Accommodation

If it is expected that buses will be bringing people to the demonstration it is wise to make preparations for this. There should be a specific area reserved for the parking of these buses while the demonstration is in session, preferably away from the automobile parking area. Also, ample space should be provided for the unloading and loading of passengers. Possibly there would be a need to have students available as guides to offer assistance in the form of direction to the passengers and the bus driver. All information concerning the handling of buses should be compiled and sent to the authorities responsible for sending the buses.

The Role of the School Safety Supervisor

While making preparations for the demonstration, the director may wish to consult with the school safety coordinator concerning the program. It is possible that the director would like to receive suggestions about the safety measures which will be in effect during the demonstration. These suggestions could include an inspection of the equipment and facilities to be used as well as advice on safety procedures for the student personnel during the demonstration. Other matters which the safety coordinator should discuss are the fire exits and extinguishers, smoking areas, adequate first-aid supplies, seating arrangements, and the advantage of having a physician in attendance for the demonstration.

The Role of the Student Supervisor

When the driver education class is helping with the demonstration, there should be an adult acting as supervisor—probably the driver education teacher. The responsibilities he would be expected to assume include the assigning of student helpers to their positions. Also, he should explain to the students what their jobs will include and the exact times that they should be at their posts. Another matter which should not be overlooked is the control of the crowd after the demonstration is over.

Guide Lines

Some of the guide lines to be used by the driver education department in the control of automobiles and the use of police protection may be as follows:

1. Preparing for the demonstration
   a. The lines of authority should be made as definite and direct as possible. Everyone should know where he fits into the organizational pattern. He should know his superiors and his proper relation to them. Good intentions or mere co-operation must be directed.
   b. A headquarters where the committee chairman can respond to emergencies should be established.
   c. An emergency service vehicle should be made available to aid motorists having operational difficulties with their automobiles. If this service can not be rendered, provide a call service to a local service station.
   d. A public address system should be made available inside the school building for:
      (1) emergency calls
      (2) reasons for vehicles to be moved
      (3) automobile lights left on
      It is recommended that this service not be misused, thereby

causing continual interruptions which inconvenience the spectators.
  e. A communications system using telephones, local band or police radios should be made available.
  f . Be certain a special parking area is allotted for doctors, visiting speakers, special guests, and emergency vehicles.
  g. Provide a special parking area for two-wheeled vehicles.
  h. Have a clear zone for loading and unloading passengers at main entrances and exits of the school building.
  i . Letter the parking area entrances and exits with clear directions for motorists to follow.
  j . Ample lighting should be made available for evening demonstrations so that motorists can clearly recognize parking directions. Manual lighting and reflectors are necessary if the parking area does not have lights.
  k. Provide proper apparel for parking lot attendants such as:
    (1) luminous gloves, vests, and jackets
    (2) raincoats
    (3) battery-powered megaphones
    (4) whistles
    (5) flashlights
  l. Fire extinguishers should be checked for readiness in case of emergencies.
2. Receiving traffic
  a. A uniform procedure for parking should be directed by students or custodial attendants.
  b. Vehicles should be parked in such a manner as to allow for a *one-way* traffic flow in the aisles of the parking lot. This could be done by forward-diagonal parking.
  c. Police assistance is recommended to aid the flow of traffic from the main arteries into the parking area.
3. Controlling during the demonstration
  a. A lot attendant should be designated to check for improper parking.
  b. A policeman and attendant should be on duty during the demonstration to protect against theft or vandalism.
  c. Personnel inside the building should be assigned to enforce fire regulations.
4. Departing procedures
  a. Have the local police stationed at intersections and traffic

lights to handle the flow of traffic into main thoroughfares after the demonstration has ended.

b. Students and custodial attendants should assist in directing traffic from the parking areas.

5. Securing procedures

It is the responsibility of this committee to see that the school building and parking areas are secured after spectators, participants, and all those connected with the presentation of the demonstration have departed. Everyone must report to the committee chairman an "all clear and secure" in the area to which he was assigned.

6. Ensuing recognition

It is the final duty of this committee to send a letter of thanks to all those who contributed to the parking and police control. A special letter of recognition and thanks should be sent to the chief of those law enforcement agencies which contributed to the success of the parking and police committee.

USE OF THE BUSINESS DEPARTMENT

The typing services of the business department, combined with the ditto and mimeograph machines, can be used to advantage in the administration of the demonstration.

Duplicating Services

Various possibilities are inherent in the duplicating field which can be used for the demonstration. Following is a list of possible helps: (1) programs—typed, dittoed, and mimeographed; (2) rosters —typed, dittoed, and mimeographed; (3) leaflets—composed, typed, dittoed, and mimeographed; and (4) posters—designed and distributed.

Typing Services

This is the area where the business department may be most helpful. The preparation of letters is a task to which few people look forward. The students in typing class may help with these tasks: (1) preparation of letters and their distribution to local service clubs and civic organizations, such as Kiwanis and Woman's Club;

(2) typing and preparing letters to the various communication media; (3) typing of name tags; and (4) typing and preparing follow-up material concerning the demonstration.

Performing General Administrative Tasks

A production of this magnitude entails a great number of administrative details such as typing of letters, communications, etc. The business department can assign certain students to do this work.

Preparation of Bulletin Boards

Much of the material for use on bulletin boards can be typewritten. The business department can prepare this material and have the students place it on the bulletin boards in an attractive manner.

Record Keeping

Proper records should be kept so that actual expenses may be tabulated and presented to the authorities. These records are invaluable to the administration in preparing next year's budget. The business students can do an excellent job in performing this task.

Using Office Machines

The preparation of financial reports often entails the use of adding machines and typewriters. The business department has these machines available for use and can assign business students to do this work. This is good practical experience for the students and at the same time relieves the physical education personnel of this responsibility.

Administration of Concessions

Concessions may be handled by the school itself or by a group from the business department. This arrangement will give valuable experience to those individuals placed in charge. This should be set up as a business operation and those persons in charge should be held accountable for all financial proceedings.

Preparation of the Budget

It is important in any endeavor to plan carefully in advance the anticipated income and expenditures, or budget. Every situation presents an individual problem. There are basic fundamental principles upon which every budget must be built. No group knows these principles better than the business department. Therefore, it is important that the physical education department enlist the services of this department in preparing the budget for the demonstration. All information relative to income and expenditures should be turned over to the business department, and the physical education department should work closely with members from that department assigned to the problem.

Keeping of Records

Records should be kept of every transaction involving expenditure of funds. The business department, because of the experience of its personnel, will be able to perform this task very well. A day-to-day expense record should be kept.

Final Audit

The business department could be a great help in keeping a record of all expenditures. In case the bookkeeping is done by the department, the director should receive a copy of the final audit at the end of the school year or after a reasonable time for all bills to come in.

Expense Reports

If the business department keeps the records, the director should receive statements at specific intervals to show how much has been spent to date under each budget item and the amount of each budget item unexpended.

Centralizing Accounting

The director, although he may be responsible for the payment of all bills, should not be in charge of the accounting procedure.

The business department may be responsible for placing the accounting procedure on a businesslike basis. This protects the director of the demonstration from charges of carelessness and misuse of funds.

Administration of the Budget

After the budget it adopted, the business department can oversee the expenditures, keep the records, etc. These records must be kept in order that the actual revenue and expenditures may be compared to the amount of money allocated to the demonstration. All bills in this case should be approved and paid through the business department.

Questionnaire for Audience Evaluation
Of the Demonstration

The success of the demonstration will depend upon how well it is received by the audience. Often this is hard to determine by the audience reaction at the time or by talking to individuals after the program. Some people are reluctant to voice their opinion for fear it will hurt their child or hurt the feelings of other people involved in the demonstration. To overcome these problems, questionnaires or checklists may be prepared so that the audience can give its reaction and opinions on an unbiased basis. The business department can take charge of this detail as the facilities needed to perform this task are at its immediate disposal.

USE OF THE MATHEMATICS DEPARTMENT

Although their number is limited, there are effective ways to make use of the mathematics department. Most of the aids offered by this department are those used in the administration of the demonstration itself.

Graphs and Charts

Graphs and charts may be used with good results. Yearly attendance totals can be maintained by the mathematics department to show either increased or decreased interest in the demonstration. Such figures can be made into graphs for presentation to interested people. They may be placed in the lobby or entrance to the gymnasium to illustrate this aspect of the program.

Another display may be made by using charts, scales, and graphs to help explain to parents the position their child holds in relation to others in this particular age group in a designated skill. Each child can be given a number so that the score and name are not easily associated. Other information can include single index numbers to represent the time spent by each individual in practicing for the demonstration and the total cost of the demonstration. An interesting graph or chart may be used to compare performances in different skills, since many times the expression of the performance of a skill in physical education may not have much meaning to the general public.

For example, scores may be applied to the amount of work required for a boy to lift heavy bar bells. This effort could be compared to putting the shot almost the length of a bowling alley. This comparison can be shown in graph form. The department may also show through graphs and charts the results of the testing program carried out by the physcial education department. The result of the A.A.H.P.E.R. (American Association of Health, Physical Education and Recreation) tests in the local school may be compared with that of the nation as a whole. After administering the Kraus-Weber test, graphs may be made to show the percentage of those boys and girls failing in the local school and on a nation-wide basis.

Bar graphs showing the percentage of the student body participating in the various activities can be made. An interesting graph can be made to show how much physical effort is required to do 10 push-ups. Charts showing calorie intake and output from various foods may be made. Comparisons in energy expended in playing a basketball game and walking a certain distance may be made mathematically.

Score Keeping

If competition is a part of the program, the math students can be used to keep score and keep running point totals. This is important in keeping the audience well informed of what is happening throughout the entire program.

Ticket Accounting

In some situations the department can be instrumental in keeping an accurate count on ticket distribution. This does not mean necessarily that tickets should be sold by the mathematics department, but rather that the tickets can be numbered and recorded.

Charting Areas

The math department can be helpful in measuring courts or specific areas for certain activities to be used in the demonstration. Another assignment might be to do a time study of the run-through of the demonstration. This study would insure the smooth running and maintenance of a schedule during the demonstration.

Results of the Kraus-Weber Tests

The following figures and percentages show the results of a testing program done at Brook-Park School. A group of children ranging from grades one through four were tested, under the same conditions and in exactly the same way. (See Fig. 7-1.)

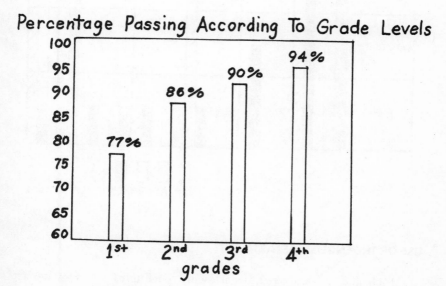

Fig. 7-1

The test consisted of six items which were devised by Dr. Hans Kraus and Dr. Sonja Weber to test muscular strength and flexibility. Experts say every boy and girl from 6 to 16, in good physical condition, should be able to pass these tests.

Of the *280* children tested, *244* passed and *36* failed.
86.8% of the children passed all of the test items.
13.2% of the children failed one or more of the test items.
43% passed all the test items on a nation-wide test.
57% failed to pass one or more of the test items on a nation-
   wide test.

Fig. 7-2 gives another example of a bar graph showing the results of Kraus-Weber tests.

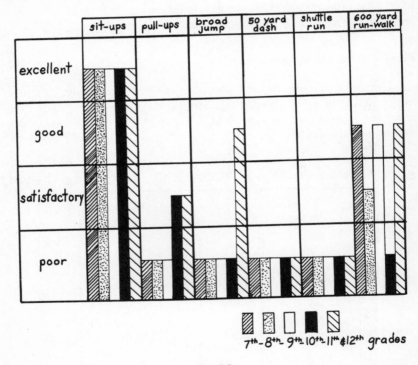

Fig. 7-2

USE OF THE ENGLISH DEPARTMENT

Much like the dramatics department, the English or language arts department can provide important and numerous contributions to a physical education demonstration. Contributions can be of the type not used directly in the production of the demonstration itself, or they can be those used in the actual performance. Those under the former category are more numerous and will be discussed first.

Prior to the presentation of a physical education demonstration, much work must be done if the full effect of the demonstration is to be felt by participants and audience alike. It is in this area that the language arts department can be of the most help. Experiences can be those which provide for practical use of skills learned in language arts class.

Invitations

Students in English classes may write invitations. This can be especially effective at the junior high school level. For example students can write invitations for their parents and relatives. Invitations can be sent to newspaper personnel, teachers, administrators, and the school board. This can be a rewarding learning experience while at the same time aiding the physical education program.

Newspaper articles

Since most classes are concerned with the use of the English language and its written form, this skill can be advanced by preparing newspaper articles telling about the physical education demonstration to be presented. These may be sent to both the community paper and the school paper. Such articles should be prepared in correct form to leave the proper impression.

Posters

Working in conjunction with the art department, the English department can help prepare unique posters advertising the program.

Radio Announcements

Publicity can be aided by having the language arts department write material for radio and school announcements. Such announcements can be used on the local radio stations and in the school public address announcements for the student body.

Skits

A skit promoting the physical education show can be prepared by the English department for presentation to the student body at a school assembly.

Research

The English department can also aid in valuable research for material to be used in the demonstration. This can include looking up sports histories and past physical education demonstrations.

Programs

Writing skills can be put to use in the production and composition of programs. Care must be taken here to work in close cooperation with physical education people so that the proper order of events is presented.

Narrator's Speech

A final aid can be to make sure that the narrator's speech is grammatically correct and is appropriate to the situation. This is especially important because the narrator will probably influence the audience to a great extent. A favorable impression created by the narrator can do much to aid a physical education demonstration. The dramatics department can work with the narrator to help him to make the correct enunciations and movements during the time he is speaking. Both the English and dramatics departments should work closely with the narrator.

Use of Constructive Criticism

Effective use of the language arts department can be made following the demonstration. Constructive criticism should always be welcomed, with the idea that the next presentation will be better than the first. This can be done effectively by having English students write a theme about the demonstration and what they liked or disliked about the program.

USE OF THE LIBRARY

The library can be of help to a physical education department presenting a demonstration. Most of the things done through the library can be done prior to the actual presentation of the demonstration.

Reference Material

Probably the most important service that the library can render is that of providing historical background and research. Students and instructors can make use of the library for reference materials concerning activities or events in the program. This information can be used in preparing for the demonstration and it may be briefly included in a program to give the audience a greater insight into physical education and its implication.

Book Covers

Another helpful service is to provide book covers to be used on the bulletin board. These book covers can be from books on sports and physical education and can add to the interest in the physical education demonstration.

Putting Books on Reserve

Enthusiasm can be engendered by giving students reading assignments from a book or magazine on activities to be included in the physical education demonstration. Insight into the significance of the activity could also be gained in this way. The librarian can help by putting all books dealing with physical education on reserve. This project could be carried out in conjunction with the language arts department.

Displaying of Materials

Assistance can be given by planning a display of materials used in the required physical education classes. Too often, the parents and the public feel that physical education is taught by the instructor's merely "throwing the ball out." The display of books on sports skills and other written materials such as notes, tests, etc, can enlighten the public as to the broad scope of the physical education program.

Librarians are often adept at such arrangement of books for display and in the use of bulletin board materials. A physical education demonstration should be accompanied by displays which accent the knowledge gained in physical education as well as the skills and fundamental procedures used.

Compilation of a History of Physical Education

The library staff may be able to assist by compiling for display a brief history of the physical education department. This summary can include the names of instructors and students, listing some of their accomplishments, and in general provide an overall picture of the department up to the present day. Information for this project may be found in all newspapers, yearbooks, administrative records, etc.

This type of information can serve as an introduction to the program or a time-filler to be used by the emcee.

Research on Authentic Costumes

Some of the activities in a demonstration will require different kinds of costumes. If the activity portrays folk dancing, special costumes which show the native dress of different countries will need to be made. The library may help by checking on the kinds of costumes used in native games and dances.

Provision of Audio-Visual Aids

In many schools, the library is responsible for such things as tape recorders, record players, amplifiers, motion picture projectors, and cameras. The library may then provide for the use of these materials, and the personnel may work closely with the members of the physical education department in helping to put on the demonstration.

Charts, graphs, and diagrams are valuable in presenting various types of data. Data on participation in school activities and data on growth can be searched out by the library and placed on charts or graphs.

Library Assignments on Acitvities

The library may provide for the students from physical education classes to be given library assignments prior to the demonstration. These assignments can deal with the particular activity the student will be performing in the demonstration. The history and the development of rules of the particular activity might be featured.

Director's Use of the Library

The director himself will wish to use the library to seek ideas for different activities that might be used in the demonstration. The school library might also contain information on methods of presenting the various activities.

Making Book Markers

Students in the physical education classes may make simple book markers and give them to the librarian. These book markers can be inserted in each book that is checked out for the two week period prior to the demonstration. This would help to publicize the demonstration. Information on these markers should include the date, time and place of the demonstration.

Collection of Texts and Other Resource Material

A great deal of effort will need to be put forth by the planning committees to obtain all the information necessary to present a demonstration of this type. The library may make a complete collection of physical education texts and other resource materials needed in planning the demonstration. This will include the latest books published in all areas of physical education.

Acquisition of Special Materials and Books

The library may obtain special materials such as costumes, books, etc. by making a special appeal through their avenues of communication. Books may be ordered through the library or borrowed from other libraries which will furnish information which would be pertinent to the demonstration.

Cataloguing of Materials

The library staff may help by cataloguing all types of physical education materials so that they are easily accessible for use in the demonstration. These materials may be used for ideas for various phases of the demonstration or for activities which might be used. Lists of these materials may be mimeographed and made available to physical education instructors that are working on the demonstration as well as to the different committees and their members.

Binding Materials

After the physical education materials which are to be used in the demonstration are gathered together and catalogued, they should be placed in folders so that they will not be torn or soiled. The periodicals should be bound for better wear and kept available for easy reference. Many ideas for the demonstration and all phases of the physical education program may be found in these professional sources.

Reference Books

The library provides easy access to reference books which may help in gathering information on the history of a particular activity which might be used by the announcer. Also this information could be made available for use by other committee members or by instructors teaching the activity.

Posters and Publicity

Illustrations and examples of posters can be provided by the library personnel which will give ideas to those people assigned to the task of making posters.

Publicity is an important aspect of any demonstration. It incompasses many areas.

Bulletin Boards and Displays

The library staff has a great deal of experience in displaying materials of all kinds. Photographs can be used for bulletin boards and window displays. These materials can be given to the library staff to use in these displays along with library materials, films, and filmstrips.

These visual aids are used extensively by schools to present ideas, depict activities, and show the needs of the various departments. The library can search out the type of film or filmstrips that may be used in an assembly program to show physical fitness as an aid to health. The library personnel may take the responsibility of ordering these aids and being responsible for their return.

SUMMARY

These are some of the ways in which the various departments of the school can help in the production of a physical education demonstration. Through the use of these departments, the demonstration can clearly be one showing many of the skills learned in all subject areas. This is especially important so that everyone can participate. When this happens, it is no longer only a physical education demonstration, but a "school" demonstration providing practical use for skills taught in the curriculum.

When asking for the help of these other departments in putting on a physical education demonstration, it should be remembered that they may need help someday. Lasting cooperation can be secured if the physical educator realizes that this is a "two-way" street.

CHAPTER VIII

Description of Activities

The American public will not support an area of education if it does not believe in it, does not understand it, or does not see its results. To the general public, physical education means varsity athletic participation. Therefore, the activities selected to be shown in the demonstration should engender greater understanding in the school and community. They should afford media of communication whereby the public will obtain a better conception of the purpose, values, and outcomes of the physical education program as it is being offered in the schools. The public must be shown that, although they are not identical, there is a direct relatonship between athletics and the physical education courses in the schools.

Therefore, the demonstration should portray the activities which are drawn from regular class work or are a direct outgrowth of the regular physical education classes. Some activities are particularly adaptable for use in a demonstration; it would be natural to select those which will fit in well in the program. They can serve also as a means of communication to the audience.

Since the general public has little understanding of the nature and values of modern physical education, activities should be selected which reflect the philosophy and objectives of the curriculum which is offered. The selection committee should keep in mind that the activity presented must be in harmony with the accepted practice of planning activities according to age level and pupil ability.

The demonstration is one way of putting into practice what is known about a curriculum. In order to have a good demonstration, it is necessary to have good curriculum. The demonstration gives the public a true picture of the actual program as it is being offered in the school. There is, however, no objection to inserting a few special activities where better students may be used in the performance of specialized skills. While it is important to use activities which are taught during the regular classes, it is justifiable to use any special skills certain students may have in order to "dress up" the program and make it more presentable and enjoyable. The objectives of the demonstration should be kept uppermost in mind and an attempt should be made to give priority to activities which are of the greatest value in meeting the needs of the students.

The selection committee should keep in mind that each part of the program must be in harmony with the age level of the group and should coincide with the criteria used in the selection of activities. These criteria should be based on time allotment, facilities available, and pupil abilities.

The activities selected should be those which can be used to advantage in the demonstration, bearing in mind the particular situation in which they will be used. The demonstration should present an accurate picture of the program. The committee must be careful that the public does not get the wrong impression that activities which are particularly adaptable to the demonstration have nothing to do with the daily work. Some such undesirable examples might be marching with flags for show, wearing gaudy costumes, etc.

The activities presented here have been used in physical education demonstrations and are well adapted for them. There is a wide choice of activities; more may be added if needed, depending upon the facilities, personnel, and general adaptability of such a demonstration to the general setup of each individual school.

The activities illustrated are not difficult to perform and can be used without a great deal of practice and long-drawn-out preparations.

CO-RECREATIONAL ACTIVITIES

Co-recreational sports may be presented to the audience in a very simple and interesting way by having all the activities going on at the same time and having the announcer explain each as the activity is being played. The arrangement on the gym floor and types of recreational activities will vary according to locality and floor space. The following diagrams will present typical set-ups. (See Figs. 8-1 through 8-4.)

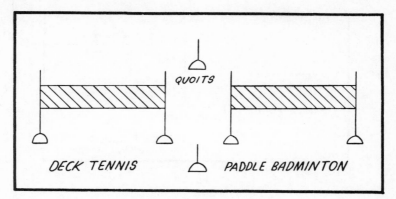

Fig. 8-1

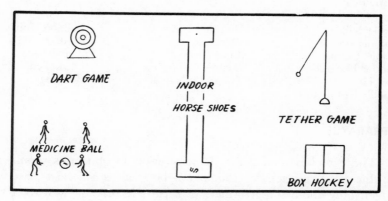

Fig. 8-2

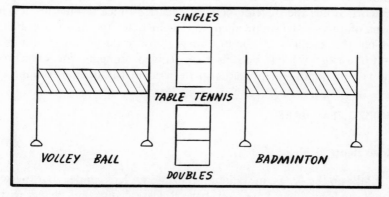

Fig. 8-3

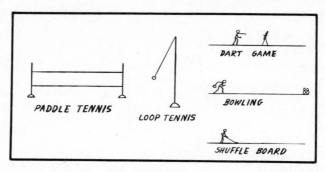

Fig. 8-4

Activities

Volleyball

Badminton

Table Tennis

Indoor Horseshoes

Box Hockey

Paddle Badminton

Shuffleboard

Dart Game

Loop Tennis

Tennis

Giant Volleyball

Balloon Volleyball

Medicine Ball

Tetherball

Deck Tennis

Bowling

APPARATUS

The exercises used for a demonstration in apparatus should not be difficult. This activity should not be used as a special feature in which only the best performers take part. It may be well to station the pieces of apparatus in different parts of the gym floor. The audience should be given to understand that the object of this type of work is not the development of expert gymnasts, but the development of physically sound men and women by means of a system in which the chances of bodily injury are reduced to a minimum.

Following are instructions to be given students for exercise on the various kinds of apparatus to be used in the demonstration.

HORIZONTAL BARS

Knee Hang

Pull up body as in chinning, bringing legs under bar between hands and hooking knees on bar. Release hands and have partner swing you back and forth. At end of swing bring head up, straighten legs, and land on feet. (See Fig. 8-5.)

Fig. 8-5

Rearway Pullover

Jumping to a hang, pull up as in chinning and flex body, bringing feet between hands. Straighten body to an inverted hang. Bring body over bar by pulling with both hands and slightly arching back. Dismount. (See Fig. 8-6.)

Fig. 8-6

Hip Circle

From front support position, bring legs back slightly before bringing them under bar quickly. Shift wrists as body comes under bar. Assume starting position. Body should be kept straight. (See Fig. 8-7.)

Fig. 8-7

Upstart

Jump to bar using ordinary grasp. Pull up as in chinning and at same time bring legs up sharply. Swing to the back, straightening body. On return bring legs up with ankles to bar. Pull down and in with arms, keeping legs close to bar. Do not bend arms more than necessary. (See Fig. 8-8.)

Fig. 8-8

Crotch Circle

Straddle bar, turning body so that it is in cross position. Cross legs and place hands in front of bar. Circle bar in windmill fashion. (See Fig. 8-9.)

Fig. 8-9

SIDE HORSE

Straddle Vault Mount

Grasp pommels and spring from both feet. Spread legs so that left foot passes over neck and right foot passes over croup of horse. Release both hands as feet pass over and land at a support rearways. (See Fig. 8-10.)

Fig. 8-10

Squat Vault Mount

Stand in side position facing horse. For man ordinary grasp jump from floor, flexing legs and bringing knees to chest. Bring feet and legs over saddle and come to side position at a support rearways. (See Fig. 8-11.)

Fig. 8-11

PARALLEL BARS

Front Dismount

Form cross support in center of bars. From long swings, legs and body are brought over bar. Hands are changed on bars and you land slightly crouched yet relaxed position. (See Fig. 8-12.)

Fig. 8-12

Forward Swing Uprise

From upper · arm hang position swing back and forth, pulling down and in with arms. Keep head up and throw out chest. (See Fig. 8-13.)

Fig. 8-13

Back Swing Uprise

From hanging position with bars underneath arms, swing body from shoulders. At end of back swing pull down with hands and lift head and shoulders. Finish in cross hanging position. (See Fig. 8-14.)

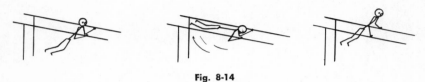

Fig. 8-14

Upper Arm Stand

From cross support bring legs above bars in a cross riding seat with thighs of legs resting on bars. Hands are placed in front of and close to thighs. Bend forward, placing outside of upper arms on bar. Bring legs up slowly, keeping them together. Arch back slightly. (See Fig. 8-15.)

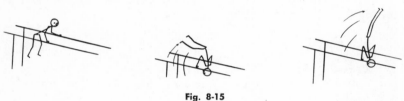

Fig. 8-15

CONDITIONING EXERCISES

These conditioning exercises can be both interesting and instructive. They should be executed in rhythm and in unison. Exercises should be picked which are not too difficult nor too exhausting. Naturally this type is better adapted to girls for a demonstration. The following exercises will portray a group which will fit in very well in the gym demonstration.

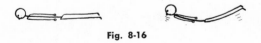

Fig. 8-16

1. Lie on stomach with arms down at side, legs straight and feet together. Lift head and legs, without bending knees, as far off floor as you can. Holding yourself in this arched position, rock backward and forward. (See Fig. 8-16.)

Fig. 8-17

2. Kneel and clasp hands at back of neck. Bend waist from right to left, left to right, and backward. (See Fig. 8-17.)

3. Sit on floor with legs out in front, knees straight, feet a comfortable distance apart. Raise arms upward, close to ears. Hold arms upward by ears as you bend trunk toward floor. Raise trunk, keeping arms by ears and reaching upward. (See Fig. 8-18.)

Fig. 8-18

4. Stretch full length on floor, back down, swing weight on shoulders and balance hips on hands. Slowly bring each leg down to floor behind you. (See Fig. 8-19.)

Fig. 8-19

5. Get on knees. Start rolling over backward until you can throw arms behind back and balance body on hands and feet. (See Fig. 8-20.)

Fig. 8-20

6. Lie flat on back with feet together. Raise left knee, bringing it to chest. Repeat with right leg. (See Fig. 8-21.)

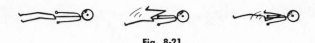

Fig. 8-21

7. Lie flat upon back with feet together. Place hands in back of head, elbows touching floor. Rise to sitting position. (See Fig. 8-22.)

Fig. 8-22

8. Sit on floor with feet wide apart. Fall forward with arms outstretched and reach as far as possible. (See Fig. 8-23.)

Fig. 8-23

9. Lie flat on back with feet together and arms outstretched shoulder height. Bring left leg over right, reaching out as far as possible without removing arms from floor. (See Fig. 8-24.)

Fig. 8-24

10. Sit on floor. Lean backward, supporting yourself with hands. Lift body forward and upward, keeping body and knees straight and resting on palms and heels. (See Fig. 8-25.)

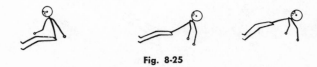

Fig. 8-25

11. Stand erect. Reach upward with arms as high as possible. Bend forward and touch floor with finger tips. (See Fig. 8-26.)

Fig. 8-26

12. Sit on floor with feet spread as far as possible and with knees straight. Using left hand, bend forward and touch right foot. Return to original position and using right hand touch left foot. (See Fig. 8-27.)

Fig. 8-27

MIMETIC EXERCISES

The leader can readily work out his own mimetics from the exercises listed below. Several illustrations are given. The main object here is to have uniformity.

Flag Raising
Discus Throwing
Standing Broad Jump
Sprinting
Punting Football
Batting
Baseball Pitching
Chopping Wood

Shot Put
Boxing
Tennis
Swimming
Tumbling
Rowing
Fencing

Baseball Pitching

Count 1—Step back facing right and raise hands over head to hold ball.

Count 2—Raise left leg slightly, bending body back and holding ball at shoulder height.

Count 3—Bring left leg high in air, bringing throwing arm back for throw.

Count 4—Bring right arm forward in throw, lunging forward on left foot. Follow through.

Count 5—Original position for repeat.

Discus Throw

Count 1—From a stride stand with feet pointing straight ahead, raise both arms sideward to right to shoulder height.

Count 2—Flex both knees and rotate body right and backward as much as possible. Right arm is swung around backward as far as possible. Do this two or three times.

Count 3—Extend legs, especially the right, and pull left shoulder and left arm backward and right shoulder forward, straightening out arm and releasing discus.

Shot Put

Count 1—On first count, face is turned to right, right arm is flexed, and fingers are cup-shaped for holding shot. Weight of body rests on flexed right leg. Left arm is obliquely placed upward.

Count 2—Move left foot to right in front of body with a momentary pause, then move left foot to right in front of body, close to floor and keeping balance with left arm. Repeat several times.

Count 3—Change position of feet in lunge forward, pushing right arm forward and swinging left arm downward.

Count 4—Return to position.

Sprinting

Count 1—Place right foot backward, with body bent in sprinting crouch. Place hands on floor resting on fingers.

Count 2—Raise hips and lean forward on fingers.

Count 3—Drive forward and run in place. Repeat.

Baseball Batter

Count 1—Pivot on right foot to stride left sideward, placing both hands at shoulder as if holding bat.

Count 2—Move bat forward.

Count 3—Replace bat to shoulder.

Count 4—Short step forward to charge position; swing bat forward parallel to floor; strike ball as right heel is raised.

Count 5—Replace left foot and hands to position. Repeat.

TUMBLING

Tumbling is a natural activity and will add considerably to the demonstration. The tumbling activities as suggested here will fit in well. More may be added in the form of the more spectacular, such as diving for distance over kneeling companions or diving for height. Other advanced tumbling feats which may be inserted are the backward somersault with a one half twist, sideward somersault, forward hand spring, forward somersault, layout forward somersault, forward double roll, bird lift, triple dive and roll, etc. Various stunts may be inserted in the program along with the tumbling acts.

Forward Roll

From standing position on mat, take full squat position with knees together, placing hands with fingers forward and palms flat outside knees on mat. Lean forward with chin against chest and push off mat with feet, landing on back of neck. Body is tucked as much as possible. Grab knees with hands as roll is executed. Come to standing position. (See Fig. 8-28.)

Fig. 8-28

Forward Dive

Forward dive is executed in much the same manner as roll except it is preceded by short run. This can be simplified by diving over rolled mats or kneeling companions. (See Fig. 8-29.)

Fig. 8-29

Backward Roll

From standing position on mat, take full squat position as in forward roll. Lean backward, pushing off mat with feet and bringing hands over head. Body is tucked as much as possible. Come to standing position. (See Fig. 8-30.)

Fig. 8-30

Cartwheel

From short run, take off from one foot with both arms raised above head, bringing them down one at a time so that they are in straight line. Swing one leg up and over body with other leg following up in a spread position. Come to stand in spread position. (See Fig. 8-31.)

Fig. 8-31

Head Spring

From short run, approach mat with hands over head, bringing them to mat. Push-off leg is brought off floor by upward action of other leg. Neck is kept stiff and as feet pass over head, push off with hands landing in semicrouched position. (See Fig. 8-32.)

Fig. 8-32

Head Stand

Take sprinting position. Place head on mat, keeping neck and arms rigid. Kick up with back leg, following with other leg. Legs are together with toes pointing upward. (See Fig. 8-33.)

Fig. 8-33

Forearm Stand

Similar to head stand except that forearms are placed on mat instead of hands. Kick-up with back leg is quite the same. Legs are kept together. (See Fig. 8-34)

Fig. 8-34

Backward Handspring

In standing position, place feet slightly apart. Bring arms downward, backward bending into sitting position. Push off with feet as arms pass over head and start their downward swing. Hands touch mat with palms down. (See Fig. 8-35.)

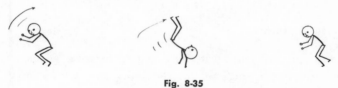

Fig. 8-35

Front Flip

From short run, jump short distance forward and upon landing spring into the air. At highest point bring arms in to body and throw head forward with chin resting on chest, making body as round as possible. As turn is completed, straighten body and land on feet. (See Fig. 8-36.)

Fig. 8-36

Handspring

From short run as in the roundoff, bring hands to mat shoulder-width apart. Throw one leg up and push off with other. As legs near mat, push with hands, landing on mat and facing in same direction as in beginning. (See Fig. 8-37.)

Fig. 8-37

Roundoff

From short run, bring arms forward and upward making a little skip just before landing on take-off foot. Bring hands to side and place them on mat one ahead of the other, shoulder-width apart. As body is brought forward, twist trunk slightly so that you come down on mat facing opposite direction from which you started. (See Fig. 8-38.)

Fig. 8-38

One-Arm Handspring

One-arm forward handspring is executed in same manner as forward two-arm handspring except, that only one arm is used. (See Fig. 8-39.)

Fig. 8-39

Kipup

Take starting position similar to that of forward roll. As back of neck and shoulders touches mat, throw lower portion of body and extend legs in a kipping motion so as to bring body forward and land on feet. (See Fig. 8-40.)

Fig. 8-40

GRAND MARCH

The demonstration may be begun or ended by using the grand march as the opening or closing activity. Everyone should be dressed in uniform gym suits to make the march more effective. The school pep song may be played and sung by the marchers. The march should not be lengthy and should be executed with snap, precision, and enthusiasm.

The following march is simple and yet effective. It is begun by having the girls march in double file on one side of the floor while the boys march on the other side. Each double file is led by a person chosen by the students and faculty as the most outstanding in character, scholarship, and posture. The files counter-march up and down the length of the floor until the boys and girls meet at the front and center and march four abreast off the floor.

Other grand march figures which can be used, but which are more difficult, are:

1. Boys form on one side, girls on the other. The first one of each line leads the line to the rear of the room, and they march down the center in two's; or players may get partners, and march in a circle around the room, coming down the center in two's.
2. The first couple goes to the right and the second couple to the left, third to the right, etc. Couples meet at the back of the room and come up in fours.
3. The three at the right turn right and the one on the left turns left, then come up the center in fours: The three on the left turn left and the one on the right turns right and come up the center in fours.
4. Four's divide into two's, going right and left when the lines meet at the other end of the room, the couples on the director's left forming a bridge by holding inside hands high, while the other line marches under—both lines marching all the time. When the lines meet again at the front of the room the couples

in the other line form the bridges, while the previous "bridges" pass under.

5. When the two lines meet at the rear of the room, the first couple of each line joins hands and skips around in a circle for seven counts. On the eighth count the couple on the left goes under a bridge formed by the couple on the right side, each couple going forward in eight counts to meet the next couple of the opposite line. This is continued through the lines until the leading couples meet again.

6. The couples meet at the front of the room forming four's—the first four turning right, the second four turning left and coming up the center in eight's, halting at the front of the room. Eight's join hands and the leader (on the right of the front line) skips into a winding formation so that attachment can be made with the second line (the last one of the first line joining hands with the one on the right of the second line.) When all the group is in line, players form a circle.

7. Players face each other and grand right and left around the circle to their partners. The leader winds up the circle by leading the players inside the outside circle. When the players are wound up, the leader unwinds outside, walking with back to players who are still winding up.

8. Two circles are formed—girls inside, boys outside. Boys make arches by lifting joined hands. Girls join hands and follow the leader in and out of the arches. Each boy takes the girl on his right and they march around the circle in two's, coming up center in fours.

9. The two inside lines form arches while the outside lines march forward, meet a new partner, and march under the arches.

CORRECTIVE EXERCISES

This activity can best be carried out by placing four boys in a group, working in pairs. Each group should have a placard with the type of corrective exercise it is demonstrating.

Kyphosis

1. Stride sitting position, hands placed loosely in front of body. Fling arms diagonally forward and upward—1. Return—2

2. Sitting position on bench, feet toeing forward.
   Raise arms sideward.
   Arms circling (backward, downward, forward, and up).

3. Sitting position on bench, feet parallel, arms bent upward grasping wand.
   Raise arms upward—1.
   Place wand behind shoulders—2.
   Return—3, position—4.

4. Stride standing, toeing forward, abdominal muscles contracted, arms sideward.
   Bend trunk forward, touching right hand to left toe, left arm extended sideward—1.
   Raise trunk, arms sideward—2.
   Reverse—3-4.
   Repeat all—5-6-7-8.
   Feet together, arms at side, stretch tall—9-10.

5. Kneeling position, sitting back on heels. Bend trunk forward until forehead is on mat near knees, arms extended backward, palms on floor.
   Slowly extend dorsal spine and head, pushing down forcibly with arms rotated to a "west point position."
   Hold—Relax.

Exercises for the Feet

1. Back-lying position.
   Push down on right heel holding foot inverted with toes curled —1.
   Relax—2.
   Same left.

2. Back-lying position, knees separated and bent to chest.
   Straighten both legs upward, steady thighs with hands, curl toes and bend ankles toward body—1.
   Hold stretch—2—3.
   Position—4.

3. Place towel on floor.
   Standing at one end, gradually pull towel toward you by using toes only.

Scoliosis

1. Stride support sitting, head bending sideward. With resistance, sit astride chair and place hands on back of chair. Helper standing behind reaches with right hand from above right shoulder of patient and places left hand on left side of patient's head.

   Bend head slowly left sideward, giving resistance with left hand. Watch for proper sitting posture during exercise.

2. Arch lying, neck rolling forward and backward. Lie on back with arms folded across chest, knees slightly bent, feet apart and resting on floor.

   Lift hips and shoulders off floor to a high arch and roll neck forward and backward. Contact with floor is at feet and head.

PYRAMIDS

The pyramids should be formed carefully and quickly and be well balanced. The movements should be done in unison by counting, for example:

> One for position in the line
> Two for preliminary position
> Three for final position
> Four for holding
> Five for dismounting

The pyramids illustrated are not difficult and are very effective for a demonstration. (See Figs. 8-41 through 8-62.)

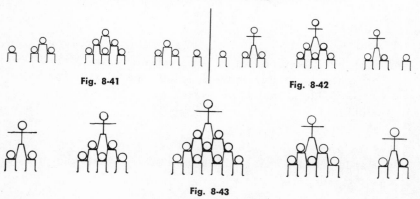

Fig. 8-41   Fig. 8-42

Fig. 8-43

Fig. 8-44

Fig. 8-45

Fig. 8-46

Fig. 8-47

Fig. 8-48

Fig. 8-49

Fig. 8-50

Fig. 8-51

Fig. 8-52

Fig. 8-53

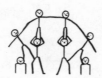

Fig. 8-54

Fig. 8-55

Fig. 8-56

Fig. 8-57

Fig. 8-58

Fig. 8-59

Fig. 8-60

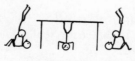

Fig. 8-61

Fig. 8-62

BASKETBALL DRILLS

Basketball Circle Dribbling Drill

The purpose of this drill is to increase ability to dribble a basketball, receive the ball, and pass the ball with one hand—in short, to improve fundamental ball handling skills of the game of basketball. Each boy may dribble the ball as the circle is formed for the demonstration or he may carry it as he runs into position. If more boys than basketballs are used, the extra boys should be spaced between the boys with the basketballs. They will receive the pass from the boy with the ball and then pass on to the next.

The leader designates the number of bounces to be taken, gives the command to begin, sets the pace, and then says "BOUNCE and CHANGE." Each dribbler then passes the ball to the man on his left. The man receives the ball, picking up the bounce, and continues right on in the same rhythm of the dribble or pass. This puts stress on the ball's being dribbled. It also helps to develop one-handed control in passing or handling the ball in short-bounce passes. The boys put one hand behind their backs to emphasize ball control. It is also good to learn to use both hands in this drill—i.e., run drill left-handed or right-handed, since game situations may call for use of either hand in receive-dribble-pass sequence; or just one-hand receive-pass may be useful. Various types of balls may be used to improve touch control as well as to set different patterns.

Basketball Dribbling Drill Diagram

O—Represents boy with basketball.
X—Represents boy without basketball. He will receive pass for drill to be continued.
→—Represents path of ball around circle.

Fig. 8-63 shows a diagram with each boy having a basketball.

Fig. 8-63

Fig. 8-64 shows a diagram for extra boys spaced in between boys with basketballs.

Fig. 8-64

Star Drill—Ball Handling

The purpose of this drill is to improve ball handling ability. Two groups enter from opposite ends of the floor. The center circles have two boys in each of eight places around the circle's edge. The outer circle will also have two boys in each of eight places in its circle's edge. More boys may be used, once the drill is learned.

The balls are passed to the boys in the outside circle and then to the inside circle, always passing to the right. This forms a star as the balls travel around the circles. If fluorescent lighting can be arranged, iridescent material can be put on the balls. With a darkened room, this will present a very colorful and effective display. It would also be very effective, when learned well, to add a ball for each line in the center circle and also one for the outer circle. This creates a double amount of movement and requires a great deal of reflex training. The drill may be run passing either to the right or the left. It may also incorporate bounce passing, chest passing, or other types. The boys may move from the inside circle to the outside circle by moving to the line to which they pass the ball.

Smaller groups may work this in the same pattern as shown in the diagram, in order to include more people. (See Figs. 8-65 through 8-70.)

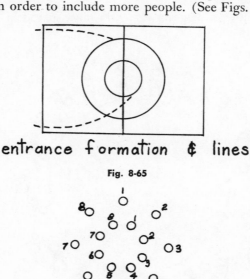

entrance formation ¢ lines

Fig. 8-65

Fig. 8-66

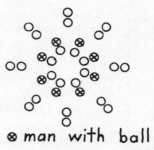

⊗ man with ball

Fig. 8-67

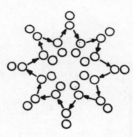

Fig. 8-68

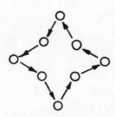

Fig. 8-69

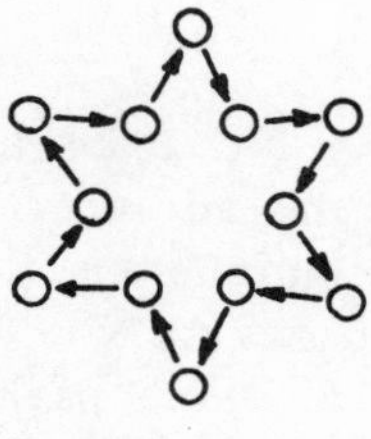

Fig. 8-70

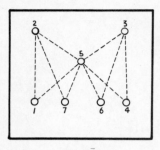

Fig. 8-71

Fig. 8-71 shows a diagram for five balls. The drill starts with 1, 5, and 3 each in possession of a ball. On the first rotation, 5 passes to 2, 3, to 4, and 1 to 5. On the second round, 2 will pass to 7, 4 to 5, and 3 to 6. On the third rotation 6 passes to 3, 7 to 5, and 5 to 2. On the fourth rotation, 2 passes to 1, and 5 and 3 exchange passes. This gives the balls to the players who had them to begin with, and the rotation may be continued.

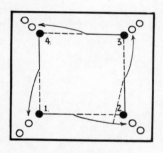

Fig. 8-72

No. 1 passes to No. 2, follows his pass, and drops in behind the receiver. No. 2 flips him a short pass and immediately cuts away as if driving for the basket. No. 1 quickly returns the ball to the cutter. No. 2 then passes to No. 3 and follows his pass for a return flip from the receiver. This is repeated.

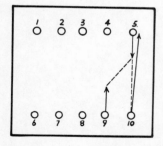

Fig. 8-73

No. 10 begins drill by passing to No. 5 who advances to meet the ball. No. 10 continues on and takes No. 5's place. No. 5 passes to No. 9 who advances to meet the ball. No. 9 passes to No. 4. No. 9 continues on, taking No. 4's place. This is repeated.

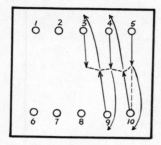

Fig. 8-74

No. 10 begins drill by passing to No. 5 who advances to meet the ball. The ball is given back to No. 10 immediately. No. 10 then passes to No. 4 who advances to meet the ball. No. 4 then passes to No. 9, etc. No. 10 will take No. 5's place, No. 5 will take No. 10's place, etc.

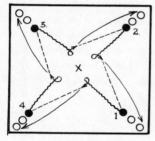

Fig. 8-75

No. 1 starts the drill by dribbling to the center, pivoting, and passing to No. 4. No. 4 then dribbles to the center, pivots, and passes to No. 3. In each instance, the passer follows his pass and takes his place at the end of the receiver's line.

MASS CALISTHENICS

Formal exercise still has a place in physical education and lends itself well to the demonstration, as it is interesting to the spectator to watch the exercises being done in unison. Music may be used or the instructor may use a count. In any event, care should be taken to keep all participants in unison. One person "out of step" will spoil the entire effect of the activity. A certain amount of explanation is necessary and important.

While the instructor is addressing the audience, the students should be lined up in a designated formation, at attention and listening to the address. After the address, the instructor leads the class in the following exercises:

1. Side-straddle hop. This is a two-count exercise. The student is standing relaxed, arms at sides, feet together. On the first count the student jumps spreading his legs and simultaneously swinging his arms overhead. On the second count he comes back to the starting position. (See Fig. 8-76.)

Fig. 8-76

2. Rowing exercise. This also is a two-count exercise. The student lies prone on the floor, hands directly over his head, feet together. On the first count he lifts his body to a sitting position and simultaneously brings his knees up so that his body from the waist up forms a 90-degree angle with the floor. His knees are as close to his body as possible. He assumes his original starting position on the count of two. (See Fig. 8-77.)

Fig. 8-77

3. Bend and reach exercise. This is another two-count exercise. The student is standing, arms and hands straight overhead, legs spread shoulder-width apart. On the first count the student bends at the waist, throws his arms between his spread legs, and touches the floor as far back as he can reach without bending his knees. On the second count he resumes the starting position. (See Fig. 8-78.)

Fig. 8-78

4. Squat thrust. This is a four-count exercise. The student is standing, arms at sides, feet shoulder-width apart. On the first count the student squats, placing his hands on the ground between his knees. On the second count the student supports his weight on his hands and arms and thrusts his legs out to the rear so that his body is as closely parallel to the floor as possible. His feet should be together. On the third count he returns to his squat position, hands between his knees on the floor. On the fourth count he rises to the starting position. (See Fig. 8-79.)

Fig. 8-79

5. Squat bender. This also is a four-count exercise. The student takes his position, feet shoulder-width apart, arms at his sides. On the first count he squats and extends his arms in front of him. On the second count he assumes his starting position. On the third count he bends at the waist, touching his toes without bending his knees. On the fourth count he assumes his starting position, hands at his sides, feet shoulder-width apart. (See Fig. 8-80.)

Fig. 8-80

6. Push-ups. This is a two-count exercise. The student takes a position with his weight resting on his legs and arms and with his body as nearly parallel to the floor as possible. The back should not be bent. On the first count the student lowers his body so that his chest touches the ground, keeping his body very straight and without bending his back. On the second count he assumes the starting position. (See Fig. 8-81.)

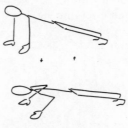

Fig. 8-81

7. Body twists. This is a four-count exercise. The student lies on the ground and lifts his legs in the air to form a 90-degree angle with his body. On the first count, legs together, he moves his legs, first to the right so that they are 6 inches from the ground. On the second count he brings them to the starting position. On the third count, legs together, he moves them to the left so that they are 6 inches from the ground. On the fourth count he returns to the starting position. While moving his legs to the right and left it is of the utmost importance that the student keep the 90-degree angle that is formed by his legs and body from the legs up. (See Fig. 8-82.)

Fig. 8-82

For most impressive results, the exercises should be performed in a military manner upon a given count. For example, while the students are at attention, the instructor says in a loud, clear voice so that all can hear, "At normal cadence, 10 repetitions of the side-straddle hop. Starting position—move!" At this command the students move in unison to the starting position of the exercise. On the command, "ready—begin!," the students should shout out along with the instructor the predesignated count that corresponds with the movement they are making. By this time there should be no doubt in the student's mind of how or upon what count he should perform a certain movement, because through rehearsal and practice this should have been taken care of. At the end of the 10 repetitions, all students should stop exercising simultaneously and on the command, "position of attention - move!," should assume the proper position.

The following exercises should be performed in the same manner. The military commands and the exercises performed by all students in unison make for uniformity, neatness, and a good all-around impression on the spectators. (See Fig. 8-83.)

Fig. 8-83

Exercise 1

Starting position—attention.
Count 1—feet astride, arms raised sideward and overhead.
Count 2—feet together, arms sideward and down to sides.

Exercise 2

Starting position—hands clasped back of head.
Count 1—trunk to left.
Count 2—trunk to center.
Count 3—trunk to right.
Count 4—trunk to upright.

Exercise 3

Starting position—deep knee bend, hands on floor, in front of
    feet.
Count 1—extend legs backward, keeping arms stiff.
Count 2—bring feet to starting position.
Halt—given as legs are extended.
    1—bring legs to starting position.
    2—position of attention reached.

Exercise 4

Starting position—feet astride, hands on hips.
Count 1—bend forward, head up.
Count 2—return to erect position.
Count 3—bend backward.
Count 4—return to erect position.
Halt—given in erect postion.

Exercise 5

Starting position—lying on back, hands clasped back of head.
Count 1—raise legs above head.
Count 2-3-4—lower legs in three slow counts.
Halt given as legs and heels touch ground.

Exercise 6

Starting position—lying on back, hands clasped back on neck,
    legs straight.
Count 1—raise feet 6 inches off floor.
Count 2—spread legs apart.

Count 3—bring feet together.
Count 4—lower feet to ground.

WRESTLING

Wrestlers should be paired up according to size for demonstration purposes. The boys should demonstrate the following prerequisites prior to demonstrating the different pinning combinations—getting behind your opponent, riding, breaking him down.

The following are examples of the way in which class instruction can be given in drill form. These commands of execution are of one take down, one escape, one break down and ride.

The Single Arm Drag

Commands:
    1—Section A.
    2—Right hand on opponent's neck.
    3—With left hand grasp opponent's right wrist.
    4—Right hand under opponent's right arm.
    5—Pull, drop your right hip, and grab opponent's right knee.
    6—Drive into opponent and flatten him down.

The Side Roll

Commands:
    1—Section A, underneath in referee's position.
    2—Pivot on your left knee.
    3—Plant your right foot out in front.
    4—Be sure to have a good base.
    5—With right hand grasp opponent's right wrist.
    6—Swing through with your right knee.
    7—Drive your legs out perpendicularly.
    8—Roll toward opponent's legs.
    9—Take an inside crotch with your right hand.
  10—Pin him with a cradle.

The Crotch Pry Break Down

Commands:
    1—Section A, riding, in referee's position.
    2—Place right knee behind opponent.

3—Lift up on opponent's inside right thigh.

4—Pull on opponent's left arm and heave him down.

5—Keep on your knees; control your balance.

6—Let opponent make next move.

7—Grasp his left wrist and drive forward.

8—Catch deeply around his waist with your right arm.

9—Ride him; keep your weight distributed.

DANCING

Dances add color and a great deal of interest to any demonstration and should be scattered throughout the program, not bunched. Advantage may be taken of special talent among the students and one or two special dances presented. Special abilities are not needed for dancing, which is the oldest of the arts, and so the majority of dances presented should involve as large a number of the students as possible. Rhythm dancing, folk dancing, acrobatic dancing and tap dancing, find their place in any program.

In rhythm dancing, anything simple can be developed by the class, demonstrating different tempos—4/4 time, 3/4 time, 2/4 time, 6/8 time; walking, running, leaping, skipping—all to music.

Folk dances are simple and adapted to large groups. Choose any that can be mastered without too much effort by an entire group. There are any number of folk dance books on the market and the instructor usually is familiar with a number of them. Old favorites include the Irish Lilt, Highland Fling, Oxen Dance, Swedish Dance, Dutch Boy and Girl Dance, Russian Dance, etc.

Acrobatic dancing can be adapted to various types of music, depending on the skill and experience of the teacher. Tap dancing and clogging are very popular in physical education classes and find their place in practically every program. Here, too, the dances presented can be selected from the instructor's own repertoire. Many instructors develop their own tap and clog dances and fit them to a current popular tune. Even though tap and clog dances are probably the most popular with the students, in a demonstration other types of rhythms and dances should be included. Social dancing classes can present a few short basic steps showing technique of instruction and should include both boys and girls. Specialty dances include the use of jumping ropes, balloons, balls, scarves, flags or pennants, etc., and can be taught to groups.

Square Dancing

For downright fun and sociability nothing can equal a Square Dance. It is the one occasion which gives everybody a chance to "get into the act." It is as typically American as our free way of life. (See Fig. 8-84.)

Fig. 8-84

Since it takes both boys and girls to put on a demonstration of this kind, the boys' and girls' physical education classes will have to be combined to demonstrate the activity.

The object of having this activity in a high school program is to provide the opportunity for every boy and girl to participate in a skill that adds stature to the social life of the individual while uniting him with a group.

In putting on this demonstration, four squares, which will consist of four couples in each square, will be sufficient.

A boy or the physical education instructor can do the explaining of the activity to the audience while the students are performing.

Each step of the demonstration and how it is to be executed are explained in detail.

The boys and girls will come out onto the floor and form four squares. The instructor or a student can describe to the spectators the various positions and moves that are basic in a square dance.

The girls should dress in long, old-fashioned cotton prints, and the boys should wear tight breeches and bright silk cowboy shirt to add a little color to the demonstration. Each person will wear tennis shoes to avoid marring the floor.

The first thing that should be explained is what is a set. A set consists of four couples who face the center of the square. Each boy stands with the girl at his right side. The head couple at HOME BASE stand with their backs to the caller.

It should be explained here that all the while the instructor is telling the people the various movements, the students can be illustrating them. This can be done to music.

Next can be explained what is meant by corners. For the boy, the girl on his left is his corner, and for his partner the boy on her right is her corner. The couples are numbered one, two, three, and four. The first couple, as has been mentioned, is the one with their backs to the caller. Couple number two is to their right, couple number three is directly across from couple number one, and couple number four is to the left of couple number one.

Next is explained what is meant by progressing in a set. This means to go visiting. Couples travel in a counterclockwise direction. Couple number one begins the figure. They move to the right to visit couple number two. After dancing with couple number two, couple number one moves on to couple number three, then to couple number four, with the same procedure followed each time.

"Honor your partner" means to bow to your partner. The boy turns toward his right, bending slightly from the waist as he bows to his partner. The girl turns toward her left and curtsies to her partner.

Next can be explained what is meant by eight hands around. This calls for all people's joining hands and circling to the left, or circling in a clockwise direction. If the caller says, "Back the other way," they just change direction to counterclockwise.

"Swinging your partner" is done as the boy and girl faces each other. The right arm of the boy circles the waist of the girl, and the girl puts her left hand on the boy's shoulder. The girl's right hand is clasped by the boy's left hand. In swinging, the girl stands with weight forward on the right foot, pushes with the left foot, and pivots on the ball of the right foot, leaning away slightly.

To demonstrate the Allemande Left the boy and girl turn away from each other and clasp left hands with their corners, walking around in counterclockwise direction until they have made a complete round, and return to their original place. Usually following this will be the Grand Right and Left. The boys will walk in a circle, counterclockwise, and the girls walk in a clockwise direction. The partners will face each other, clasp right hands, and walking past each other, give the left hand to the next person, the right hand to the next, the left hand to the next until they return to their original place.

The last thing to demonstrate will be the Promenade. Facing in a counterclockwise direction, standing side by side, partners cross arms, joining right hand with right hand, left hand with left hand (skater's position), and march once around the set until reaching original places.

Having completed the explanation as students demonstrate the steps, the instructor should step away from students and a complete dance should be done.

The music will have to be supplied by records. There could be a caller if there is an experienced caller among the student body; but if this cannot be done, then records can be supplied with the caller's announcements on the record.

Remember, Square Dancing really moves along, so it is important that the people putting on the demonstration have some skill in it.

This demonstration should last no more than five to eight minutes because there will be other activities after this one.

The Virginia Reel

Players form two lines, facing each other—boys on one side, girls on the other. Players join hands down the lines and with four steps march toward their partners, make a bow on the last step, then back to original position with four steps. This is repeated. Players drop hands and do the following:

1. Meet partners in center, swing around with right hands joined and back to place.

2. Swing around with left hands.
3. Swing around with both hands.
4. Do-si-do—walk around partner passing right shoulders.
5. Do-si-do—passing left shoulders.

Leaders join hands and slide down center and back. Each one leads his own line outside to the foot of his line. There the leading couple form a bridge and the couples pass under. The leading couple stays at the end of the line while the first couple under the bridge become the leading couple. This continues until the first couple get back to the head of the line. There may be two to five leading couples if there are a great many players or the players may be divided into groups of ten or fifteen couples.

Virginia—Hunt the Squirrel

"First couple lead out for the squirrel"; the first couple bow to the couple on their right.

"Hunt the squirrel"; the lady goes around the lady and the gentleman around the gentleman, then the lady around the gentleman and the gentleman around the lady.

"Swing your opposite," the gentlemen swing the ladies with both hands, and following this procedure the first couple proceed around the squirrel.

This movement is repeated progressively around the square until the head couple have returned to place. Meanwhile the other couples are called out successively until the last couple have returned to place. The call used to start each couple, after the first, is: "Next couple out."[1]

Lady Round the Lady

"First couple lead out on the head"; the first couple balance to the couple on their right. The calls are chanted with the music and the action suited to the words.

"Lady round the lady and the gent go slow."

"Lady round the gent and the gent don't go."

The lady circles the opposite lady and the gentleman follows her slowly; the lady circles the opposite gentleman, completing a

---

[1] Journal of Health and Physical Education, September, 1947, "Square Dance Figures of Tidewater, Virginia," Carolina B. Sinclair.

figure eight, and meets her partner as he completes his circle around the lady.

"Join hands and circle four."

"Break and swing your partner round the floor."

The two couples form a circle moving clockwise, break and partners swing, the first couple moving on to the next couple.

The figure is danced continuously until all couples have returned to their places. Each couple in turn responds to the call: "Next couple out."[2]

Kansas (Quadrille Formation)

I. A. Couples 1 and 2 only.
        Form a circle and swing once around.
        Grand right and left in group of four.
        Join hands and circle right to place.
    B. Everybody does this part:
        Swing your partner.
        Allemande left (swing corner).
        Swing your partner.
        Grand right and left (until you meet your
            partner across circle).
        Promenade to place.

II. A. Couple 1 repeat I,A with couple 3.
     B. Repeat I,B.

III. A. Couple 1 repeat I,A with couple 4.
      B. Repeat I,B.

IV, V, VI. Repeat with couple 2 as leaders, etc.

Calls used:

"Jump up and never come down
Swing your partner round and round."

"Ice cream and lemonade
Grab a partner and promenade."

"Swing your man, swing your pa,
Swing the man from Arkansas." (Partner)

[2] *Ibid.*

Alabama—Four Hands Crossed

First and second couples make a small circle facing in. Others in the circle stand and watch.

I. Men join both hands across circle. Ladies join both hands below men's hands. Circle around to the left once.

II. "Ladies bow." Ladies bow heads and men lift joined hands over ladies' heads and put arms in back of ladies. Circle around to left once.

III. "Gents bow low." Men bow and ladies' arms go over their heads and around the back. Circle around to the left once.

IV. "Swing your corner."

V. "Swing your partner."

VI. "Couple up."

VII. "Do-si-do."

VIII. "Swing your partner." Couple number 2 swing back to place while couple number 1 swing on to dance with couple number 3.

X. Repeat until each couple has been around the room.[3]

ARCHERY

This activity will prove both interesting and entertaining but will necessitate some planning and work. It may be conducted as a contest between the girls and boys, different groups of girls or boys, mixed groups, or classes. To make it more interesting, place different colored balloons on the target. A running score should be kept and announced at frequent intervals. Do not let it drag or last too long.

ROPE TUG OF WAR

Teams line up facing each other, grasping own end of the rope, with tape on the rope directly over the center line. At the starting signal all men pull, and the team pulling the middle of the line over the six-foot restraining line wins. (Restraining lines six feet apart on either side of the center line should be drawn on the floor.) If neither team succeeds within a given period, the side having the center of the rope on its own side wins. (See Fig. 8-85.)

[3] American Country Dances by Edythe Saylor, Journal of Health and Physical Education, October, 1934.

Fig. 8-85

GOLF TECHNIQUES

There are three types of grips that are used most commonly in golf. The natural grip is one in which the hands are placed on the club independent of each other, similar to the position of a baseball player's hands on his bat. In the overlapping grip, the little finger of the right hand is lapped over the forefinger of the left hand and the thumb of the left is extended down the shaft, so that the pad of

Fig. 8-86

the thumb of the right hand rests on it, while the thumb of the right extends obliquely across and around the shaft, coming in contact with the tip of the right forefinger. The interlocking grip is the same as the overlapping except that the little finger of the right hand interlocks with the forefinger of the left hand. (See Fig. 8-86.)

In demonstrating golf techniques, take the following material in order because it more nearly follows the order of play. The technique of using each club cannot be thoroughly discussed here. However, in a demonstration it will be more important to show the use of each club in order. It may be well to show the stance along with proper swing technique. Place rubber mats on the floor to drive from, using cotton balls.

Driver	Mid Iron	Mashie Niblick
Brassie	Mid Mashie	Niblick
Spoon	Mashie	Putter
Driving Iron	Spade Mashie	

ROPE JUMPING

There are many drills which can be worked out in rope jumping. It is well to follow a definite idea or pattern so that the audience can follow along as the pattern unfolds itself. To begin the drill illustrated here have the boys' group enter from one corner of the gym and the girls' from the opposite corner. Both single lines will meet in the middle of the gym as shown in Fig. 8-87, and each person will be jumping his rope in rhythm with the person in front of him. The first girl and boy meet and go directly up the center of the floor. As they approach the end of the gym the girls will go to the right and the boys to the left.

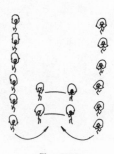

Fig. 8-87

After reaching the end of the room, both girls and boys will turn, facing each other about three and a half yards apart, thereby forming partners, as in Fig. 8-88. When all couples are facing each other, ropes are placed in jumping position. The odd-numbered couples will then jump forward doing a do-si-do and return, followed by the even-numbered couples' going through the same procedure. Odd-numbered couples will then move forward and jump a circle around each other and back in place.

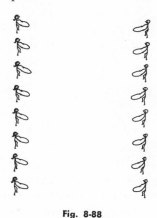

Fig. 8-88

After all are back in place, the boy on the end hands one end of his rope to his partner and they begin turning the rope. While this is being done, couple 2 jump around the outside of couple 1, stop jumping, and run through the rope being turned by couple 1. After couple 2 have run through the turning rope, they do the same as couple 1. This procedure is continued until the last couple have run through all the turning ropes. It should be emphasized that the ropes must be turned in rhythm and the couples must not stop once they have started through. The couples turning the ropes should adjust the turning so as to help the couples running through. If there is a miss the couple should take their place at the end of the line.

After the last couple have run through, all ropes are halted. The first couple jump the rope together, keeping time to the music. When couple 1 have jumped the last rope they go to the left, swinging the ropes to the side, as in Fig. 8-89. The next couple follow, but go to the right instead, etc., with each couple alternating to the left and to the right. This makes two double lines moving up

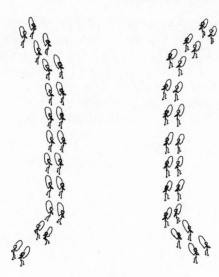

Fig. 8-89

each side of the floor. Upon reaching the end of the floor, couples 1 and 2 will turn toward the center, making a group of four. The four abreast begin jumping in unison down the floor followed in the same fashion by couples 3 and 4, etc. (See Fig. 8-90.) When she has

Fig. 8-90

reached the end of the floor, the girl doubles the rope she has, holding the handles in the left hand. She then takes in her right hand the loop which the girl on the left gives her. After the last girl has completed this she leads the group to a large single circle using the square dance step. After this is completed, all stop and take a jumping position. All then jump forward at a given signal. One half of the girls then jump backward as in Fig. 8-91. One girl takes her

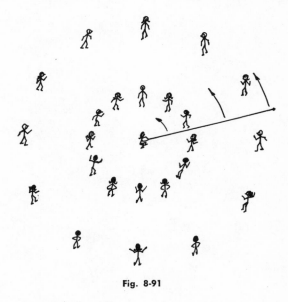

Fig. 8-91

place within the smaller circle and starts swinging her rope in a large circle close to the floor forcing the participants to jump over the rope as it passes beneath them. The smaller group then jumps back forming one large circle and an exit is made by crisscrossing with boys and girls in the same lines. (See Fig. 8-92.)

In Fig. 8-93, an equal number of boys and girls enter the gym from opposite corners. Both single lines meet in the middle of the gym. They then turn and go directly up the center of the floor, each jumping his rope in unison with the person in front of him, in cadence and in time to the band music that is being played. The boy and girl in the lead go to the end of the court so that the entire group is well spaced on the floor, as shown in the diagram. As the leaders reach the end of the court, each person turns to the outside; this will leave the boys and girls facing in the opposite direction with

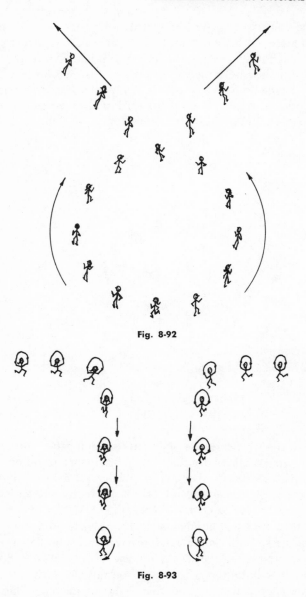

Fig. 8-92

Fig. 8-93

enough space in between so that the ropes do not touch during the routines, as in Fig. 8-94. During all these maneuvers all persons are jumping in time to the music. At a given signal the music and jumping are stopped, and the groups are made ready for the following

Fig. 8-94

routines which are all done in cadence and in time to music. The rope jumping should stop at the end of each routine. Students should then proceed according to the following instructions:

1. Cross the arms at the elbows and turn the rope with the hands far out to the sides of the body. Do this 50 times in unison before proceeding to the next routine.
2. Alternate, putting the heel of one foot out in front as the jump is carried out. This must be done in unison, starting with the heel of the right foot extended on the first jump on a designated signal. Alternating from right to left, the jumps may be continued as many times as desired.
3. Place the left foot in front of the right foot. Using a rocking motion on the jump, hop on the front foot, then on the back foot for a designated number of times. After the number specified has been completed, place the opposite foot forward and repeat the routine.
4. Place the feet together. At a designated signal, jump placing the feet apart approximately two feet parallel to the body. On the next jump bring the feet together to the original position. Alternate this routine for a specified number of times.

5. Stand on the right foot with the left leg extended and big toe pointed forward. Hopping on the right foot, tap the little toe of the left foot on the floor in unison with the other jumpers and in time to the music.

6. Stand on the right foot with the left foot forward. Hop on the right foot swinging the left foot forward. Do this in time to the music and in unison with the rest of the group a designated number of times.

7. Stand in place. While jumping in place, in unison, and in time to the music, turn one-quarter turn to the left with each jump. Do this until three complete turns are accomplished.

8. Stand in place on one foot with the other foot extended behind. Tap the toe of the back foot at each hop, in time to the music.

9. Stand on both feet with ankles crossed. Hop in time to the music using both feet.

10. Stand with both feet together. Hop or jump in unison and in time to the music, keeping the feet together.

Fig. 8-95 shows a different version of a rope-jumping drill, with the girls and boys entering the gym in the same way as in Fig. 8-93 and jumping side by side. As they reach the center of the court,

Fig. 8-95

the boys turn to the right at a 90-degree angle and the girls turn left similarly. This procedure is carried out until the last person reaches the position where the first person made the original turn.

At a designated signal the boys proceed in a wide arc to the right and the girls to the left until a complete turn is made. (See Fig. 8-96.) Each group at this time moves forward to the end of the court, which means that the boys and girls will be at opposite ends of the court. Each group then follows the inside person back up the center of the court until the boys and girls are again opposite each other.

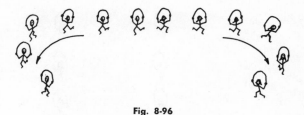

Fig. 8-96

Each girl puts her rope aside, and she and a boy jump together in cadence to the music, with the inside arm of each around the waist of the other. The free hand holds and swings the rope. The tempo of the music begins slowly and increases until it is very fast and a mistake is made. The boys and girls leave the floor in the same manner in which they entered.

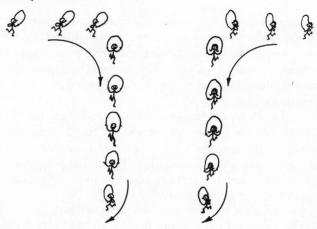

Fig. 8-97

Fig. 8-97 shows the participants coming onto the court in the same way and using the same procedure as in the previous drill. They skip side by side to the center of the court, keeping time to the slow rhythm of the music.

After reaching the center of the court, both the boys and girls make a right turn while still jumping in time to the music. (See Fig. 8-98.) The first four boys swing to the right, turn, and are then followed by the first four girls. These girls are followed by the last four boys, then by the last four girls. This results in four groups of four, moving and jumping behind one another.

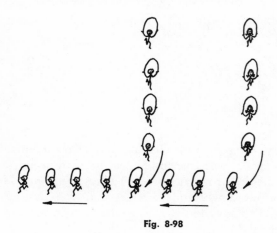

Fig. 8-98

Each group makes a left turn, followed by another left turn as they reach the end of the court. As they reach the other end of the court, the group does a to-the-rear march maneuver in unison. After reaching the middle of the court, a squad left procedure brings them in to a straight line, as in Fig. 8-99. All these maneuvers should be done in time to music.

In Fig. 8-100 an equal number of boys and girls march in from opposite sides of the floor and proceed to the middle of the floor. They line up opposite each other about 10 yards apart. At a designated signal and in cadence, they begin jumping rope in time to the music and start interchanging positions in zigzag fashion, working from one end to the other.

The boys and girls enter in the same manner as in the above drill from opposite sides, jumping rope in time to the music and in step with the person ahead of them. They proceed to line up about 10

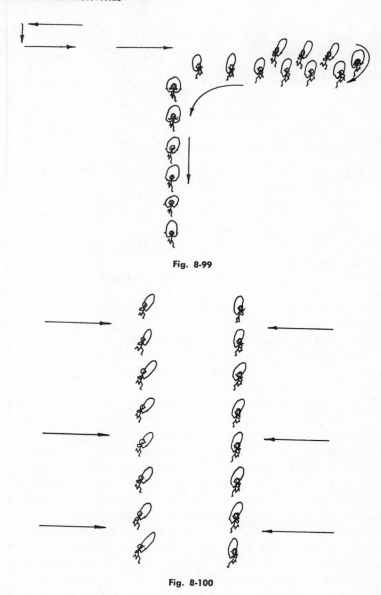

Fig. 8-99

Fig. 8-100

yards apart and, at a designated signal, begin jumping to opposite corners.

The boys and girls enter the gym from opposite sides of the gym, all jumping rope in cadence to the music. The girls proceed to the center of the floor where they make a large circle, all the time jumping the rope and moving in the circle.

The boys, having entered from the opposite side, proceed to the center, and form a circle around the girls, moving in the opposite direction. One group will be moving in clockwise fashion and the other counterclockwise. At a designated signal, the group moves off the floor in the same manner in which they entered.

Other drills which may be used are:

1. Have four boys and girls form a single line, jump to the center of the floor, and go through a definite routine. This may consist of eight hops with both feet, then eight steps, eight hops on the right foot, eight hops on the left foot, eight front crosses, and then a jump back to position.
2. Have another group do the same thing, but swing the rope backwards.
3. Have two girls do a tap routine while jumping.
4. Have two boys do a set of doubles and crosswings, combining the two while doing one jump.
5. Have one boy do whirlwind jumping while running around the gym. Various swings may be made.

RELAYS

Relay races are activities which provide fun and excitement to children of all ages. They provide an opportunity for all to take part in an activity and share equally in the result. Relays which provide for practice of game skills may be used as lead-up activities to the actual game. They may be used as an entire lesson or as a fill-in where only a few minutes are available. It is important in conducting the relays for a demonstration that too many participants are not used. This will result in many of the players standing idle while waiting their turn to participate. The relays should not be so complicated that the audience cannot grasp the intent immediately. They should, therefore, be kept simple and explained quickly, and any team that breaks a rule should be disqualified.

There are many types of relays. Some require complicated equipment and certain facilities. Some are more adaptable to indoors than others. Some have more spectator appeal than others and it is with these facts in mind that the following relays are offered for use in a demonstration.

The most important thing in presenting relay races to an audience is to justify its place in the program. The spectators should be told why relays are a part of the program. Emphasize that they are not just fun activities. They are games which are suitable to a small area and offer activity for many students at one time. It should be explained that competition is important to youngsters, and relays give the students an opportunity to compete.

In order for the audience to determine the team that is ahead or leading, it is well to identify the last man on each team to compete. This may be done by tying a colored handkerchief around his arm. Also, all other members of the winning team may throw up their hands, jump in the air, and yell when their last member has finished. This creates a great deal of enthusiasm. Teams may also use different-colored jerseys.

The secret of any type of demonstration is to keep it moving and to offer variety. Do not include relays which are so complicated that the spectators lose interest. Be sure that there is little time lapse between races. Allow just enough time to inform the audience what the teams are to do. To highlight the demonstration, it might be possible to pick a team from the audience and have them compete against the boys from the class in one of the easier relays. In this way, they will see that even though a relay looks easy or amusing, it still has value in the physical education program.

Fig. 8-101

Cricket Walk Relay

Contestant squats with arms stretched around inside of legs and outside of ankles with hands grasping top of feet. He then walks forward to a designated point and makes return trip walking backward. (See Fig. 8-101.)

Walrus Walk Relay

Contestant places himself face downward on floor, knees together, with weight resting on hands and toes. Legs and arms are kept straight. He then walks forward on hands to a designated point, dragging his feet and keeping body straight.

Crab Walk Relay

Contestant takes sitting position on floor with knees bent and hands on floor behind hips. He raises hips until trunk is straight. He then moves forward to a designated point and backward to original spot. Body must not be allowed to sag but must be kept straight. (See Fig. 8-102.)

Fig. 8-102

Reverse-Crab Relay

Position of participant is same as in crab relay except that player moves forward with hands and feet.

Scooter Relay

Scooter commonly used in elementary school may be used and will present a challenge to contestants and many laughs for audience. Contestants may assume various positions on scooters.

Sitting Scooter

Contestant sits on scooter with a leg on each side. He moves scooter backward by pushing with feet.

Standing Scooter Relay

Contestant places one foot on scooter and uses other foot to propel scooter forward.

Kneeling Scooter Relay

Contestant kneels with one knee on scooter and uses other foot to push scooter forward.

Backward Scooter Relay

Contestant places one knee on scooter with his back to starting line. He uses other leg and foot to push scooter backward toward finish line.

Zigzag Scooter Relay

Contestant sits or kneels on scooter. He propels scooter forward and around chairs that have been placed in straight line between him and finish line.

One-Legged Relay

Contestants are evenly divided into two, three, or four lines. Each contestant is given a short rope with which he ties his ankles together. At given signal, first person in each line moves forward, by jumping, to a designated point and returns. As soon as he returns to his original position, he touches off his teammate who progresses on same route as first contestant. (See Fig. 8-103.)

Fig. 8-103

Kangaroo Relay

Contestants are evenly divided into two, three, or four lines. Contestant at head of each line places a towel between his knees. At a given signal, he jumps forward to a designated area and returns. He then gives towel to teammate who follows same procedure. If towel is dropped, contestant must return to starting position. This may be done using various other objects in place of towel.

Run and Sit Relay

There may be as many contestants as desired as long as each line contains an equal number of players. At a given signal, contestant at head of each line runs to a designated spot or line and sits on floor with feet raised. He taps feet together three times, gets to feet, and returns to original position. Each teammate follows the same procedure.

Jumping Relay

Contestants are evenly divided into two, three, or four lines. Contestant at head of each line is given a baseball bat. At a given signal, he runs to a designated spot or line and returns. As he returns to original position, he grasps one end of bat in one hand and next person in line grasps other end. They place bat low and parallel to floor, each on either side of line of teammates. They then move to back of line and return, forcing teammates to jump over bat. After return jumping is done, person who was second in line follows same procedure as first contestant. This is carried on until all contestants have gone through this procedure. If either person lets go of bat, they both must return to head of line. (See Fig. 8-104.)

Fig. 8-104

Coat and Hat Relay

There may be as many contestants as desired in this relay as long as there is an equal number on each participating team. Each team is provided an old coat and hat. Coat and hat are placed on floor beside first contestant. At a given signal, first player in each line puts on coat, buttons it completely, puts on hat, and runs to a designated spot and returns. He then takes off coat and hat and gives them to teammate who repeats procedure.

Run and Throw Relay

Any number of players may participate in this relay. Lines of players are formed with equal number of players in each line. First player in each line is given a soft ball. At a given signal, he runs as fast as he can to a line 40 to 50 feet away, turns, and throws ball to teammate who is second in line. Same procedure is followed until everyone in line has caught ball and run to line. If ball is dropped on throw, it must be returned to thrower, who again will throw it to player in line. Ball must be caught before player may advance to line.

Front-to-Front Relay

Contestants form two or more lines with equal number in each line. First two contestants in each line face each other. At a given signal, first partner jumps and straddles his partner hip high and claps his hands around partner's neck. Second partner places his hands around thighs of first partner, thereby holding him in a sitting position. As soon as this is accomplished, second partner moves to a designated area where they exchange positions for return trip to starting line.

Obstacle Relay

Contestants are required to overcome certain obstacles. These obstacles may be non-contestants who assume different positions in line with each file of players. One person takes a position so that runner must crawl between his legs, another so that he must leapfrog over him, another so that he must dive through his legs, etc. Any number of obstacles may be used.

Upside-Down Walk Relay

Contestants form two or more lines with equal number in each line. First player in line faces second player and does a hand stand grasping partner's feet. Partner in turn grasps ankles of person doing handstand. At a given signal, they move forward to a designated area where partners exchange positions and return to starting line.

Caterpillar Walk Relay

Contestants are evenly divided into two, three, or four lines. First player in line assumes a position with hands and feet on floor and rump high in air. Second player lies along the first man's back, facing in same direction. Knees are open, bent, and crossed over his partner's seat. First contestant keeps rump high and knees and arms fairly straight. Top man has most of his weight resting on his hands which are directly in front of hands of underplayer. At a given signal, contestants move forward with hands and feet in unison, as a caterpillar walks. This can be done using two, three, or more players. Added players take positions similar to second player. The more players there are, the more difficult the stunt. As players reach designated area, they change position for return trip back to original starting position.

Turkey Walk Relay

Contestants form two or more lines with equal number in each line. Second person in line grasps first person as for a wheelbarrow, except that he grasps high around stomach. Player designated as wheelbarrow, clasps legs around waist of partner and hooks one foot over ankle of other leg. He is now facing floor. He then raises himself up so that he is able to place hands on knees of partner. He keeps head up and looks forward. Partner leans back to gain proper balance. At a given signal, he moves forward to a designated area where partners exchange postions and they move back to starting line. Next two in line follow same procedure until all have finished.

Forward-Backward Relay

Contestants are evenly divided into two, three, or four lines. First two players stand back-to-back and straddle a baseball bat, grasping bat with both hands. At a given signal, player facing forward

Fig. 8-105

moves forward toward a designated line. Partner follows, walking backward. Both contestants are in crouched position. As they arrive at line they remain in same position, only reversing walking procedure for return trip to original position where they touch off another couple on team. This couple obtains bat from first couple and repeats same performance. This continues until all have completed stunt. (See Fig. 8-105.)

Dizzy-Izzy Relay

Contestants are evenly divided into two, three, or four lines. Contestant at head of each line is given a baseball bat. At a given signal, he places end of bat on floor with handle up. He then grasps end of handle with both hands and places forehead on top of handle. He then circles bat three times, being sure to keep bat on floor and forehead in contact with bat. At end of three turns, he runs, carrying bat to a designated point, and returns; there he gives bat to teammate who repeats performance until all have had an opportunity. (See Fig. 8-106.)

Fig. 8-106

Wicket Walk Relay

Contestant takes hold of both ankles, keeping knees straight. He then walks forward to a designated point and returns, touching off teammate, who repeats performance until all have had an opportunity.

Twister Relay

Contestants form two lines of equal number. First two contestants face each other in a partner situation and so on down line. Contestant joins right hand with left hand of partner. They then lift opposite legs over clasped hands at same time, turning back to back to place both feet on floor. They keep turning, lifting other leg, and come back to original position. They continue this maneuver until they arrive at a designated point and then return to original take-off point. At this point, the others who have formed partners continue action until a team winner is determined.

Two-Man Carry Relay

Contestants form two or three lines composed of equal number of players. One of the players sits on floor with bent knees and hands clasped under knees. Two of the other players lift him by grasping his arms between shoulder and elbow. They carry him to an established point and return, whereupon they exchange positions until all have had an opportunity of being the carried and the carrier. (See Fig. 8-107.)

Fig. 8-107

Man-Passing Relay

This relay may include any number of players as long as sides are equally divided. Players of each team face inward and grasp hands with teammate facing them, thus forming two lines with players in each line standing shoulder to shoulder. At a given signal, first two players in line release hands and one of them jumps face down with arms over head and extended into arms of players in line. He is then passed up to other end by his teammates in a bouncing movement. As he reaches other end, his teammates help him alight. He then runs to head of line, touches player who had held hands with him, and then returns to foot of line. Second player follows same procedure as first, and as he reaches end of line he runs to head and touches third man, then returns to foot, where he joins hands with original partner.

Cardboard Relay

Teams are selected and stand in single file behind a starting line. Two large pieces of cardboard are given to first contestant in each line. At a given signal, he puts one piece of cardboard on floor and steps on it. He then places other one in front of him, steps on it, reaches back for first piece and places that in front of him, etc. He continues this maneuver, without stepping on floor until he reaches a designated point and returns to touch off teammate who goes through same procedure. (See Fig. 8-108.)

Fig. 8-108

Couple Cardboard Relay

This relay is carried out in same manner as cardboard relay except that two people participate as partners. One person has duty of placing cardboard while other moves forward by stepping on them. Winner is decided in same manner as in regular relay.

Skin-the-Snake Relay

Two or more teams may compete with as many players on a team as wanted, as long as numbers are equal. Players stand in line with feet well apart. Each player reaches between legs with right hand and grasps left hand of player in back of him. At a given signal, line moves backward with rear or last player lying on back still holding hands with player in front of him. As each player moves back over player in back of him, he also lies on back. As he lies down he should keep legs and feet close to body of teammate in front of him. This procedure continues until all players are lying down. At this point, rear man rises and procedure is reversed. Team that has all players standing with hands still clasped wins. (See Fig. 8-109.)

Fig. 8-109

Sack Relay

Contestants are equally divided into teams and line up in straight lines. Any number of players may be used. First contestant in each line is given a gunny sack. At a given signal, he puts both feet in sack and holding it up with hands he jumps toward goal line and back.

Upon return, he gets out of sack and gives it to teammate who is second in line. Teammate follows same procedure, as does everyone else until all have done so and winning team is determined. (See Fig. 8-110.)

Fig. 8-110

Chicken-Walk Relay

Contestants are divided equally into two or more teams. Team members are placed in lines. Each member squats with feet together, knees spread. He clasps hands in front of ankles and around thighs. He moves forward as fast as he is able, taking short steps as his movements will be hampered by his position.

Kangaroo-Jump Relay

Contestants are divided equally into two or more teams which are lined up in single file. First two team members in each line are given a piece of cardboard about 1 foot square which they place between their knees. At a given signal, first contestant in each line moves forward in long jumps to a designated point and returns. He touches hand of teammate who is next in line, and this teammate completes same maneuver. Meanwhile, first contestant hands his cardboard to next teammate and goes to end of line. As a team finishes, members jump into the air and yell, thereby signifying a winner. (See Fig. 8-111.)

Fig. 8-111

Backward-Run Relay

Contestants are divided equally and are placed in straight lines with backs toward line toward which they are to run at a given signal. Contestant moves backward to this line and returns, touching off a teammate. This procedure is continued until all have finished and a winner is declared. (See Fig. 8-112.)

Fig. 8-112

All-Fours Relay

Contestants are placed in straight lines with same number of players in each line and on hands and knees. At a given signal, first contestant in each line moves forward on hands and feet to a designated spot and returns, touching off teammate who is second in line. (See Fig. 8-113.)

Fig. 8-113

Backward-All-Fours Relay

This relay is same as all-fours relay, except that contestants move backward instead of forward.

Sweep-Up Relay

Teams are formed with equal number on each team. Each team is given five table tennis balls, a broom, and a dust pan. Balls are placed on floor in front of first contestant in each line. At a given signal, he attempts to sweep balls into dustpan, run to a designated spot, and return. After doing this, he dumps balls in front of teammate who is second in line. Teammate follows same procedure, and this is continued until last player has crossed starting line.

Turtle Relay

Contestants squat and place hands behind knees, with right hand grasping left wrist. They then move forward to a designated area and return while maintaining this position. Straight lines should be maintained and equal number of players should be on each team. Winner is determined when all players on a team have finished.

Player-Under Relay

Contestant runs to a designated area and returns. Upon returning, he drops to all fours and crawls through legs of teammates, who are standing in straight line with feet spread apart. Upon reaching rear, he rises, runs to front of line, touches off next player in line, and goes immediately to rear of line. This continues until all have finished and a winner is determined. (See Fig. 8-114.)

Fig. 8-114

Under-Weave Relay

This is done in same manner as player-under relay except that players face to side and perpendicular to runner. Players stand in wide stance with feet touching next person's. At a given signal, first player in line runs to line which is about 20 feet away, returns, and crawls through legs of second player in line from front, third player's legs from rear, etc. Upon reaching end of line or last player, he runs to front of line and touches off next player, then returns to end of line. Second player follows same procedure as first, as do others until all have finished.

Back-Support Relay

Players of each team line up in a column, paired off. Front man of first pair sits on floor with feet on starting line and trunk inclined backward. His partner grips him under arms and stands behind him. At starting signal, front man arches back, and, with weight supported on feet and by partner, he moves to distance line. Behind distance line partners exchange positions. After first pair cross over starting line, next pair proceed. (See Fig. 8-115.)

Fig. 8-115

Pilot Relay

Two or more teams with equal number of players may participate. Players are grouped in threes, the two end-men with backs

Fig. 8-116

to starting line. Elbows of three men are interlocked. Middle man runs forward; two outside men run backward. They run to turning point and start back, this time with middle man running backward and two outside men running forward. Next set of three players starts when first set crosses starting line. Team finishing first wins. (See Fig. 8-116.)

Indian-Club Relay

Equipment needed is one hula hoop and three Indian clubs for each team. Divide class so that same number of boys and girls are on every team. When whistle is blown, first person in each group runs to hula hoop and places Indian clubs outside of hula hoop. Person then runs back to own line and touches next person in line. This person runs to hula hoop, places Indian clubs in center of hula hoop, and returns to line, touching next person in line. This is continued until everyone has taken a turn. Winner is first team finished and standing in a straight line with right hands raised.

Wheelbarrow Relay

Players are divided into two teams and line up in two straight lines. Front boy in each line gets down on all fours and his legs are grasped by boy in back of him so that in order to go forward he must "walk on his hands." A certain distance must be traversed and then position is reversed for return trip. (See Fig. 8-117.)

Fig. 8-117

Horse and Rider Relay

Two or more lines of an equal number are formed. At a given signal No. 2 boy in line will jump upon back of boy in front of him (No. 1 boy). The "horse" then carries him to goal line where a change is quickly made reversing position of horse and rider. Horse then runs to finish line where next horse and rider repeat performance. (See Fig. 8-118.)

Fig. 8-118

Broom Relay

Lines are formed with equal number in each line. No. 1 player is given a house broom and at a given signal No. 2 player sits on brush part of broom placing feet and hands on handle. No. 1 player pulls him to a designated line and back and then second player pulls third, etc. (See Fig. 8-119.)

Three-Legged Relay

Players are divided into teams of equal number. They pair off in two's, and each pair is given a strap or short rope which is used to tie their inner legs together at ankles. At a given signal they run to a predetermined line and return, whereupon next pair is touched off. (See Fig. 8-120.)

Fig. 8-119

Fig. 8-120

Back-to-Back Relay

First two players stand back-to-back. At a signal they link elbows. Front player lifts other upon his back and runs to a designated line where he lowers player. Player who was carried then takes his turn and lifts first player and returns to starting line, where he touches off next pair. (See Fig. 8-121.)

Fig. 8-121

Centipede Race

Group is divided into teams of equal number. Players on each team line up in file, one behind the other. Each player attaches himself to teammate in front of him by placing his arms around teammate's waist and clasping hands together. At a given signal, each line moves forward in step, as fast as possible, to a designated line and returns. If anyone falls or loses his grip, team is disqualified.

Circle Relay

Two or more circles are formed with equal number of players in each circle. Players then lie face downwards with heads facing toward center of circle and about two feet apart. At a given signal a player jumps up and steps over each individual player as fast as he can, returning to original place and position. As soon as first player steps over, player next to him jumps up and does same thing. First side to finish wins. (See Fig. 8-122.)

Human-Chair Relay

Teams are formed with equal number on each team. At a given signal two team members form a chair by facing each other, grasping their own left forearm with right hand, midway between wrist and elbow. Each then grasps the other's right forearm with left hand. Third player sits in chair and is carried to a designated line and back, whereupon second and third players carry fourth, and so on. (See Fig. 8-123.)

Fig. 8-122

Fig. 8-123

Boat Relay

This relay is enjoyed by both spectators and participants. Each team of five or six players straddle a long pole facing rear and cox-swain takes his position at end facing front. It is duty of coxswain to keep his crew in step and to direct them.

Over-and-Under Relay

Lines are formed with equal number of players in each line. A volleyball or basketball is passed at a given signal between legs of first player and taken from his hands by player in back of him. No. 2 player in line passes or hands ball over head to No. 3 player in line. This is repeated until last player in line receives ball. He then carries ball to head of line and process is repeated until person who started at head of line regains his position at head. (See Fig. 8-124.)

Fig. 8-124

Tumbling Relay

This relay is played by executing several tumbling stunts such as forward roll, backward roll, hand spring, hand stand, etc. Lines are formed as in other relays with equal number of participants on each side.

Animal Relay

Lines are formed with same number of boys in each line. At starting signal, boy at head of each line races to a designated spot and imitates some animal by either noise or action and returns. Animals like the goat, donkey, rooster, duck, cow, etc., may be imitated.

Dressing Race

Boys come in fully dressed in street clothing with gym suits underneath. Each boy takes off outer clothing and deposits it in huge pile along with every other boy. Boys then line up at starting line and at a given signal race to pile, find their clothing, put it on, and get back to starting line. Winner must be fully dressed with shoes tied and clothing buttoned.

GAMES OF LOW ORGANIZATION

Games which have an appeal to the audience should be used in the demonstration. The games should not take up too much time. The success of the demonstration depends on its variability and the precision with which it is run off, not by the extraordinary feats of the performers. The games described are interesting to both participant and observer and will fit in well in the demonstration.

Dead Man

Eight to ten pupils sit closely together in a circle with legs pulled up and with arms held forward and upward. In middle stands a par-

Fig. 8-125

ticipant who makes himself stiff from head to foot. He lets himself fall backward and by pushing or shoving he is passed from one to another around circle. Person who lets dead man fall must take his place. (See Fig. 8-125.)

Swat Tag

All participants except one form circle standing about 1 foot apart with hands in back of them. Person not included in circle is given knotted towel or handkerchief or newspaper. He then walks around circle and places towel, handkerchief, or newspaper in hand of someone in circle. This person then turns upon player to his right and beats him while he is running around circle to original position. Beater then walks about circle and places swatter in someone else's hand. (See Fig. 8-126.)

Fig. 8-126

Cock Fight

Participants are divided into pairs. Each participant raises left foot behind and grasps it with left hand. Right hand must be kept

Fig. 8-127

behind back. At a given signal each attempts to upset the other by bumping with his body. (See Fig. 8-127.)

Elbow Tug of War

Two teams line up partner-fashion, 2 feet apart, and link elbows back-to-back on center line. At a given signal each participant attempts to lift opponent on his back and carry him across a line 10 yards from center line. Team carrying greatest number of opponents over its line wins.

Three-Deep

Players form in pairs, making double circle. One person is appointed to be "it" and another to be chased. Person being chosen

Fig. 8-128

jumps in front of a pair and "it" attempts to tag runner. Runner becomes safe when he goes in front of a couple and stays there. Player at rear of this new couple may be tagged by "it" unless he runs out of way. (See Fig. 8-128.)

Indian Wrestle

Two participants lie on backs with heads in opposite directions and bodies close together. On count of one, leg nearest opponent is lifted in vertical position. On count of two, leg is brought back to floor and on count of three, player hooks opponent's leg and attempts to roll him over backward. (See Fig. 8-129.)

Horse-and-Rider Fight

Two teams are formed with equal number on each team. Larger boys are selected as horses and smaller boys as riders. Riders are carried on backs of horses and teams are lined up on opposite sides of gym. At a given signal the two teams advance forward and riders

Fig. 8-129

attempt to pull opposing rider from his horse. If horse falls, both horse and rider are disqualified. (See Fig. 8-130.)

Jump the Rope

A large circle is formed with one boy in center. He is given a long rope with an old tennis shoe tied to one end. This shoe is swung around in a circle about knee high by grasping other end of rope. Players in circle must jump over shoe as it approaches them. If shoe strikes them they must drop out. (See Fig. 8-131.)

Fig. 8-130

Fig. 8-131

Hand Wrestling

Participants lie on stomachs facing each other. Clasp hands with elbows touching floor and about 3 inches apart. On a designated signal each tries to force other's arm down to floor without raising his elbow from floor. (See Fig. 8-132.)

Fig. 8-132

Broncho Busting

Participants form into groups of two and these two should be of equal size and weight. Broncho bends down so that hands are placed on knees. Rider sits on broncho's back but is not allowed to wrap legs around his waist. Broncho tries to buck rider off but must keep hands on knees. (See Fig. 8-133.)

Square Pull

Each of four players has a rope about length of a jump rope. These are tied firmly together at one end; at other, each rope is tied into a loop knot to serve as a handle. Each player puts one hand in handle. The four stride out in four opposite directions as far as ropes will stretch. Two yards farther out from each player an Indian club or other object is set up which he is to try to pick up. Game consists of a tug of war, each player trying to pull other far enough in his direction to enable him to pick up his club. One who first does this wins.

Fig. 8-133

Soccer Circle Ball

Players stand in circle facing inward, feet wide apart and touching feet of neighbors. One player is designated as kicker and stands in center of circle with a soccer ball on floor in front of him. He kicks ball in an effort to send it between legs of any man in circle. In blocking ball, players may use any soccer techniques such as foot trapping, or heading, but may not block with hands. Any player who allows ball to pass either between his legs or between himself and his neighbor on right, changes places with kicker. If kicker does not succeed on his sixth try, he changes places with last one to block ball.

Dribble Tag

Boys who are to participate in drill shall enter gymnasium from one entrance, each carrying a basketball. All boys except one shall line up across mid-court line. Other boy shall stand under basket at one end of court. At command from instructor, boys start dribbling and they may dribble anyplace on basketball floor so long as they do not go out of bounds. Boy under basket is "it" and he attempts to tag one of other class members with his free hand. As soon as he does, individual tagged is "it" and he attempts to tag someone else. Drill continues in this manner for a period of time predetermined by instructor.

Rules of drill are:

1. Anytime a boy double dribbles, loses control of ball, palms ball, travels, or steps out of bounds, he is automatically "it." He raises his hand at spot where violation occurred until all boys recognize him as being "it." He then attempts to tag another boy.
2. No boy can touch boy who has just touched him.
3. *Ball must be dribbled continuously.* No boy can stop dribbling and stand holding ball. Number of participants may be unlimited.

As soon as time period is over boys take basketballs and walk off gymnasium floor through door which they entered.

Horse-and-Rider Pull

Contestants take positions similar to horse-and-rider relay. Teams may be formed or contest may be on individual basis. Two lines are drawn about 20 feet apart, and contestants take positions between lines. At a given signal, riders grasp right hands and horses move forward in an effort to pull opposition across line. If this is accomplished, winner moves to designated area for winners. If any part of rider touches floor, he is immediately disqualified. (See Fig. 8-134.)

Push Ball

This is an excellent team game and is adaptable to gymnasium demonstration. It is thrilling and a vigorous activity. The push ball is a large ball that can be inflated to approximately 6 feet in diameter. Any number of contestants may play. Two lines are established about 20 feet apart with ball placed between lines. At a given signal, players of both teams who are lined up behind lines move forward and

Fig. 8-134

attempt to push ball over opponents' goal line. There should be no rough tactics, and all efforts should be directed toward pushing ball and not interfering with an opponent's efforts by pushing or pulling him. Ball may be pushed up into air. If this happens, game is carried on same as if ball were on floor.

Bag Boxing

This activity may be conducted on a team basis, and number of participants depends upon equipment and space available. If only a limited number of boxing gloves are available, turns may be taken in their use. Contestants line up facing each other in groups of two, depending upon amount of equipment available. Each contestant has on one boxing glove and is standing in a gunny sack which he holds up with free hand. At a given signal, he moves forward and attempts to force opponent to fall or to drop hold on sack by hitting him with boxing glove. He is allowed to hit only on body. Winner goes to winner's area, and glove and bag are given to next two contestants. This continues until all contestants have participated and winner is determined.

Horse-and-Driver Boxing

This activity may be conducted on a partner or a team basis. Number of participants is determined by amount of equipment available. Contestants are paired, and one is designated as horse and other as driver. A 12-foot rope is placed from back of neck over shoulders and under armpits of horse. Driver grasps ends of rope or reins so that he will be able to drive horse. Horse has on pair of boxing gloves and is blindfolded. Driver steers horse with reins and horse hits straight out with gloves in an attempt to hit other horse. No slugging is allowed. If an opponent is hit a specified number of times, he is declared loser, opponent being other "horse."

Horse-and-Rider Boxing

This activity may be conducted on a team basis if enough equipment is available. Team members may be identified by arm bands or colored jerseys. One person is horse and other is rider. Rider sits on shoulders of horse and wears boxing gloves. At a given signal, each rider attempts to unseat other riders by hitting them on body. No head blows are allowed. Opponents may be paired up or rider may attack anyone and everyone. As soon as a rider is unseated, he retires to side line and winner to winning area, providing opponents are paired up. If contest is on a team basis, winner turns to another adversary and this continues until one team no longer has any rider on a horse. Once unseated, the rider cannot remount.

Rooster Fight

This activity may be conducted on an individual or team basis. Contestants are divided into groups of two. These two sit on floor facing each other with feet touching and knees slightly bent. Arms are folded across chest. At a given signal, each participant attempts to overbalance the other by raising feet and striking soles of feet against soles of adversary. He may either be tipped over backwards or fall sideways. He must not use hands to help prevent his overbalancing but must keep them folded across chest at all times. (See Fig. 8-135.)

Fig. 8-135

Jousting

This may be organized as a dual or team activity. If it is organized on a team basis, team members should be identified. If it is on a dual basis, champion of each round challenges one of other winners. Equipment required consists of two stools upon which contestants stand on long horse upon which contestants sit. Two poles are used, jousting ends of which are padded with towels. At a given signal, contestants attempt to dislodge opponents. Dropping pole or falling off stool or horse disqualifies an opponent. Team winner is decided on number of individual winners.

Tail Snatch

Contestants are divided evenly into two teams. Team members are each given a piece of colored cloth, about 1 foot long, and 2 inches wide. A different color should be given to opposing team members. Participants place end of these pieces of cloth under their belts behind so that they resemble tails. At a given signal, players attempt to snatch off tails of opposing team members. Contestants must confine their running to a designated area which is determined before contest starts. There should be no holding, pushing, shoving, or rough tactics. Contest may be continued until one team has all tails, or it may be run on a time basis and team that has most tails after a definite time is winner.

Scooter Hockey

Number of contestants participating in this activity will be dependent upon number of scooters available. Each player on team is provided with a scooter and either a broom or baseball bat. A volleyball or basketball is placed between two teams. At a given signal, players attempt to hit ball across opponents' goal.

Fill the Vacancy

Participants form a large circle and each person is given a number. Players are facing in and are numbered consecutively. One player is placed in middle. At a given signal, he calls out three numbers and these numbers must not be greater than those held by players. Players whose numbers are called exchange places immediately. Player in middle must stand on one leg in middle of circle while he calls numbers. As soon as numbers are called he attempts, by hopping on one leg, to move into one of places vacated before one of players whose number has been called is able to do so. If he is successful, player whose place he took is then designated as middle player.

Individual Dodge Ball

Contestants form a large circle with one player appointed to take his place in center. Players forming circle are given a volleyball

Fig. 8-136

with which they attempt to hit player in center below knees. Player in middle may move about freely as long as he stays within circle. Ball may be passed, batted, or rolled to any player in order to move it into a better position for an attempt to hit player in middle. (See Fig. 8-136.)

Number Call

Contestants are placed in a circle and each is given a number. One player is stationed in circle with a volleyball. He calls out one of numbers given to players and drops ball on floor from as high as he can reach over his head. Player whose number is called rushes forward and attempts to catch ball before it hits floor a second time. Ball may also be thrown in air.

Grab the Stick

Contestants are paired up in groups of two. Each group is given a short stick about 2 feet long and as big around as a broomstick. One player holds stick at each end about waist-high. Other player places his open hand directly above stick with intention of grabbing stick. Second player holding stick lets go of it. Purpose of stunt is to test reflex action of contestants.

Protest the Pin

Players station themselves in a large circle with one player and a bowling pin in center. Players around circle try to knock pin over, using a volleyball. Player in center attempts to prevent them from doing this. Players may pass the ball to one another and across circle at any time.

Ball Fight

Two contestants are placed in a large circle. A basketball or medicine ball is given them and both wrap their hands around ball. At a given signal, each player tries to wrench ball from grasp of other. No tripping or rough tactics are allowed. Contestants must stay in circle or they are disqualified. Person taking ball from other is winner but he must not step out of circle in obtaining ball.

Balloon Fight

Teams are selected with equal number on each team. Teams are identified by arm bands or jerseys, or they may be given different colored balloons. Balloons are tied to back belt of each player and players from opposing team attempt to break balloon. After a player's balloon is broken, he is automatically disqualified and moves to losers' area. This continues until all balloons from one team are broken. No rough tactics are allowed and area to which players are confined must be clearly indicated.

Stick Twister

Contestants face each other in groups of two. Each contestant grasps a stick which is held between them at chest height and parallel to floor. Hands are placed wide apart on stick and at a given signal, each tries to force right end of stick down so that it touches floor. No jerking of stick, pushing, or pulling is permitted.

One-Legged Wrestle

Two contestants face each other, standing on one foot and with right hands joined. At a given signal, each contestant attempts to force his opponent to lower upraised foot to floor. Neither contestant should touch his opponent with his free hand. (See Fig. 8-137.)

Fig. 8-137

Arm Wrestling

Contestants face each other as partners down line. These partners stand with right feet forward and inside of ankles touching. Bodies are facing slightly in opposite direction. Right hands are clasped and forearms and elbows of right arm are touching. Left arm may be at side or behind back. At a given signal, each contestant tries to force partner's arm sideward and downward to such an extent that he gives up his beginning position.

Bend the Arm

Contestants form in groups of two with one behind the other and slightly to his right, both facing in same direction. Contestant in front stands with left arm at side, and right arm straight out sideward, parallel to floor, with elbow straight. Partner behind him grasps opponent's wrist in right hand, with left hand on opponent's upper arm near shoulder. At a given signal, he tries to force opponent to bend arm. Both stand with feet well spread.

Open-Hand Boxing

Contestants are arranged in partner formation, facing each other. Each contestant grasps partner's left wrist with right hand. At a given signal, each contestant tries to hit partner with right hand.

Rope Pull

Two contestants face each other, having a short piece of rope between them. Partners grasp ends of rope while standing side by side, each with right foot forward and about 1 foot from partner's. Each contestant grasps end of rope and, at a given signal, attempts to pull partner forward far enough to enable puller to pick up, with free hand, a rumpled piece of paper which has been placed at equal distance behind each player. First to pick up paper wins.

Hand Pull

Contestants face each other in groups of two partners. They stand facing each other with one player bending arms across chest in such a fashion that fingers of both hands are touching at finger point. Partner grasps wrist of opponent and attempts to pull fingers apart.

Two-Legged Wrestle

Same as above with opponents facing each other, hands joined and both feet on floor. Contestant forces partner to raise one foot.

One-Handed Wrestle

Contestants face each other in groups of two. Each person places right foot forward one step with outside or inside of ankle against outside or inside of opponent's ankle. Clasping opponent's right hand, contestant tries to force him to lose his balance by pulling forward or sideward, or pushing backward. Neither foot should leave the floor. (See Fig. 8-138.)

Fig. 8-138

Cock Fighting

Opponents sit facing each other with knees bent. Hands are clasped under knees, and contestants balance themselves on buttocks. On a given signal, each tries to roll other backwards, using feet only.

Leg Lift

Opponents sit facing each other. Feet are spread about 2 feet apart and arms are folded. Left leg is placed over opponent's right leg and right leg is placed under left leg of partner approximately between ankle and knee. At a given signal, each tries to lift opponent's leg, at same time keeping own on floor, and tip him over from his sitting position. Legs should be kept fairly rigid and knees should not be bent.

Waist Wrestle

Contestants stand facing in opposite directions, side by side. Feet should be slightly spread with left foot in advance of right foot. Body is bent forward. Each grips other around waist with both arms. At a given signal, each tries to lift other off floor.

Elbow Wrestle

Opponents sit facing in opposite directions, back-to-back. Knees are bent and feet are resting on floor. Left elbow is locked over right elbow of opponent with right elbow locked under his elbow. At a given signal, contestant tries to force elbow of his opponent to floor in a sideward motion.

One-Legged Tug of War

Contestants face each other as pairs. Opponents raise right legs forward and interlock feet. Foot is placed behind ankle. At a given signal, using leg grip, each contestant tries to pull opponent forward over a designated area or line.

Reverse Tug of War

Contestants face each other in groups of two. Partners stand back-to-back bending over with knees slightly bent. Partners reach back through own legs and grasp each other's right hand. After obtaining a firm grip, each, on a given signal, attempts to move forward past a designated area or line. Other arm may be moved about freely. If hand grip is broken, contestants move out of contesting area so

Fig. 8-139

that audience's attention may be concentrated on those still competing. (See Fig. 8-139.)

Stick Wrestle

Contestants stand back-to-back in groups of two. Each group
has a stick about 3 feet long and 1 inch thick. A broom stick or a
baseball bat will suffice. Stick or bat is held directly over heads of
partners, at arm's length, and each partner grasps stick with palms
facing foward. One foot should be slightly in advance of other in
order to obtain more balance and leverage. At a given signal, contestants pull forward and downward without moving feet out of position until one opponent loses position or relinquishes hold on stick.
Losers should step to one side of floor and winners to the other.

Squat Tug of War

Contestants line up in pairs. Both partners squat and take hold of
end of a towel with both hands. At a given signal, each tries to pull
the other off balance so that he either falls or lets go of towel. Towel
may be jerked or pulled in any direction in attempt to overbalance
opponent. Losers move out of area and winners go to winners' area.
Contestants must remain in squatting position at all times. (See Fig.
8-140.)

Fig. 8-140

Wrist Wrestling

Contestants form in groups of two and assume a horizontal position, resting on hands and toes as if they were about to do push-ups. They face each other with heads about 3 to 6 inches apart. Each partner attempts to grab opponent's wrist in such a way that it will cause opponent to collapse because he no longer has hand on floor for support. Winners go to winners' area.

Steer Riding

Contestants form in pairs. One partner assumes a position on all fours, with only hands and feet touching floor. He is the steer. Partner straddles him, sitting as far back on steer's rump as possible with his back toward head of steer. He may not clamp his feet together. Steer attempts to dislodge rider from this position by bucking and twisting.

Medicine Ball Balance Throw
From Sitting Position

Contestants face each other in pairs, sitting with feet together. Bottoms of contestant's feet are in contact with those of his partner. Contestants throw a medicine ball back and forth, trying to overbalance catcher. Number of participants will depend upon number of medicine balls available for use.

Medicine Ball Balance Throw
From Squatting Position

Same as above except contestants are in squatting postion. As soon as a contestant is overbalanced, he removes himself to a predetermined losing area and winner goes to winners' area.

One-Legged Fight

All contestants are divided into two teams of equal number. Teams wear different colored shirts so that they may tell each other apart. Team members stand on one foot with arms folded across chest. At a given signal, contestants hop toward their opponents and by bumping them try to upset them so that, in order to regain balance, they must put foot which they are holding in air on floor. Players who are eliminated move to side of floor, leaving winners still in contention. Contest continues until only those players representing one team are left. One player may eliminate as many as he can and two or more players may attack one player. There should be no kicking or pushing, and team that eliminates all its opponents wins. (See Fig. 8-141.)

Fig. 8-141

Circle Wrestling (A)

A circle or circles approximately 10 feet in diameter are drawn. Two contestants are placed in each circle facing each other. At a given signal, each contestant attempts to throw opponent out of circle. All fair wrestling tactics may be used, but there should be no roughness. If any part of contestant's body touches outside circle, he loses contest.

Teams may be chosen, and if this is done, they should be identified by wearing arm bands of different colored jerseys. Winner of each contest should go to a previously established area. Winning team is determined by number of individual winners.

Circle Wrestling (B)

A circle 20 feet in diameter, or smaller if desired, is drawn on floor. Two contestants are placed in circle facing each other, and each holding the other by upper arms. At a given signal, each attempts to force the other out of circle by pushing, pulling, or twisting of body. Tripping and unnecessary roughness are not allowed. If contact with each other is broken, contest begins over again. Teams may be used, or this may be strictly on an individual basis.

Circle Wrestling (C)

Same as above, except that a bowling pin is set in middle of circle, and contest is started by having contestants with hands on shoulders begin on either side of pin. Object is to force one of contestants to knock over pin. Same rules apply as those in previous contest.

One-Legged Circle Fight (D)

Same as above except contestants stand on one foot and grasp other foot in front with both hands. Same rules apply as those above.

Backward Pull-Away

Contestants are placed back-to-back with elbows locked. Lines are established approximately 10 to 12 feet in front of each contestant. At a given signal, each contestant attempts to pull opponent over line. Both contestants must pull at all times and not do any pushing or jerking. As soon as opponent is pulled over line, he goes to losers' area, which has been designated previously, and winner to winner's area. Teams may be chosen, and if so, colored shirts may be worn to designate different teams. A winner is decided on number of players in winners' area from each team.

Kangaroo Fight

Contestants are paired off with equal number on each side. Each contestant is given a baseball bat which he places behind knees. He places arms under bat and grasps legs below knees. This leaves him in a squatting position. From this position, and at a given signal, he hops toward opponent and attempts to bump him off balance. If either opponent is forced to release grasp, he is declared loser and must retire to losers' area, while winner goes to winners' area. Teams may be established, if desired. (See Fig. 8-142.)

Fig. 8-142

Elimination

Two lines are drawn about 20 feet apart and parallel to each other. Teams are formed with equal number on each side and are identified by arm bands or colored jerseys. At a given signal, each team attempts to carry, drag, push, or pull opponents across opponents' goal line. They, of course, try to avoid being dragged over their own goal line by opponents. No striking or kicking is allowed. Two or more players from one team may attempt to carry one player from other team over goal line. If desired, this game may be limited to just one opponent against another.

Shoulder Push

Contestants are paired off with equal number on each side. Contestants face each other in center of two lines which are drawn about 20 feet apart. Contestants lean forward and place hands on shoulders of opponents. At a given signal, each contestant attempts to push opponent over his goal line. Both contestants must push only. There should be no pulling. Every contestant must stay in front of opponent or between opponent and his line at all times, so that he will be in a pushing position. As soon as an opponent is pushed over his line, he moves over to the losers' area. The winning team is determined by counting the number of winners against the number of losers. This, too, may be carried on by individual pairs of contestants. (See Fig. 8-143.)

Fig. 8-143

One-Legged Wrestle

Any reasonable number of contestants may take part. Contestants form in groups of two facing each other and standing on one foot. At a given signal, they hop forward on one foot with other foot raised in front of them. Using front foot, each attempts to force opponent off balance so that opponent must put upraised foot on floor. He must not kick but must use foot in a pushing motion. (See Fig. 8-144.)

Fig. 8-144

Bat Pull

Contestants line up in groups of two, each group having a baseball bat. Two contestants face each other and grasp ends of bat. At a given signal, they attempt to pull each other over a predetermined line. They must keep both hands on bat, and back up as they pull. They must not jerk bat in an attempt to break hold of opponent. As soon as a winner is determined, he moves to winners' area. Teams may be selected and a team winner determined as long as there are equal numbers participating.

Wrist Pull

Contestants are paired off with equal number on each side. Two lines are drawn about 20 feet across. Contestants face each other in middle of floor. Each contestant reaches forward with right hand and grasps wrist of opponent. At a given signal, he attempts to pull opponent across line which is in back of him. Contestant must pull forward at all times and must keep his back toward line in back of him. As soon as an opponent is pulled over his line, he moves over to losers' area and winner goes to winners' area. Teams may be established and winners may be declared by counting losers against winners. Each contestant must be identified with mark of his team.

One-Legged Tug of War with Rope

Contestants stand with backs to each other in groups of two. Partners have a short piece of rope about 6 feet long between them. Rope is tied around ankle of each contestant. At a given signal, each attempts to pull the other across one of two lines which have been drawn 20 feet apart. Contestant may put hands on floor as he is not required to stand upright. Teams may be organized and team that wins will be determined by number of individual winners it has. As soon as a player is pulled across goal line, he removes himself to losers' area and winner goes to winning area.

Rope Pull and Pickup

Contestants are paired up with equal number on each side in groups of two. Each group is given a rope 6 feet in length. Contestants stand with backs toward each other and ends of rope tied around one ankle. A towel is placed equidistant from each contestant. At a given signal, each contestant tries to pull the other toward towel and pick it up. Winners go to a selected area and are counted to determine team winner.

Long-Horse Boxing

This activity may be conducted on an individual or team basis. Two players sit facing each other on long horse. Each has on a pair of boxing gloves. At a given signal, each player attempts, by hitting opponent, to knock him off horse. Only body blows are allowed. It is a foul to strike opponent in head unless opponent ducks in such a way so that it is unavoidable. Mats should be placed around horse and spotters may be used so as to prevent an accident from a fall. If game is played from a team standpoint, winner will go to area designated for winners. Team winner is determined by number of individual winners on each team.

Four-Man Tug of War

Contestants are divided into four teams. Four contestants, one from each team, form a square with team members grasping a corner of a rope that has been tied together. Distance between each player should be at least 6 feet. Directly behind each player, at a distance of 6 feet, a towel is placed on floor. At a given signal, each player, by pulling on rope, attempts to pull other players toward him far enough to allow him to pick up towel. Winners go to a designated area by number or by color of jersey he wears. Team winner can then be determined.

Steer Tying

This activity may be conducted on a team basis. Each contestant has a partner from opposite team. Each contestant is given a rope approximately 4 feet long. Contestants stand facing each other, and at a given signal each tries to tie ankles of opponent together. All unnecessary roughness should be avoided; slugging or striking opponent is against rules and draws a forfeiture of contest. All winners go immediately to designated winners' area where a team winner is determined.

Kneeling Wrestle

Contestants face each other, kneeling on both knees. At a given signal, they grasp right hands and, by pushing and pulling, attempt to throw each other off balance. Knees may not be moved from floor and no part of body except knees and feet may touch floor at any time. Teams may be formed, and winner determined by number of individual winners on a team. (See Fig. 8-145.)

Captain of the Mat

Two teams are formed, with each team selecting a captain. One captain takes his place in center of mat, surrounded by teammates.

Fig. 8-145

At a given signal, other team members attempt to displace captain and replace him with their own. Whenever any part of player's body goes off mat, he is considered out. Captain of attacking team may be determined on a time basis. Pushing and pulling is allowed but there should be no striking or kicking. Rough tactics should not be allowed.

Reach the Goal

Two teams are selected and face each other on their respective goal lines about 25 feet apart. Players are identified by wearing different colored jerseys. At a given signal each player grasps his left foot, which is behind him, with right hand. Each tries by hopping on one foot to reach and cross opponents' goal line. If player falls or touches upraised foot to floor, he is eliminated. Players may attempt to force this situation by butting with shoulder, but free hand may not be used. Play continues until all players have either reached goal or been eliminated. Team winner is determined by number of players who reached opponents' goal.

Pole Pull

Contestants are divided into teams with equal number on each team and even number of teams. Procedure is same as it is for rope tug of war except that a vaulting pole is used. If there are more than two teams, an elimination pull may be conducted. (See Fig. 8-146.)

Fig. 8-146

Pole Push

Same procedure as above is used except team members of one team attempt to push members of the other across a designated line instead of pulling them. (See Fig. 8-147.)

Fig. 8-147

Feet-Together Boxing

Contestants are divided into two teams and then into groups of two, one from each team. Each person is given a set of boxing gloves, and a short rope with which he ties his feet together. At a given signal, he attempts to knock opponent off his feet using only body blows.

Winner goes immediately to winners' area. Number of contestants will be determined by number of boxing gloves available, although it is possible to have several groups and these groups take turns using gloves.

Bird Fight

A circle is drawn, diameter of which may be determined by number of participants. Team members are identified by colored jerseys.

Each participant bends forward and grasps ankles with hands. At a given signal, he attempts to upset opponent or shoulder him from circle. This is continued until a winner is determined; this, of course, is when all members of one team are out of circle. (See Fig. 8-148.)

Fig. 8-148

Pillow Fight on the Long-Horse

This activity may be conducted on an individual or team basis. Two players sit facing each other on long horse. Each is given a pillow, and at a given signal, each participant attempts to knock opponent off long horse by hitting him with pillow. Procedure is same as long horse boxing except that contestants may strike each other on any part of body in their effort to dislodge their adversary. If game is played on a team basis, winner goes to winning area.

Pull Across

Two teams are formed with proper identification. A line is drawn on floor, and members of teams stand on opposite sides of line directly across from opponents. On a given signal, they reach across line, grasp opponents by hand, and attempt to pull them across line. Winners go to winning area so that a team winner may be determined. Any part of body touching across line indicates a loser.

Horse and Rider Reach the Goal

Two lines are drawn 20 feet apart with horses and riders composing each team stationed behind their goal line. At a given signal, horses and riders advance toward opponents' goal and at same time, attempt to unseat opposing riders. Largest number of riders to reach opposing goal line wins contest.

Back-to-Back Wrestling

Contestants form teams which are properly identified. Contestants pair up so that each person has an opponent from other team.

Fig. 8-149

They stand back-to-back with elbows locked together. At a given signal, each tries to lift the other off his feet. Team winner is determined by number of individual winners. As soon as an opponent is defeated, he moves to losers' area and winner to winners' area. (See Fig. 8-149.)

Tire Boxing

Two teams are formed and each contestant is furnished a pair of boxing gloves. If enough are not available, participants should take turns in using gloves. Tires are placed close together, and a contestant from each team stands inside tire. At a given signal, each tries to upset the other or force him to step outside tire by hitting him on body. No head blows are allowed. Winners go to winning area and are counted to determine team winner.

Backward Push-Away

Contestants are placed back-to-back with elbows locked. Lines are established approximately 10 to 12 feet in front of each contestant. At a given signal, each contestant attempts to push the other over line by pushing backward. He is not allowed to pull at any time, so he must keep himself between his opponent and his line at all times so that he will be able to exert a pushing position. As soon as an opponent is pushed over his line, he removes himself to losers' area, and winner goes to winners' area. Teams may be established, and if this is done, they should be identified by wearing different colored jerseys. Winning team is determined by counting number of winners against number of losers.

Cage Ball

Use a 36-inch cage ball. All students file in and form a circle. Here they sit on floor, and assistant throws ball into play. Players from each team try to kick ball over heads of opponents.

Volleyball, Baseball, Basketball Game

Players are divided into two equal teams. Play area includes a baseball diamond at one end of gymnasium and a basketball goal at the

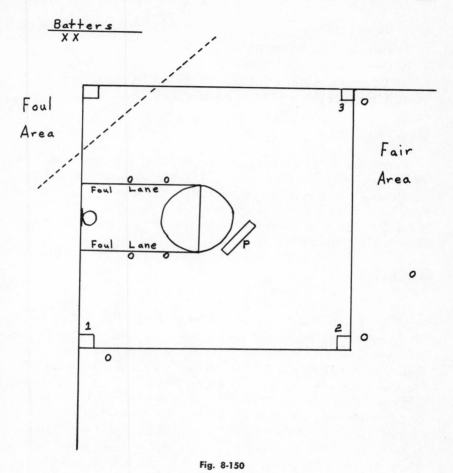

Fig. 8-150

other. (See Fig. 8-150.) Length between baseball bases will depend on age and skill of children playing. Each team has a pitcher, a catcher, fielders, and two to four players playing near foul lanes by goal. Pitcher, standing in pitcher's box, throws a volleyball to batter, who in turn attempts to serve it with a volleyball serve in fair territory. If he serves ball fairly, he runs for first base and so on around bases as in baseball, object being for batter to reach Home before fielding team can score a basket. Fielders are to relay ball to players near basket. Three outs retire a team. A point is scored for team at bat when a batter reaches Home before a basket is made by fielding team.

Batter is out when:

1. He fails to touch all three bases.
2. He fails to use volleyball serve.
3. A basket is made by fielding team before he reaches Home.
4. After three attempts, he fails to serve ball in fair territory.

Human Tug of War

Center line of gym is used as a dividing line. Boys are divided into two equal teams in single lines, facing each other on opposite sides of dividing line. Each man places arms around waist of opponent in front of him. Two leaders of opposing teams grasp each other around waist. On signal, each team attempts to pull opponent over center line. Pulling time should be 30 seconds.

Push Ball

Players: 10 to 25 on a side

A large cage ball is placed in center circle of basketball court. Two opposing captains stand 1 yard away from ball. Rest of players are 15 feet back from ball in their half of floor. At whistle, captains immediately play ball, by advancing toward it. Their respective team members come to their assistance. Object of game is to propel ball over opponents' goal line by pushing, rolling, passing, carrying, or using any other means except kicking ball. When ball goes out of bounds, teams line up at right angles to sideline and 1 yard apart at point where ball went out of bounds. Ball is tossed between two teams. When ball becomes tied up in one spot for 10 seconds, ball is declared dead and is put in play as for an out-of-bounds situation.

A goal counts 5 points and scoring team gets a chance to score an extra point. Ball is placed on opponents' 5 yard line as teams line up across floor, width of ball apart. On whistle, ball is put in play for one minute, and, if driven across line, team scores one point.

Number Basketball

Group is divided into two teams of any number. Each team is lined up along sidelines of basketball court. Each team counts off, beginning with one and running through to last boy. Team's basket is determined.

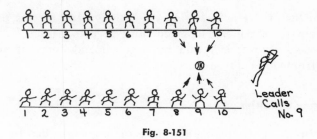

Fig. 8-151

Leader calls out a number and that boy from each team becomes center and runs out to get ball. Boys on his right and left also come out and they play three against three in regular basketball until a score is made or whistle is blown for them to go back in line. Leader then calls another number. (See Fig. 8-151.)

Circle Sit

"Circle sit" is a stunt that may be performed by large or small group of participants; however, the larger the group the more difficult it is to perform. Participants form a large circle facing in same direction approximately 1 foot apart from one another. At a given signal, everyone simultaneously seats himself on knees of person to his rear. If stunt is performed properly, everyone in circle will be seated comfortably on knees of person behind him and he will likewise be supporting person in front of him.

Tumble-Tussle

This is a wrestling match between as many participants as wanted. Participants are paired up, seated on floor with backs together. Knees are slightly bent and hands are clasped under knees. While in this position, participants' wrists and feet are tied with short ropes. Both boys are now quite helpless with backs to each other. At a given signal, each tries to knock the other over.

Balloon Squash

This can be a coeducational game or be confined to one sex. In either event, teams can be chosen so that different colored balloons may be used to distinguish players. Each participant ties a blown-up balloon to his or her ankle, using color designated for his team and leaving enough of balloon loose on floor to be squashed by another player's foot. Contest is begun by a signal and continues until all balloons from one team are broken.

Ping-Pong with Bottles

A variation of the regulation game of ping-pong can be done by placing three coke bottles on each side of net. One bottle is placed in middle of table about 18 inches from net. Other two bottles are placed about 10 inches in from side edge of table and about 1 foot opposite each other.

Game is played by regular rules of ping-pong. Ball is played off bottles just as if they were part of playing surface.

Scooter Ball

Equipment needed:

6 to 24 gym scooters
1 cage ball
4 Indian pins
smooth playing surface

Number of players:

6 to 24
6 on each team ideal

Object of game:

To advance a cage ball over opponents' scoring line.
One to three points for a game, depending on length of time available.

Method of play:

Players from each team line up at opposite ends of playing area facing each other. Cage ball is placed in center of floor and at a signal players advance toward ball on their scooters and try to move ball across opponents' goal by throwing, pushing, or carrying it. Opponents attempt to take ball away and reverse action to other end of floor.

Rules:

1. Players must sit on scooters at all times.
2. Players must not kick ball.
3. Players must not hit ball with closed fist.
4. Ball must cross line between bowling pins to score point.
5. Two bowling pins are used at each end to designate end lines.
6. Failure to observe above rules means expulsion from game.

FIRST-AID DRILL

Fireman's Carry

"One" places left arm between legs of "two" so that crotch of two is at shoulder of "one." "Two" leans forward until he lies across "one's" shoulders. "One" straightens up, lifting "two" off ground. "One," using hand of arm through "two's" crotch, grasps wrist of "two's" arm which is hanging over his shoulder. Retaining this position, "one" runs forward. (See Fig. 8-152.)

Fig. 8-152

Cross Carry

"One," standing in front of "two," leans forward. "Two" bends forward until he is lying across middle of "one's" back. "One" then places one arm around two's knees and one around "two's" shoulders and straightens up, lifting "two" from ground. Retaining this position, "one" runs forward (See Fig. 8-153.)

Fig. 8-153

Single Shoulder Carry

"One," standing in front of and facing "two," assumes semisquatting position. "Two" leans forward until he lies across "one's" left shoulder. "One" clasps his arm around "two's" legs and straightens up, lifting "two" from ground. Retaining this position, "one" runs forward. (See Fig. 8-154.)

Arm Carry

"One," standing beside "two," bends his knees and lifts up "two" by placing one arm below his thighs and the other around the small

Fig. 8-154

Fig. 8-155

of his back. "Two" places his near arm around "one's" shoulders and clasps his other hand. Retaining this position, "one" runs forward. (See Fig. 8-155.)

Fireman Drag

"One" lies on back, arms extended backward. "Two" ties "one's" wrists together with a piece of cloth. "Two" straddles "one" and places head between "one's" arms. "Two" then crawls forward, dragging "one." (See Fig. 8-156.)

Fig. 8-156

ATHLETIC POSES

An exhibition of living statuary presents a colorful activity and one which will be enthusiastically received. Naturally the poses in a demonstration of this type will portray modern athletes. Care should therefore be taken in the selection of the individuals. Those persons possessing symmetrical physical development as well as poise and interpretive ability should be chosen.

It is necessary for the individuals to practice these poses very carefully. The background should be of black cloth if possible and a blue flood light should be thrown upon the subject. The lighting effect is very important. The posers should remain perfectly still. It will add color to the act to have the band play softly during the performance. Careful rehearsing is important. Popular poses are discus throw, basketball throw, etc.

The Marble White make-up is probably the best for this purpose and is by far the safest. A sufficient amount for one individual is made by using the following formula:

Heat 1 pound of shortening until it becomes a liquid. Add 1 pound of zinc oxide and mix well. Allow the mixture to cool and form a paste. It should then be applied to the body of the poser, using the hands for spreading. Do not apply too thickly. After applying the paste, place a pound of Number one Stein's White Powder in a muslin sack. Dust the entire body with sack and the result will give a white marble effect. The poser should be careful not to breathe the powder. A swimming supporter may be used under the make-up.

A wig can be made in various ways. One way is to take a white felt hat, cut off the brim in such a way that the hair will be completely covered. Glue can be placed on the hat and cotton stuck on so as to resemble hair. Another method is to use shaving cream placed in the hair.

STUNTS

The suggested stunts are particularly adapted to a demonstration as they require little equipment and involve competition. They are interesting and will create amusement, yet, at the same time, show the general public a sample of the type of program carried out in the physical education department.

Bone of Contention

Any reasonable number of contestants may take part in this activity. Students pair off into groups of two. These two contestants sit on floor facing each other, with legs extended and shoe soles touching. Each contestant bends forward and grasps a stick which is held directly over toes. At a given signal, each contestant tries to pull the other off floor so that he loses his footing. Contestant must not let go of stick, lose balance, or be pulled up, as this constitutes a loss. (See Fig. 8-157.)

Crane Dive

Place a small piece of cardboard approximately 6 inches above floor. This can be done by using a small block of wood which can be carried out on to floor by contestants. Contestants stand and balance on one foot, then lean forward, raising other foot backward.

Fig. 8-157

By bending forward and using arms for balancing, contestant attempts to pick up cardboard with teeth and return to original position without losing balance.

Full Squat

Contestant places both hands behind back, grasping left wrist with right hand. He then squats by bending knees until he is able to pick up a piece of paper from floor, using fingers of left hand. Head should be erect and back straight.

Dutch Jump

Contestant stands with feet approximately 1 foot apart and parallel with body, bent forward. He then springs into air, throwing legs forward and upward, keeping knees stiff, and touches toes of both feet with fingertips.

Finger Feat

Contestant places elbows at shoulder height with hands in front of chest and close to body. Fingers of right hand should be touching those of left hand. Another contestant stands in front of him, grasps his wrists, and attempts to pull his fingers apart.

Human Ball

Contestant sits on floor with knees drawn up close to body. He puts arms between and under thighs and clasps hands together in front of ankles. While holding this position, he rolls on side, back, and returns to sitting position.

Heel Click

Contestant jumps into air and clicks heels together twice before touching floor.

Seal Flap

Contestants line up in straight line, supporting their weight on hands and toes, with face downward. They push off with hands, as body is thrown upward, and attempt to clap hands before returning to starting position. (See Fig. 8-158.)

Fig. 8-158

U. Sit

Contestant sits on floor with legs extended forward. He then rocks back on buttocks and at same time raises both legs off floor, keeping arms sideways at shoulder height. He keeps this position for as long as possible. (See Fig. 8-159.)

Fig. 8-159

Jack Knife

Contestant lies on back with arms and hands at sides. He raises upper part of body, at same time keeping legs perfectly straight. This will place all weight on buttocks. He then attempts to touch toes with fingers. (See Fig. 8-160.)

Fig. 8-160

Jump Foot

Contestant forms a loop by grasping right foot with left hand or, if he prefers, left foot with right hand. He then jumps into air and attempts to place foot he has been standing upon through this loop. (See Fig. 8-161.)

Fig. 8-161

Long Reach

Contestant stands with toes on a line drawn upon gym floor. Using a piece of chalk, he places a mark on gym floor as far as possible from line. He must return to original position without moving toes from line.

Mercury Stand

Contestants stand on either foot and bend body forward until at right angles with supporting leg. Arms should be out to side

Fig. 8-162

for balance. Head is up, back arched, and upraised leg in line with trunk of body. Toes of free foot should be pointed. Contestants hold pose for as long as possible, and as each contestant fails he drops out of line. Contest continues until only a winner remains. (See Fig. 8-162.)

Bear Hug Wrestle

Contestants face each other, with each contestant having a partner. They stand with bodies bent forward. Left leg of each contestant is placed forward and arms are placed around opponent as in an embrace with left arm under right arm of opponent and right arm over left arm. At a given signal, each tries to swing the other off his feet.

Long-Legged Sitting

Contestant sits on floor with legs spread apart and hands grasping ankles. A piece of crumpled paper is placed directly between legs at ankles. Keeping knees straight, contestant leans forward until he is able to grasp paper with his teeth.

One-Legged Balance

Contestants all face in one direction in straight line. At a given signal, they balance on one foot with opposite foot on knee of supporting leg. As each contestant fails, he steps back out of line so that only successful contestants remain in line. Contest is continued until all have failed. This may also be done with eyes closed. (See Fig. 8-163.)

Fig. 8-163

Angel Rise

Player lies on back with knees bent so that soles of feet rest on floor about 1 foot apart. Another player steps up onto his knees and by reaching back, grasps hands of person lying on back. His back will be toward person lying on floor. Players then throw their weight forward and by so doing, person lying down is brought to his feet and person standing on his knees is thrust forward while still maintaining his position.

High Kick

This stunt requires two players. One player stands in front of partner and holds hand out palm down at a height he thinks is

Fig. 8-164

beyond ability of kicker to kick. He lowers hand until partner is able to kick hand. Procedure is then reversed. (See Fig. 8-164.)

Slow Slide over Back

Partners stand back-to-back with hands overhead. They reach back and clasp hands. One player then bends over slowly, keeping back fairly straight and bringing arms forward until partner's back is against his own. He continues to bend, slowly, keeping arms straight until he brings partner up on his back and lets him slide down slowly so that his hands touch floor. Both players then do a handstand.

Somersault over Back

Partners work together. Standing back-to-back and grasping hands, one partner bends forward and pulls other up over his back. As partner is brought over his back, he, the partner, brings knees to

Fig. 8-165

chest in a somersault movement and lands on feet, facing partner. (See Fig. 8-165.)

Through the Stick

Performer holds a stick (about handle size and 4 feet long) with both hands behind back and palms facing forward. He brings stick up over head and down in front of body, brings right foot up and around right arm and through—between hands and stick—, then places stick flat on floor. Performer raises stick with left hand over head and down over back, lifts left foot off floor, and steps backwards through stick.

One-Legged Squat

Performer stands on one foot, extending other foot in front, with knee straight. He lowers body into squatting position on supporting leg, then comes back to original position without touching floor with hands or other foot. Hands may be placed straight out in front of contestant or to side. (See Fig. 8-166.)

Fig. 8-166

Chinese Get up

Two participants face each other as partners. They sit down on floor back-to-back, with knees drawn up and elbows locked. At a given signal, they lean against each other and slowly stand. They then sit down slowly to original position.

Three-Man Scramble

This stunt may also be carried out by as many players as are wanted, depending upon number of mats available. Participants are divided into groups of three. These three lie face downward on mat about 1 foot apart and all facing in same direction. At a given signal, middle player rolls to his left and assumes position occupied by player to his left. In order for him to do this, player to his left rises on hands and feet and springs over him to position formerly occupied by middle player. He lands in middle position and immediately rolls to his right where he assumes position occupied by that player, who also rises on his hands and feet and springs over him to position formerly occupied by middle player. Player now in middle position rolls to his left, etc. This routine can be continued for as long as desired. (See Fig. 8-167.)

Fig. 8-167

Camel Walk with Rider

This stunt necessitates three players. First person assumes a front position with weight of body resting on hands and toes. Arms and legs are held stiff and rump is held high in air. Second person assumes a similar position directly under him facing in opposite direction. Feet of both players are well spread. After both have assumed this position, they grasp ankles of partner and raise themselves off floor as far as possible. Third sits astride back of first player, with his back toward the head. They then move forward.

This is a very difficult stunt and a great deal of help must be given by third player in getting second player in position.

Head Stand

Performer places head on mat. Hands are placed so that he will not fall forward or sideward. Balance is important. (See Fig. 8-168.)

Fig. 8-168

Triple Forward Roll

No. 1 lies on back with knees drawn up and feet on floor. No. 2 stands with feet astride No. 1's head. No. 1 grasps ankles of No. 2. No. 3 grasps ankles of No. 1 and throws up his feet so that No. 2 can grasp them. No. 3 rolls forward. (See Fig. 8-169.)

Fig. 8-169

Knee and Shoulder Balance

No. 1 lies on back with legs drawn up and feet on floor. No. 2 places hands on knees of No. 1 and comes to stand with shoulders supported by No. 1. (See Fig. 8-170.)

Walking on Hands

This takes a great deal of practice. Back should be slightly arched and feet kept together. Various obstacles may be set up to make activity more spectacular, as indicated in picture. (See Fig. 8-171.)

Dead Man Carry

No. 1 assumes a rigid position on floor on back. Nos. 2 and 3 pick him up by head and feet.

Fig. 8-170

Shoulder Hand Stand

No. 1 squats with one foot ahead of the other so that he is balanced. No. 2 places hands on shoulders of No. 1 and comes to a hand stand. No. 1 rises to feet. This can be very effective if done by a large number of students. It takes practice and should not be attempted by those individuals who do not have ability to complete stunt.

Inverted Hand Walk

No. 1 places hands on feet of No. 2 and comes to a hand stand. No. 2 grasps his ankles and walks forward. (See Fig. 8-172.)

Fig. 8-171

Horse Walk

No. 1 rests on hands and feet on "all fours." No. 2 straddles No. 1 with his back toward No. 1's head. He clenches his feet, bends forward and grasps No. 1's heels. No. 1 walks forward on all fours.

Monkey Walk

No. 1 rests on hands and feet on "all fours." No. 2 puts legs around No. 1 and clenches his feet around his back. No. 2 then grasps No. 1's hips. No. 1 walks forward on all fours.

Squat Stand

Performer rests hands on floor bringing weight over them in a squat balance. Weight should be well centered.

Fig. 8-172

Front Flip

Performer takes a short run, springs into the air and at highest point, brings arms close to body and brings head forward. As he completes turn, he straightens body and lands on feet.

Double Wheelbarrow

No. 1 grasps No. 2 by ankles as No. 2 rests on hands. No. 3 places feet so that they can be held by No. 1. No. 2 walks forward on hands. (See Fig. 8-173.)

Elephant Walk

No. 1 stands with feet spread apart. No. 2 faces No. 1, jumps upward, putting legs around No. 1's waist. No. 2 then bends backward,

Fig. 8-173

placing hands on floor between No. 1's legs. No. 1 bends forward until hands are on floor. No. 2 then places hands on heels of No. 1.

Forearm Stand

Participants make a V-shaped triangle with forearms. Using heads as balancers, they push off with feet to a stand, keeping feet together. Hands are cupped with head resting in hands. (See Fig. 8-174.)

Head Stand (Clap)

Everything is done same as in regular head stand with exception that balance is maintained while hands are struck together and returned to floor.

Back Pitch

The "flier" lies on back on mat with hands on mat and at side of head. Legs are raised and knees are bent. Thrower stands at his feet facing him and grasping his ankles. Thrower lifts flier by ankles and throws him up and away. As he is lifted, flier pushes up with hands and snaps legs down, assuming upright position.

Fig. 8-174

Wrestler's Bridge

Participant lies on back on mat. Knees should be bent and feet placed about 2 feet apart with soles down. Hands are placed just above head in a palms-down position with thumbs touching each ear. Back, neck, and head are arched while hands and feet force trunk of body off mat.

Back Bend Walk

Participant starts with wrestler's bridge. While in this position he walks backward on hands and feet.

Seal Walk

Participant assumes stoop-falling position (push-up) with fingers pointing backwards and thumbs pointing forward. Toes are pointed forward, with arches of feet resting on mat. Body is pulled forward as arms and feet are dragged. Hips sway from side to side.

Knee Walk

Participant assumes a position on knees on mat with body in upright position. He then grasps both ankles with hands. Maintaining this position, he walks forward on knees.

Armless Rise

Participant assumes horizontal position face up on mat. He crosses arms over chest and attempts to rise by moving feet under buttocks. He must not move arms from folded position as he comes to standing position.

Sit Through

Participant assumes horizontal position face down and parallel to mat. Hands are placed at sides of body in palms-down position. Arms are straightened forcibly and with a sudden flexing of hips and knees, participant jumps through arms, coming to sitting straight-leg position. Fall may be broken by using arms.

Thigh Balance

Two participants stand facing each other at arm's length. No. 1 places left hand behind neck of No. 2 and left foot on No. 2's thigh. To enable him to do this, No. 2 bends knees slightly and places feet slightly apart. He then supports No. 1 by bracing himself and placing right hand behind and above No. 1's knee. No. 1 then steps to a stand on thighs of No. 2 and he in turn transfers his other hand behind and above No. 1's knee to help support him. No. 1 arches back and leans forward with head thrown back. Both are facing in same direction.

Spin the Top

Participant stands in upright position. He jumps in the air and while in the air attempts to make a complete circle, landing in starting position. Axis of rotation is center of body. A thrust of the arm in direction of movement is an aid. Head should also be turned in direction of movement.

Crab Walk

Participant assumes a position on all fours with back facing mat. He then walks backward, forward, or sideward on all fours.

Hop, Step, Jump

Participant places both feet parallel to a line. He then springs forward and lands on one foot. He continues his movement into a long step. A violent thrust of the arms is executed to add height, momentum, and distance. Lead foot of step movement now becomes take-off foot for next movement which is the jump. Jump is executed and participant lands on both feet.

Forward Roll (one leg)

Participant does forward roll from one foot coming up on same foot. Legs are kept apart as in striding position.

Forward Roll (ankles)

Participant grasps ankles and does forward roll without releasing grasp on ankles. Most difficult part of this activity is to regain feet after roll. Mechanics are same as in forward roll without using hands.

Forward Roll (thighs)

This is same as preceding roll except that hands are placed under buttocks.

Safety Roll (shoulder roll)

Participant runs forward into dive turning head and shoulder under and to side, breaking fall with arm. He lands on back of shoulder blade and rolls diagonally over back and buttock muscles to a slant.

Fish Flop-Chest Roll

Participant does a hand balance. He then lowers weight of body slowly with arms, holding chin up and slipping chest forward slightly. He lands on chest and rolls down onto stomach, thighs, knees, and then feet. Body arch should be held until toes touch mat.

Mule Kick

Participant stands erect. He dives forward, landing on hands and keeping arms rigid. He then kicks feet outward and backward to resemble a mule kick.

Snap Down

Participant does a hand balance. Knees are slightly bent, and as body falls off balance, knees are forcibly extended and legs are snapped down, flexing at hips. There should be just enough knee bend to keep from jarring them when landing. Participant should push hard with hands, arms, and especially with shoulders. He should land with arms out and even with shoulders.

CLOWN ACTS

Clown acts always have a place in a demonstration. They can be put on without a great deal of preparation or practice, providing you have two or three outstanding tumblers or gymnasts. The instructor can help them work up the acts, and they can practice by themselves until they know what is expected of one another. The clown acts will of course be more successful if the participants dress the part. Just to look at an individual dressed as a typical clown is funny enough, and almost anything he does is amusing. It is perhaps best that two work together on this activity. Many of the acts can be original. Some which have proven successful are given here.[4]

No. 1 slaps at No. 2's cheek as No. 2 slaps his hands; they reverse the procedure, with No. 1 swinging his hand within a few inches of No. 2's cheek, stopping it. No. 2 slaps his hands together as No. 1's hand comes close to his cheek. (See Fig. 8-175.)

---

[4] Health and Physical Education Journal, South Chicago Dept. Y.M.C.A., Jan., 1931, "Clown Tumbling Stunts," L. L. McClow.

Fig. 8-175

Clown makes forward roll, rising high in the air after coming off feet. Clown shakes buttocks while in air. (See Fig. 8-176.)

Fig. 8-176

No. 2 lies on floor, face up. No. 1 stands with feet straddling No. 2's head. No. 1 jumps up and comes down as though to land on No. 2's head. This is done several times. (See Fig. 8-177.)

Fig. 8-177

No. 1 pulls No. 2 up by seat of pants and kicks him. No. 2 falls forward into a roll. (See Fig. 8-178.)

Fig. 8-178

No. 1 lies on back with face turned to side. No. 2 runs across No. 1's face and body very lightly. (See Fig. 8-179.)

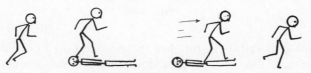

Fig. 8-179

Clown springs upward and forward with legs and arms as stiff as possible. (See Fig. 8-180.)

Fig. 8-180

Two clowns do a double roll forward, bringing each other stationary while high in the air. (See Fig. 8-181.)

Fig. 8-181

Clown takes a forward roll and, hitting on buttocks, rolls forward. (See Fig. 8-182.)

Fig. 8-182

No. 1 stands on edge of table, waving arms and pretending to fall backward. As he falls, No. 2, who is *looking toward audience* and *directly in line with No. 1*, turns just in time to catch No. 1 and push him back onto table. (See Fig. 8-183.)

Fig. 8-183

Clown runs and dives forward on stomach on top of table, sliding off other side. As he lands, he does forward roll coming up onto his feet. (See Fig. 8-184.)

Fig. 8-184

Clown runs forward as if to jump over chair. He stops suddenly, jumps into the air so that he comes down on chair in sitting position. (See Fig. 8-185.)

Fig. 8-185

Clown balances himself on chair. (See Fig. 8-186.)

Fig. 8-186

Clown runs forward and dives over chair in a forward roll. As he comes out of roll he brings with him a newspaper which is lying on floor and then stands and reads paper. (See Fig. 8-187.)

Fig. 8-187

No. 1 sits on chair reading newspaper. No. 2 runs forward and dives over chair in forward roll. As he is in the air he takes paper from No. 1's hands, continuing forward roll. As he comes out of forward roll onto feet, he stands and reads newspaper. (See Fig. 8-188.)

Fig. 8-188

Clown Act—I Wanna Be in the Band

A very clever pantomime act involving two clowns and a person dressed as a band director may be worked out with the help of the dramatics, music, and home economics departments. This act will also give some recognition and attention to the band, as the success of the act depends a great deal upon the musical accompaniment.

MATERIALS AND MAKE-UP OF THE PARTICIPANTS

The humor of any clown act depends a great deal on the clowns' costumes; therefore, every effort should be made to have appropriate dress for the participants. One person should be dressed in a very funny clown outfit, one in a clown-like band uniform and one in a band director's uniform. The face make-up can be applied by the dramatics class. Here again originality is important.

PROPS

The main prop is a cardboard box large enough for one clown to get completely inside of it and be fairly comfortable. A large enough opening should be made in the top of the box so that the clown is able to stick his head through it. Another opening should be made in the side of the box large enough for the clown to get in and out of the box. A curtain should be attached to the opening so that, after the clown is in the box, he cannot be seen. The box should be open at the bottom.

A long-handled hammer with a soft fake head attached to the end of it is needed, along with two cornets, and a mannequin head made up exactly like the clown who will be in the box.

THE CLOWN ACT

The pantomime act itself should be well rehearsed so that the participants are familiar with the actions of each other. The act opens with the two main participants, one dressed as a clown and the other dressed as a bandsman, walking in slowly, arguing about their ability to play the cornet and which one will be selected to play in the band. After much argument and threats to each other they try to prove who is the better by both taking turns playing the cornet. The audience is then well aware that the person dressed as the clown is the best player. However, he is told by the bandsman that he cannot play in the band because he is not wearing a band uniform.

The bandsman or poor player then shows the audience that he knows he is the poorest player and that he is thinking of some solution to his problem. Suddenly he gets the idea that he can put the clown, who is the good player, in the box and have him do the actual playing while he himself makes believe he is the one doing the playing. He will in this way fool the band director into letting him play in the band.

The big problem for the bandsman is to get the clown to consent to his scheme and then to get him into the box. Quite a scramble takes place before this is accomplished. In the process the bandsman picks up the hammer and deals the clown several devastating blows. He finally gets him into the box. As soon as the clown is in the box, he sticks his head through the hole and starts to protest. The audience will laugh at this, but will not be expecting what is to follow. The bandsman picks up the hammer again and tries to keep the clown in the box and out of sight by hitting him on the head. Each time he is hit, the clown disappears into the box, but each time he again sticks his head out of the box and is hit by the hammer. The fourth time, he sticks up the fake head of the mannequin which has been concealed in the box. The bandsman puts a great deal of motion into his windup and really hits the fake head. The head rolls off and breaks up on the floor. The bandsman finally gets the clown to stay in the box. The two then agree to try to fool the band director and proceed to work out a set of signals for the band tryout. If the bandsman taps the box two times the clown in the box will start playing. If he taps the box only one time the clown in the box will stop playing. They practice the act before the audience until is it perfected. The poor player then goes and gets the band director. He tries to impress the director with his ability as a cornetist and finally convinces him to come over to the table and listen to him play.

The director removes his hat and places it on the box. The bandsman then moves over to the box and kicks it twice causing the clown in the box to start to play. The bandsman acts as though he is doing the playing. The director is very favorably impressed and starts to take him over to the band. Meanwhile the clown in the box has not stopped playing, because he has not been signaled to stop, so the bandsman must go back and kick the box one time to stop him. During all this time he must make believe he is playing while the director is trying to pull him away from the box toward the band.

Both of them then start toward the band but when they are almost there the band director realizes that he has left his hat on the box and goes back to get it. While reaching for the hat he stumbles and accidentally kicks the box twice, causing the clown in the box to start playing.

The band director then realizes that he has been duped and suddenly lifts up the cardboard box, revealing the clown, who still keeps playing for a short time after the box has been removed. Finally realizing that he has been discovered, the clown jumps up and runs off the floor.

The band director then goes over to the bandsman, grabs him by the coat and the seat of the pants, and escorts him from the floor.

The act should last about 10 minutes.

Emmett Kelly and His Friend (Clown Act)

This simple clown act was originally done by Emmett Kelly when he was a member of the great Ringling Brothers Circus. Also it was presented twice on the Ed Sullivan show. It is quite simple to fit this act into any high school physical education demonstration.

The key to the success of this act is the manipulation of the spotlight, for so much depends upon how this is used. It is necessary, therefore, to select with great care the person who is to direct the spotlight. The only other props necessary for the act are a broom and a 4 x 6 mat.

The person selected to be the clown should have some acting ability or experience and he should be fairly tall. His clothing should not be that of a typical clown, but should be similar to that of a tramp —extremely tattered and torn. This clothing can easily be made by taking a suit which is several sizes too large and tearing it almost to shreds, being careful to keep all pieces in place. Small patches of bright colored cloth should be sewed on the coat and pants. The shoes should be as large as possible with the toe open so that loose papers may be picked up as the clown walks slowly about the gymnasium. This maneuver always draws a laugh from the audience. Another way in which the clown can be used is to hand out suckers to the kiddies at intermission and at the end of the show.

The dramatics department should be called upon to make up the clown. A picture of Emmett Kelly may be obtained from the library. The clown's facial expression is very sad, and of course this fact is important to the act. His appearance will have a big effect on the success of the performance. (See Fig. 8-189.)

Fig. 8-189

The operator turns off some of the lights in the gymnasium, leaving just enough light for the clown to be clearly visible. He enters through the regular main entrance and walks slowly to the center of the gymnasium. The spot man throws a small ball of light behind the clown making it appear that it is following him as he walks about. The clown should stop once or twice in his walk and kick and motion at the ball of light as if he is trying to chase or drive it away. It jumps away from him, and he acts as if he is extremely puzzled by the actions of the friend who keeps following him. As the clown nears the center of the gymnasium, he finds a broom which he picks up, and he slowly creeps toward the ball of light. He slowly raises the broom over his head and brings it down with tremendous force upon the light. Just as this is done, the spot man enlarges the light so that it places the clown in a large circle of light. The clown cannot understand this turn of affairs and makes this known to the audience. He walks slowly around the floor but the light follows him, keeping him in the center. He then tries to tiptoe out of the spotlight and just as he puts his foot down outside of the light the spot man moves the light so that he finds himself again in the center of the light. The clown is very upset and extremely puzzled, but he picks up the broom again and starts beating the light. With each blow the light becomes smaller and smaller. These blows are well spaced and when the ball of light becomes very small the clown starts sweeping it in the direction of the mat. He picks up the corner of the mat and carefully sweeps the ball of light under it. Just as he does this, the spot man snaps off the spotlight and turns on the house lights, and the act is over.

The length of the act depends upon the clown and his acting ability. The entire act should not take over ten minutes. This performance is always well received by an audience.

Other Acts

There are other clown acts that can be used, one of which may be the use of stilts. This is always an entertaining activity and can be worked in with others as a comedy act. For example, after the boys have performed the feat of walking on their hands as shown in Figure 8-171, the clown may follow them while walking on the stilts as shown in Figure 8-190.

Another act may show several clowns being pursued by a policeman, or the policeman may be in charge and be trying to have the clowns perform certain skills, as shown in Figure 8-191. The participants should, in this case, be dressed in comical uniforms that go along with the act.

MARCHING

A place should be made in every physical education demonstration for marching. The marching may be either simple or complex, de-

Fig. 8-190

pending upon how much preparation the instructor wishes to give to it. The drill should be well thought out and there should be musical accompaniment, as the quality of marching will be vastly improved by it. Here are a few sample drills which may be used in a demonstration. They are not difficult and can be added to or improved upon wherever necessary.

Fig. 8-191

Formations: Squads of Sixteen

Two groups of eight enter gym from each end corner, marching straight ahead to opposite corner and alternating as they march through each other's line in center of gym. (See Fig. 8-192.)

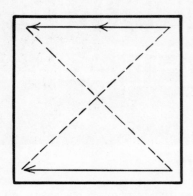

Fig. 8-192

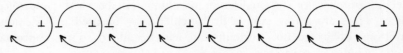

Fig. 8-193

Marchers count off by fours and twos from right to left. No. 1 circles around No. 2 in eight counts, coming back to original position.

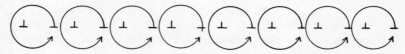

Fig. 8-194

No. 2 circles around No. 1 in eight counts, coming back to original position.

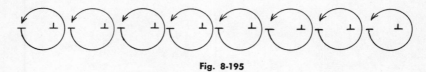

Fig. 8-195

No. 1 circles around No. 2 in opposite direction from that in Fig. 8-193.

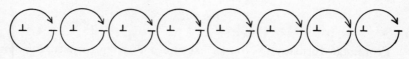

Fig. 8-196

No. 2 circles around No. 1 in opposite direction from that in Fig. 8-194.

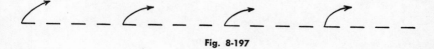

Fig. 8-197

Using No. 4 as pivot, marchers quarter wheel to the right.

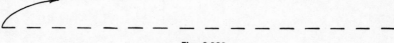

Fig. 8-198

Using No. 4 as pivot, marchers half wheel to the right.

Fig. 8-199

Using No. 4 as pivot, marchers full wheel to the right.

Star Formations

Using center men (No. 4's) as pivots, marchers execute a full wheel to the right, then about face and to the left.

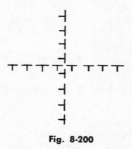

Fig. 8-200

From star formation, No. 4's execute a quarter turn to the left. They do this four times, coming back to original position.

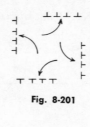

Fig. 8-201

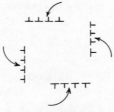

Fig. 8-202

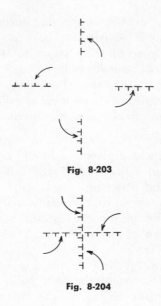

Fig. 8-203

Fig. 8-204

No. 4's full wheel to the left.

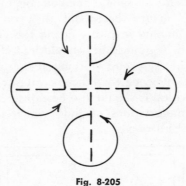

Fig. 8-205

SELF-DEFENSE

The self-defense (judo) demonstration should be given on a 60' x 60' ensolite mat. The purpose of the self-defense demonstration is to bring a better understanding of judo to the general public.

It will be necessary to do more planning for the presentation of this type of activity; therefore, the descriptive talk about the activity should be given by the physical education instructor in order that he may ad-lib or further explain a given skill during the demonstration. A student may do this if he has worked with the physical education activity sufficiently to be fully aware of what is going on and to understand the various techniques involved.

The following information should be given to the audience so that it is completely informed as to what is taking place during the activity and what its purpose is in the program.

1. An introduction of the students and instructors.
2. An introduction and explanation of the activity.
3. The purpose and objectives of the self-defense unit in the physical education program.
4. The value and purpose of the "daily warm-up exercise." The value of warming-up for the specific activity.
5. A full explanation of the drills, breakfalls, flips, principles of leverage, take-downs and counters.
6. A full explanation of the judo position and judo match.
7. An occasional mention of the floor formations and the effort that is made to make full use of the facilities available for this type of activity.

The warm-up exercises should include jogging around the mat, alternately running on the heels and then on the toes (double circle formation). Running in place, facing the center of the circle, may also be included. A gym leader should lead all the exercises with all of the members of the group working at the same time. It should be explained to the audience that these exercises are preliminary to the actual judo activities. It should also be explained that the activities shown here are demonstrations of judo which are taught to large groups in actual class situations.

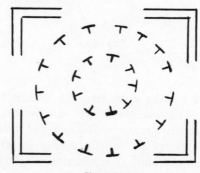

Fig. 8-206

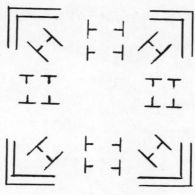

Fig. 8-207

The types of exercises given here are typical for preparation for the judo activities. They will show the audience what types of exercise are needed before beginning the rigorous judo activity. Figs. 8-206 and 8-207 show the position of the participants on the mat for the most effective use of the facility and the space, in order to take care of as many students as possible at one time.

Extreme care should be taken to avoid giving the audience the wrong impression of the sport of judo. Many people are of the opinion that judo is a brutal and maiming activity and should not be included in the physical education program. The selection of judo throws should, therefore, be made with care to give the public the correct impression. The difference between judo and karate should be explained to the audience.

1. *Stretching exercises* (4 counts)
   Windmill, 20 side straddle hops, 10 burpees, 6 count push-ups, trunk rotation, neck roll, groin stretcher. Front and rear bridging, curls.
2. *Two-man "belly slapper" drill*
   Place hands alternately on stomach, shuffle feet first left then right, alternate hands, deliver light blows to midsection of partner.
3. *Two-man "shoulder slap"*
   Same as above, but place hands on shoulders and alternate.
4. *Belly hand-off with medicine ball*
   Everyone in one circle facing in. Teacher in center tosses ball to a boy who returns it.

5. *Relay formation* (work across mat) (See Fig. 8-208.)
   a. Forward rolls
   b. Sideward rolls (both ways—alternating)
   c. Backward rolls

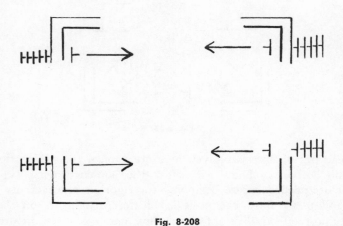

Fig. 8-208

6. *On-guard position drill*
   From prone position, jump to feet with body balanced, arms
   out in crouch. Repeat from hands and knees position. (See Fig.
   8-209.)

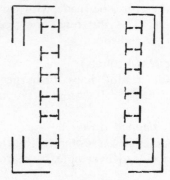

Fig. 8-209

7. *Circle Drills—Breakfalls*(To center and back)
   a. Standing shoulder rolls
   b. Front forearm breakfall—from knees

Front forearm breakfall—from stand
Running front breakfall
c. Sideward breakfall
d. Backward breakfall—from a squat
Backward breakfall—from a jump
Running backward breakfall
8. *Flips* (Two-man drills)
a. Sideward roll flips
b. Front flip toss (half-speed)
c. Fireman carry and roll
d. Flip-toss (full-speed)
e. Hip-toss No. 1
f. Hip-toss No. 2 (See Fig. 8-210.)

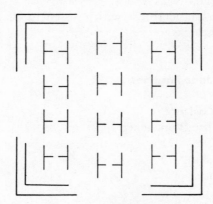

Fig. 8-210

Leverage Demonstration

1. Single wrist grab on forearm—step into opponent's forearm to break grasp.
2. Double wrist grab—reach in with free hand, grab, and lift up quickly.
3. Both wrists grabbed—step forward, swing forearms down sharply, and carry arms out with elbows straight. (Work against thumb-side of grip.) Step into opponent using top of head, butt chest, and lift legs at knees, with head tipping the balance. (*Always assist partner in falls! Passive resistance!*)
4. Wrist-breaker come-along—police method of subduing and transferring prisoners in a crowd.

Advanced Wrestling Take-Downs and Counters

1. Double leg tackle and counter
2. Forward and backward trips
3. Ankle take-down
4. Arm drag and fake arm drag, ankle pick-up, or back heel.

Additional Holds and Counters

1. Breaking a scissors hold
2. Counter and break full-Nelson
3. Breaking strangles (rear and front)
4. Guillotine and breaks
5. Breaking overhead thrust with crossed hands into straight and reverse wristlocks

Demonstration of Judo Positions

1. Posture and balance
2. Position of hands on jacket
3. Balance
4. Posture breaking
5. Nonresistance
6. Contact
7. Body mechanics

Judo Demonstration

After all the fundamental steps of self-defense are explained and all the drills are completed, the audience should have a better understanding of judo.

At this time all boys should clear the mat and sit around the outside edge. The best four pairs will then demonstrate judo matches for one minute. The boys should officiate the matches. The pictures show several holds and falls used in judo. Fig. 8-211 is the "floating knee wheel," and Fig. 8-212 the "flying scissors." These can be easily shown in a demonstration and will be of extreme interest to an audience. Fig. 8-213 is a mat position for matches.

Fig. 8-211

CROSS MAT TUMBLING

Cross mat tumbling is just what the name implies—tumbling on mats that are crossed. The mats are placed so as to form a cross, and, as the participants alternate in the exercises, it appears that there will be a mix-up in the center. However, with the proper timing and practice, this will not happen. It is interesting to the audience because they are constantly expecting a mistake to be made and the drills to break down. They are always amazed when this does not happen; consequently, it is both thrilling and amusing to both the spectators and participants.

Fig. 8-212

A group of 30 youngsters would be ideal for such a demonstration, which would start by having two lines of alternating boys and girls march out from the opposite entrances on the sides of the gym. (See Fig. 8-214.)

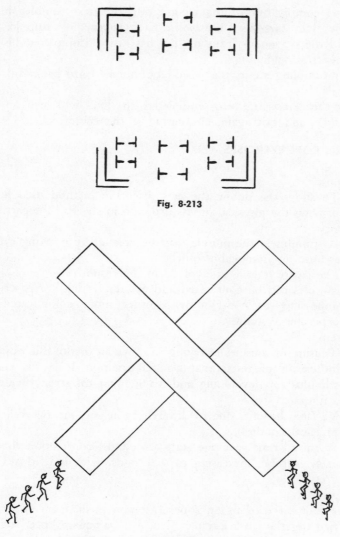

Fig. 8-213

Fig. 8-214

Each line would march across two mats that are crossed in the center of the gymnasium. When the last person in each line has reached the end of the mat, the line will stop and all will about-face.

Now, the first person in either line will proceed to do front rolls until he or she reaches the end of the mat. While the first tumbler is coming out of the second roll, the next tumbler in the other line will start his front rolls. Each succeeding tumbler will wait until the person in front of him has nearly completed his second roll before beginning.

Other tumbling stunts that could be included are back rolls and cart wheels.

After the demonstration is completed, the lines will turn towards the entrance, and exit again, alternating at the center.

ISOMETRIC ROPE EXERCISES

I. Purpose
  A. To show the public the new scientific method used in improving the physical fitness program in the P. E. department.
II. Theory
  A. A stimulus in the muscle may be created by exerting a force against an immovable object.
  B. The entire muscle is involved in the response.
  C. Muscles can be contracted and exerted which are practically impossible to contract with other more complicated and expensive systems.
III. System
  A. Tensing of muscles in trying to move an immovable object.
  B. Indication of tests: that one contraction a day is enough stimulus for developing and maintaining the strengthening of a muscle.
  C. Variable benefits due to differences in age, mental ability, or physical condition.
  D. Required time: average start 6 seconds' contraction time for each exercise, increasing to 9 seconds, with individual's progress.
IV. Apparatus
  A. 8-foot piece of nylon rope, 1/4 inch in diameter, with ends tied together in a circular piece with a square knot, and two rubber handles 5 inches in length and 5/8 inch in diameter placed on the rope so that they will slide.
    1. The flexible handles make it possible to lengthen or shorten the rope by knotting it to the desired length.
    2. No weights or any other heavy objects necessary.
    3. Can be used by anyone almost anywhere and is easily carried.

V. Period of time required for demonstration
   A. One-half to three-quarters of an hour
VI. Formation for demonstration
   A. Alignment for 30 students: All 30 line up, facing audience as
      shown in Fig. 8-215. The participants perform any exercise
      they wish.

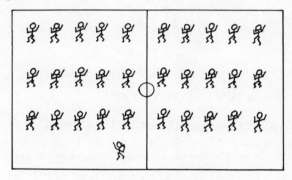

Fig. 8-215

Exercise Description

THE BACK LIFT

Handles of rope are grasped with palms facing in toward body.
Rope should be placed under arches of both feet which are spread
approximately 2 feet apart. Legs should be bent slightly, back
straight, and head up. Participant should exert a pull up, keeping arms
slightly bent at elbow. (See Fig. 8-216.)

Fig. 8-216

BACKWARD ARM PULL

Handles of rope are grasped with palms facing backward, arms
straight at side of body and rope in front of body. Body should be
bent slightly forward at hips, and arms should be kept straight. Force

should be exerted by pushing arms backward and upward. (See Fig. 8-217.)

Fig. 8-217

BEHIND THE BACK OUTWARD PULL

Rope should be doubled and grasped with hands in a position behind back. Palms should be facing in toward body. Participant should exert a pull out and away from body. (See Fig. 8-218.)

Fig. 8-218

BEHIND THE BACK PULL

Handles of rope are grasped with hands behind back and with palms facing out laterally to body. Rope should be placed under feet,

Fig. 8-219

which are spread approximately 2 feet apart. Participant should keep hands together and exert a pull upward. (See Fig. 8-219.)

LEAN OVER SIDE ARM PULL

Participant bends over, keeping knees straight. Handles of rope are grasped with palms facing in toward feet, which are spaced about 2 feet apart with rope under them. Pull should be exerted out and up with body remaining bent at waist. (See Fig. 8-220.)

Fig. 8-220

CURLS

Handles of rope are grasped with palms facing up, elbows close to sides of body and arms bent at a 90-degree angle. Knees should be slightly bent. Rope should be placed under buttocks, and a force should be exerted upward in a curling motion. (See Fig. 8-221.)

Fig. 8-221

FRONT ARM PULL

Grasp rope after it has been looped, placing hands in front of chest and palms facing inward toward and against chest. Pull is outward with elbows placed in a position parallel to floor. (See Fig. 8-222.)

Fig. 8-222

REVERSE CURL

Handles of rope are grasped with palms facing down, elbows close to sides of body and arms bent at a 90-degree angle. Knees should be slightly bent. Rope should be placed under buttocks and force should be exerted upward in a curling motion. (See Fig. 8-223.)

Fig. 8-223

OVER THE HEAD ARM PULL

Rope is grasped by handles and held over head with arms extended and forward, elbows slightly bent, and palms out. Exert pressure down and out. (See Fig. 8-224.)

Fig. 8-224

LATERAL ARM LIFT

Rope is grasped by handles, with arms hanging and rope in front of participant. Pressure is exerted out and up with arms. (See Fig. 8-225.)

Fig. 8-225

ARM PULL

Rope should be looped and grasped with palms facing in and in front of chest. Elbows are slightly bent and pull is exerted out, using muscles of shoulders and upper arms. (See Fig. 8-226.)

Fig. 8-226

ARM PULL (no loops)

This exercise is done same as one above, except that rope is not looped. (See Fig. 8-227.)

Fig. 8-227

FORWARD ARM LIFT

Handles of rope are grasped with palms facing back, arms straight and rope behind participant and under buttocks. Force is exerted forward and up, keeping arms straight. (See Fig. 8-228.)

Fig. 8-228

MILITARY PRESS

Grasp handles of rope, which has been placed around shoulders and under arms. Elbows should be behind and outside of rope with palms of hands facing forward. Arms should be spread so that hands are at right height to maintain correct arm bend of 90 degrees. Pressure is exerted up and out. (See Fig. 8-229.)

Fig. 8-229

BACKWARD LEG LIFT

Participant loops rope around ankles with one leg ahead of the other in striding motion and with enough pressure on rope so that it is taut. Pressure is exerted backward with back leg. Keep both legs straight. (See Fig. 8-230.)

Fig. 8-230

DOWNWARD PUSH

Handles of rope are grasped with hands at sides, and arms bent. Rope is placed behind head and resting across shoulders. Lower portion of rope is in small of back and force is exerted downward. (See Fig. 8-231.)

Fig. 8-231

FORWARD LEG LIFT

Participant loops rope around ankles with one leg ahead of the other in striding position and with enough pressure so that rope is taut. Front foot is extended forward, keeping knee straight. (See Fig. 8-232.)

Fig. 8-232

THE FORWARD PUSH

Participant grasps handles of rope with palms facing down. Rope is placed over head and across shoulder blades. Arms are raised so that they are parallel to floor. Arms are slightly bent so that rope is under elbows. Hands are forward and outside shoulders. Pressure is exerted outward from chest in attempt to straighten arms. (See Fig. 8-233.)

Fig. 8-233

KNEE SPREADER

Participant loops rope around outside of knees while sitting on floor. Knees are spread apart so that rope is taut. Feet are together with knees drawn up so that heels are about 1 foot from buttocks. Force is exerted outward by both knees. (See Fig. 8-234.)

Fig. 8-234

LATERAL LEG LIFT

Participant loops rope around ankles with feet spread apart far enough so that rope is taut. Pressure is exerted sideward by pressing one leg outward while standing on other leg. (See Fig. 8-235.)

Fig. 8-235

UPPER LEG LIFT

Participant loops rope and stands on it with one foot. Other end is placed over instep of other foot which is brought forward with knee bend. Force is exerted by lifting front leg forward and upward. (See Fig. 8-236.)

Fig. 8-236

HEEL LEG LIFT

Participant loops rope and stands on it with one foot. Rope is placed around back of heel just at base of Achilles' tendon. Leg is slightly flexed and pressure is exerted by forcing leg backward. (See Fig. 8-237.)

Fig. 8-237

FENCING

Although it is gaining in popularity, there is at the present time relatively little secondary school fencing. This is due to a large extent to a lack of interest and to the absence of qualified personnel to teach the sport. However, fencing does provide an activity which will captivate an audience and send them away impressed with the activity, if it is properly presented and administered.

The layman spectator does not understand the directing and judging of this sport. Consequently, before the demonstration, he should be given, in leaflet or verbal form, some basic information about the rules and techniques of fencing. This activity is adaptable to either the boys' or girls' program. (See Fig. 8-238.)

Fig. 8-238

TESTING

Testing is an important phase of the physical education curriculum. It is not understood by many people, however. The following segments will provide the purpose and understanding of a test. They will demonstrate to the public the general make-up of a test and the procedures used in administering it.

The Zone Run

This is to test the individual's reaction, speed, agility, and endurance.

The student starts behind the line marked in tape on the floor and runs to the other end of the line marked #7. He must touch the floor beyond the line with one foot and return to the starting line. This he repeats, back and forth, for 20 seconds. His score is determined by the number of zones he has passed in the allotted time.

The demonstration is set up with four boys participating. While one is running, two other boys will be stationed at the end lines so it will be easier for the runner to distinguish the lines. The other boy will be located in the middle of the zone to aid the instructor in counting the zones passed. (See Fig. 8-239.)

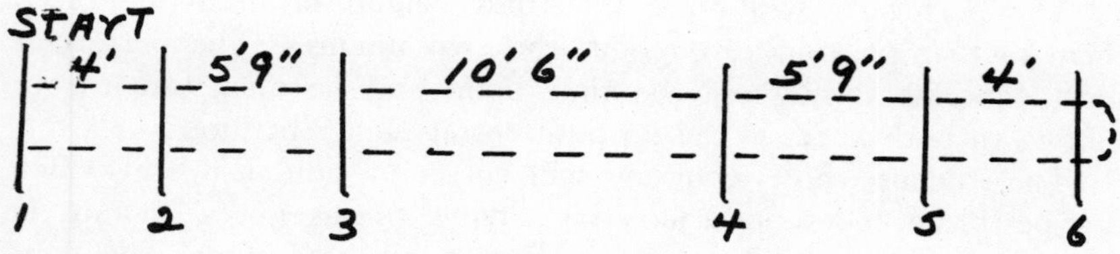

Fig. 8-239

Three Consecutive Jumps

This activity tests the individual's leg strength, agility, and coordination.

The student will approach the starting line and place both feet behind the line, but as close to the line as possible. When he is ready, he will make three jumps. Jumps must be consecutive, and the feet must be kept together to eliminate the running steps. The distance will be measured from the back of the starting line to the back of the rear foot or any part of the body that touches the floor at the conclusion of the third jump.

Students will aid the instructor by measuring the distance of each jump. Three trials will be given and the best effort of the three will be recorded as the individual's distance. (See Fig. 8-240.)

Fig. 8-240

Two Minute Sit-ups

This is an endurance test to determine how many sit-ups the student can perform in a period of two minutes.

For demonstration purposes, as many pairs of students may be used as wanted.

One student of the pair will be the performer and the other will hold the performer's feet and count the repetitions accomplished. The performer will place himself in a supine position, with knees flexed and feet flat on the floor. The other student will hold or anchor his feet to the floor.

The performer will place his hands behind his head and keep them in that position throughout the two minutes. The performer must continue throughout the time limit, and he must touch both elbows to both knees in the up position on each repetition.

The student who is counting will not count any sit-ups in which the performer does not touch his elbows to his knees, or any in which he releases his hands from behind his head. Once the continuous motion stops the performer is considered finished.

ROLLING TIRE SCOOP THROW

Divide players into two groups. Line up groups facing each other about 20 feet apart. Assign a player from each group to act as a tire roller; two rollers stand in the center area, one at each end. (See Fig. 8-241.)

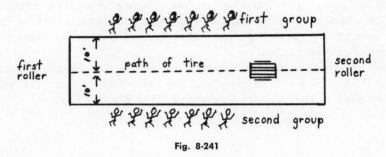

Fig. 8-241

Each player in the first group to throw has a scoop and a ball. Players in the second group do not have to have scoops and balls, and can take turns using equipment with the first group. Each player of the first group, using his scoop, attempts to throw the ball through the tire as it is rolled past. Scoops are tossed over to the second group (if every player doesn't have one). Then the second roller sets the tire in motion and the second group tries to throw the ball through it.

The rollers then join their respective groups and two other players act as rollers. Continue the game until each player has acted as a roller. Each ball tossed through the tire counts one point. The player or team with the highest score wins.

MEDICINE BALL EXERCISES

Although the use of the medicine ball has been discontinued in many of the physical education programs, it still is a very worthwhile activity and one which, if encouraged, would regain its popularity. It provides a good activity for a demonstration because of the fact that few people are familiar with it. It also provides enough action to create interest. It is a humorous activity, providing many laughs.

Equipment needed for the following exercises is six medicine balls. Divide the students into six groups of four each. Make sure each group has an odd number. (5,7,9,11). Each group has one medicine ball. (See Fig. 8-242.)

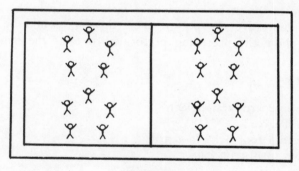

Fig. 8-242

1. Pass ball with both hands to person directly on right. When passing ball, step off with right foot and aim ball at receiver's chest.
2. Use same exercise as No. 1, except ball should be passed to second person on right.
3. Hold ball above head, stretch back and throw ball to person on right.
4. Use exercise as in No. 3, except ball should be passed to second person on right.
5. Sit on floor and hold ball with both hands over head, lean

backwards, and throw ball to person on right.

6. Use same exercise as in No. 5, except ball should be passed to second person on right.

There are many more exercises that can be used. Two or more balls can be used in each group, so that the activity can be made very complicated. The main purpose, however, should be one that shows the benefits derived from the use of the medicine ball in the physical education classes, and there are many indeed. Care should be taken that the activity does not develop into a comedy act.

HIGH ELEPHANT VAULTING

High elephant vaulting is a variation of the Swedish vaulting box. Basically, it involves a running approach to a 2-foot take-off from the springboard, working over the top of extended parallel bars to the mats on the opposite side. The stunts that are utilized are the various vaults characteristic of the horse and other apparatus.

The closer the performers follow each other over the apparatus, the more impressive the performance. Spacing should be just suf-ficient to allow the preceding performer to clear the landing area.

Equipment

1. Springboard (trampolet)
2. Parallel bars
3. Seven 5-foot by 8-foot mats
4. Two small trim bats

Preparation

1. Two mats are placed lengthwise over top of extended bars.
2. One mat is placed under springboard.
3. Four mats are placed in a pile on side opposite springboard. (Top mat should be canvas.)
4. One small mat is placed at either end of parallel bars.

Participants

Any number of participants may be used, but a minimum of

eights is recommended. Some degree of tumbling skill is required. (See Fig. 8-243.)

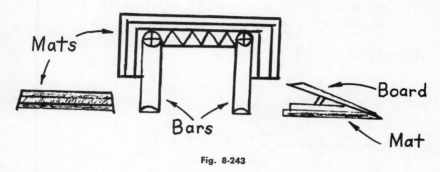

Fig. 8-243

Teaching Precautions

1. Spot performers from matted side of bars grasp upper arm as needed.
2. During practice, spotter may take a seat on top of parallels.
3. All performers should be sure to work on same side on flank and rear vaults. (This prevents being kicked in head.)
4. Positioning of hands on mat should be watched. Some stunts require working from the far bar or a near hand position.
5. Performers must be careful not to duck heads too soon during progression. They must get heads higher than mat.

Program of Stunts

1. Vault to hands and knees, stand, and dismount.
2. Vault to stand and dismount.
3. Flank vault.
4. Rear vault
5. Straddle vault over kneeler.
6. Shoulder roll.
7. Headspring.
8. Handspring.
9. Cart wheel.
10. Swan dive. (Boys must keep heads up; six boys should be used as catchers.)
11. Finale—the pile-up. One boy lies parallel and on top of bars. All others do flank vault, placing hands on back of bottom

man. One boy is added to pile each time through, or sooner if preferred. When there are five or six on pile, one boy hits into pile with glancing blow. All boys then roll off mat onto floor, but with caution.

SERPENTINE RUNNING

This activity is similar to marching except that the participants run instead of walk. It is a very colorful activity because of the

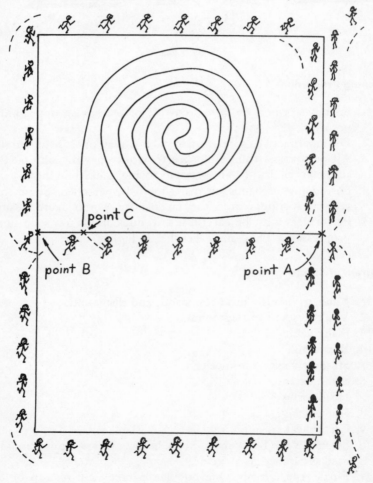

Fig. 8-244

constant movement of the participants and the intricate design used, which give the viewer the impression of a serpent moving across the floor.

The individual leading the group is the key person because he must gauge the distance the lines should be apart and also when to make the turn as he arrives at the center of the circle. This maneuver is very important and unless it is done correctly it will spoil the effect of the entire activity. The following points should be observed:

1. Boys and girls should enter gymnasium by running to basketball side line and proceeding to point A.
2. At point A, boys and girls form one line by alternating and following center line to point B.
3. At point B, boys and girls separate, boys going to right and girls to left. They continue running along basketball boundary line until they reach point A again. They now alternate and form single line to point C.
4. At point C, first person turns right as he continues running. Everyone follows him, and they form a large circle. As he runs, he continues to make smaller circles. He reverses direction near center of circle and comes out of circle running between lines that are running toward center. (See Fig. 8-244.)

PHYSICAL FITNESS RUN

Conditioning exercises which play an important part in any physical education program are necessary before progressing into more strenuous physical education activities. Many times these exercises are viewed as being monotonous, with little real meaning attached to them.

In an effort to make conditioning more meaningful and less monotonous, and to add competition, the physical fitness run can be used as a conditioning medium. This event provides for individual and/or squad competition. This is an especially exciting event in a physical education demonstration.

Ideally, the physical fitness run can be performed simultaneously by two six-man squads, either indoors or outdoors. The directions given are for indoor competition. Events that may be included in the run are: sit-ups, push-ups, standing broad jump, reach and jump, and running. Variations may be made as the instructor desires.

Equipment

1. Four markers for the corners of the gym floor (sand-filled bleach bottles)
2. One reach-and-jump board
3. Two standing broad jump boards

Personnel

1. One starter
2. A judge for each event to assure its proper execution. He must watch closely to note improper execution for the purpose of increasing speed.

Procedure

1. Both teams should progress around gym in counterclockwise direction.
2. Team A starts at point 1A from sitting position (see Fig. 8-245) and Team B from point 1B from sitting position (see Fig. 8-246.)

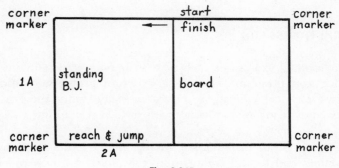

Fig. 8-245

3. Team A follows steps listed below:
    a. One and one-fourth complete laps around gym—no passing.
    b. One standing broad jump per person at point 1A. Each participant must wait turn.
    c. One-fourth lap around gym—no passing.
    d. One reach-and-jump per person at point 2A. Each participant must wait turn.

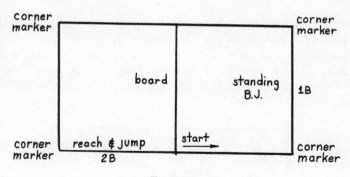

Fig. 8-246

e. One-half lap around gym—no passing.

f. Ten sit-ups by each person, all done simultaneously.

g. One-half lap around the gym—no passing.

h. Ten push-ups by each person, all simultaneously.

i. One-half lap around gym—no passing. Everyone must then be seated in squad order at original starting point.

4. Team B follows steps listed below:

a. One and one-fourth complete laps around gym—no passing.

b. One standing broad jump per person at point 1B. Each participant must wait turn.

c. One-fourth lap around gym—no passing.

d. Ten sit-ups by each person, all simultaneously.

e. One-half lap around gym—no passing.

f. One reach-and-jump per person at point 2B. Each participant must wait turn.

g. One-half lap around gym—no passing.

h. Ten push-ups by each person, all simultaneously.

i. One-half lap around gym—no passing. Everyone must be seated in squad order at original starting point.

VOLLEYBALL DEMONSTRATION

Volleyball, which may be played on the basketball court, is an excellent activity to demonstrate. The fundamental skills may be shown, such as serving, setting up, and spiking.

First, four boys bring out the volleyball nets. These boys could be the student intramural staff. The boys in the demonstration could be an all-star team selected from the previous year's intramural program or the top two teams in the program.

After the boys enter from their respective sides, they take their positions. One group will be the servers. After serving the ball, the first contestant will retrieve the ball after the defense returns it, then pass it to the next man in his line. He then falls in at the end of the line. When every man on that side has served the ball, the other group become servers.

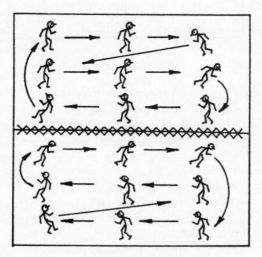

Fig. 8-247

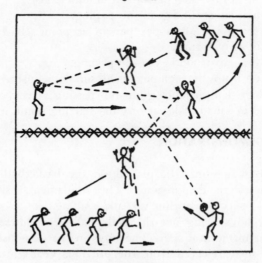

Fig. 8-248

After the ball is served, the other group returns the ball as in game conditions. No 1 passes to No 2, who is the set-up man. He, in turn, hits the ball very softly to the spiker. The spiker will then, using good form and a legal shot, spike the ball over the net. The group rotates in order.

At the conclusion of the skill demonstration, the time remaining in the half may be used in a scrimmage.

The faculty director of the intramural program should be at the public address system. He can explain the rules of the game, the objectives sought in volleyball, and some of the statistics of the previous volleyball programs. (See Figs. 8-247 and 8-248.)

SYMPHONY IN MOVEMENT

This number may be called "Symphony in Movement," "Rippling Rhythm," or the like. It involves boys and/or girls in mass calisthenics. There should be a total of 64 students. If both boys and girls are included, there should be an equal representation of each sex. Half of the group enters from one side of the gymnasium and half from the other; they form eight rows—boys and girls in alternate rows, if the group is a mixed one.

The group counts off by four's from the front of each row, and the exercises are done in staggered rhythm. An example of this is an arm sideward movement. A count of four brings the arms over the head, with four counts to return to the sides. On the count of one, No. 1's start the exercise, while No 2's start on the count of two, No. 3's on the count of three, and No. 4's on the count of four. In 16 counts, the arm movement will have been completed twice by No. 1's. No. 2's will finish on the count of 17, No. 3's on 18, and No. 4's on 19. When this exercise is done correctly, the person standing in the front of each line will seem to have eight arms.

Another exercise, deep knee bends done to a four count, will give the group a waving motion. Other exercises can be adapted to this staggered rhythm to give other effects. After completion of the exercises, the group will file out in the same manner as they entered.

POLE DRILL

The pole drill can be a very interesting activity for the demonstration. While it may not be thought of as a regular daily activity performed by the average physical education class, it is definitely a rhythmic activity and should be treated as such. If done correctly to music, it may be used to show the audience how uniformity of movement is taught and to demonstrate the importance of rhythm in the teaching of physical skills.

Arrange for five with each pole.

The drill should be done to music, the tempo depending on the movements of the drill.

Description of the pole: wood - 7 feet long and 1½ inches thick, painted the school colors. (See Fig. 8-249.)

Fig. 8-249

The drills may be worked out according to the ability of the performers.

COMBATIVE EXERCISES

These are exercises in which one person exerts his strength and skill against another person in an effort to overcome the power and exertion of his opponent through various means and positions.

These exercises can be demonstrated with or without implements or materials. There are numerous ways and means of demonstrating combative exercises, but only one will be shown.

Combative Exercises Without Implements

The physical education class members should be divided into partners of equal size and weight. Exercises should be done to music which is coordinated with the moves in the exercise. The position of the class on the floor can be arranged to suit audience seating or the needs of the type of exercises used.

This example of combative exercise will have music accompaniment and should be worked out with the music committee so that appropriate music is used.

Example A:
1. Two boys face each other in front forestride. No. 1 holds No. 2 at wrists with overgrip.
2. Hold.
3. No. 1 forces No. 2 from frontarm outward to closearm.
4. Hold.

Example B:
1. Same as Example A.
2. Hold.
3. Close-heel-stand—closearm, hands open.
4. Hold.

Example C:
1. Etc.

ROPE CLIMBING

Rope climbing is an exercise that will build strength and agility and, of course, is a good conditioner. A certain amount of safety precaution is necessary as there is an element of danger involved in an activity of this kind. It does, however, lend itself very well to a demonstration because of this very element of danger, which is intriguing to the audience. It also satisfies the desire the average youngster has for climbing and competing.

Great strength in the arms is not required for this stunt. The muscles of the back and legs should be strong to relieve the burden of the arms.

In teaching the climb, the preliminary steps are as follows:

1. While standing, cross feet. First, place one foot on top, then place other on top. Choose which postion is more comfortable. Leg that is best is placed behind and is referred to as rear leg; the other, front leg.
2. Rope is then firmly grasped in both hands as high as possible, keeping elbows straight. While standing on front foot, lift rear leg upward with knee and ankle bent and toes pointing upward. In this position, rear leg is brought in contact with rope in such a way that rope rests outside ankle and inside knee. Put weight

on arms, keep elbows straight, cross front foot over rear foot, and hold rope tightly between outer surfaces of ankles and bony inner surfaces of knees. Body is now in sitting position with legs extended forward. Rope is grasped between ankles and knees. Hips are bent. Arms are reaching up to grasp rope. Also, elbows are kept straight.

3. Next, straighten knees and hips, keeping firm leg grip. Arch back and bend arms, so that body is close to rope.

4. In second position, body is extended close to rope with ankles, knees, and hands gripping rope firmly, and elbows completely bent.

5. Final step consists of shifting arms upward to a new hand grasp as high up as can be reached, with elbows straight. All steps should now be repeated in order to go up rope to height at which a tape has been placed for the stop. In coming down rope, leg grip is gradually released as hands alternate, making descent slow and gradual.

Faults to be avoided are relying on arms too much and not reaching up high enough for next grip.

Drills

There are many drills that may be worked out to make rope climbing interesting to the spectators. The routines may be started by bringing the boys in from both sides of the rope. When the students are in position, the safety points should be explained and shown. Then the different types of climbing should be demonstrated.

The drills should be conducive to greater enjoyment of a demonstration.

SCOOTERS DEMONSTRATION

Gym scooters are relatively new in physical education. This new medium is readily accepted by the student body and when used properly can add much to the physiological part of the program.

Twenty-four boys, with scooters in hand, enter the gym floor from one end and line up in four squads of six. (See Fig. 8-250.)

On command, each squad separates into halves and proceeds to opposite ends of the gym, facing each other; this makes three members of each squad at each end of the gym.

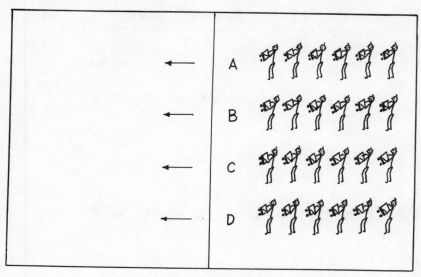

Fig. 8-250

Relay Race

Each boy lies face down with the lower region of the abdomen on the scooter. He propels himself by using his arms only, in the manner of the front crawl stroke in swimming.

The race starts from one end of the gym and as each boy finishes, he stands up, thereby indicating that the next person in line should start. The winning squad is the first to have all six players on their feet. After the race is over, the boys regroup in squads of six and leave the gym in single file (A first, followed by B, etc.).

VERTICAL JUMP

Before this part of the demonstration is begun, it should be explained that this exercise is used as a testing device, and not just a drill to provide exercise and activity.

To begin the drill, a line of boys enter the gym from one corner of the gymnasium and a line of girls from the other corner, as shown in Fig. 8-251.

Bleachers

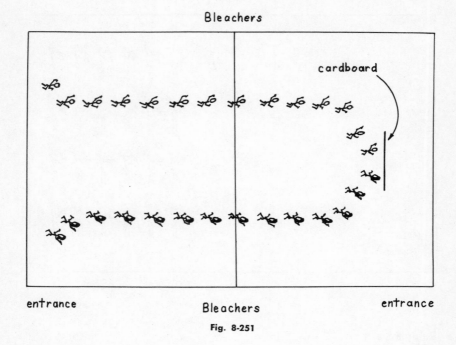

entrance   Bleachers   entrance

Fig. 8-251

Equipment

A strip of cardboard 4 feet wide, and painted black on each side, is needed. The cardboard should be fastened at the top and bottom by wood stripping. It should be suspended from the ceiling by ropes so that there is a range of height from 6 to 10 feet from the floor, and should run lengthwise down the center of the gymnasium. The students are dressed in gym uniforms of the school colors. A public address system is a must.

Purpose

To demonstrate the vertical jump with and without the use of scientific principles. Newton's first and third laws are involved and should be presented. The purpose is to correlate good physical education with sound scientific principles.

Procedure

At a command, each student takes three standing vertical jumps and marks each on the cardboard with chalk. Then, at a second command, each student takes one step before jumping and, just before reaching his height, extends the free leg down vigorously and pushes downward sharply with the free arm. The student takes three jumps in this manner, and marks each jump.

Conclusion

By the body's center of gravity being raised more, the last three jumps should be visibly higher than the first three.

OFFICIAL'S CODE OF HAND SIGNALS

During the course of the program, there may be short intervals of time between demonstrations which need to be filled so that the entire show may operate smoothly. The suggestion offered here may provide a means by which the audience's attention can be directed away from the necessary movement and preparations for the next demonstration.

A student or instructor, dressed in a sports official's uniform, may present a short demonstration to the audience which would explain and illustrate the official code of signals used by the referee in an athletic contest. Depending on the time of year in which the demonstration is presented, the type of signals illustrated would be primarily the signals used in the particular seasonal sport.

To add effect and efficiency to this demonstration, a spotlight may be focused on the demonstrator and a public address system should be used. As an example, the official illustrating the basketball referee's signals may be stationed beneath the goal at the end of the gymnasium. While two basketball players dressed in uniform show how the infractions are committed, the proper hand signals are given by the referee. Some of the basketball signals illustrated by the demonstrator could include:

1. Start the clock
2. Stop the clock
3. Jump ball

4. Holding
5. Charging
6. Illegal use of the hands
7. Technical foul
8. Traveling
9. Illegal dribble
10. Bonus situation
11. Goal tending

BOWLING TECHNIQUES

During any physical education demonstration, it is well to include in the program a unit concerning the carry-over activities taught at the junior-senior level.

One of the most popular sports, bowling, would be well received, since most people are interested in it.

Demonstration

In gymnasiums, plastic balls and pins are usually used. The students should demonstrate the four-step approach. This can be done in a group or as singles. Then the students may participate in a game of bowling. The techniques which are taught should be explained and the equipment which is used should be on display. The method of scoring may also be explained. This type of demonstration may well be used by the spectators as a "participating" or "trying out" activity after the demonstration is over.

SOCCER TECHNIQUES

This demonstration is set up primarily to give the public a general interpretation of the basic drills and maneuvers that are used in soccer. The unit on soccer in the physical education program will cover such areas as history, equipment, fundamentals, scoring, and players and their positions. These areas will be touched upon briefly, depending upon the allotted time in the program.

The demonstration will cover briefly the fundamentals for putting the soccer ball in play by dribbling, kicking, and striking or pushing it with any part of the body except the hands and arms.

Definitions

Kicking—This may be done with the top of the instep as in regulation football, with the inside of the foot, with the outside of the foot, or with the heel.

Dribbling—This is a series of short, controlled kicks made by a player who is advancing the ball; it is generally accomplished with the inside or outside of the foot.

Trapping—This is the stopping and taking possession of the ball. It is accomplished with the sole of the foot by simply stepping lightly on the ball; or with both feet by clamping the ball between the legs and the ground if the ball is a high fly or a high bounder.

Volleying—This is meeting the ball before it hits the ground, either with the foot or knee. The foot volley is used to gain distance and change direction.

Half Volleying—This is meeting the ball just after it hits the ground, usually with the instep or inside of the foot.

Soccer Drills

Fig. 8-252 shows that the first man in Line A will roll the ball to the first man in Line B who kicks it without trapping the ball. The ball will be kicked with the toes pointed downward and inward. This will put the ball in play with an instep kick. The first player in each line will go to the opposite end of his line after he has participated in the drill.

The first man in Line A will bounce the ball to the first man in Line B, who will return the ball to the second man in Line A with a half-volley kick.

The first man in Line A will pass the ball to the first man in Line B who will return the ball with a volley kick.

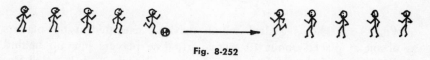

Fig. 8-252

Fig. 8-253 shows a drill which is primarily used for dribbling the ball for speed and accuracy. The first man in Line A will approach the ball and kick it with the inside of his right or left foot. He will alternate with each kick—first the inside of his right foot and then the inside of his left foot. The kicks should be approximately 5 to 7 feet in length. When he reaches the boundary line he will turn around and bring it back to the second man. The second man in line will trap the ball and put it back into play. He will go down and come back and so on, until the last person in the line has taken his turn.

Fig. 8-253

Fig. 8-254 shows a drill which can be used in the practicing of trapping the ball and kicking with accuracy. Player A will pass the ball to his left to B who will trap the ball and pivot to his left with his foot on the ball and kick it to the man on his left. This will continue around the circle.

This exercise can be done first clockwise and then counterclockwise.

Fig. 8-254

Fig. 8-255 shows a drill which may be executed using players as obstacles placed about 10 feet apart. The players line up behind one another in Lines A, B, and C. The first man in each line dribbles the ball to the right side of the first obstacle and then the left side of the next obstacle. This is done until the players reach the last obstacle, and then they turn around and return in the same manner. After the first man passes the last obstacle he gives the ball to the second man in his line and goes to the end of the line. The second man traps the ball and begins the obstacle race.

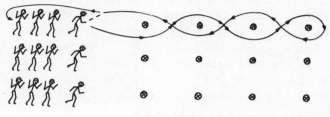

Fig. 8-255

These are just a few of the many drills which an individual can utilize in teaching proper handling of the soccer ball for a demonstration on soccer. These drills can be conducted on the gym floor, with the narrator in the center of the floor explaining each drill and its function in the proper methods of soccer ball control and handling. (See Fig. 8-256.)

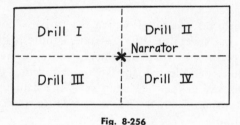

Fig. 8-256

FREE THROW SHOOTING CONTEST

Contestants

One champion may be selected from each of the physical education classes and enough runners-up to have 12 contestants.

Scorers

Members of the freshman basketball team.

Introductions

Each boy will come on to the court as the announcer calls his name. The total number of free throws made by each boy will be announced as will the name of the winner.

Procedure

Six baskets should be used. Two contestants will shoot at each basket. One boy shoots 15 free throws while the other boy rebounds, and then the two boys switch positions. A freshman basketball player keeps score at each basket. All 12 boys will shoot 15 free throws. The boy who makes the most of the last 15 free throws will be the winner. In case of a tie, each of them will shoot again until he misses. The boy with the highest number of successful free throws is the winner.

CHOREOGRAPHY

Choreography is experimentation with movement evolving from an idea. It is necessary to have music accompaniment for this movement. The girls would perform in this activity.

Once an idea has been worked out for the dance, the music is decided upon to accompany it.

A theme must be presented which, in turn, is communicated in part at least to the spectator. For instance, should a group decide to do a dance depicting excitement, then a piece of music suggesting excitement should be selected for accompaniment. The group will realize in the discussion for the selection of the dance, that the dance itself will need to be defined and explained so that the movement can be decided upon.

The procedure to be followed to create the dance may be as follows:

1. Decide on a theme and the type of communication or movements to be used.
2. Define the dance and decide on its limitations.
3. Gather ideas that suggest the gestures necessary to communicate the movements to the spectator.
4. Experiment with all the movements.
5. Select the most appropriate and expressive movements which will depict the idea.
6. Design the dance into patterns of movement.
7. Perfect the dance.

As an example, in developing the theme of the excitement of a child over the approach of a parade, one thinks of the child darting to and fro, watching and waiting, jumping up and down, clapping and waving the hands, imitating a drummer or trumpeter, and following the parade as it moves along. The dancers experiment with these ideas in class, then stylize the gestures, vary the themes, and finally, after careful selection of the movements, combine the most appropriate and exciting ones into a complete pattern of movement, resulting in the complete dance. The dancers then perfect the routine until the techniques involved become habitual, and they are able to project themselves into the part.

SCOOTER HOCKEY

This is a very exciting game to be used in a demonstration, primarily because it has not been seen by many people. Participants should carefully abide by rules so that there are no injuries and so that the game goes along smoothly. A brief description of the game, its purposes, and objectives should be presented to the audience before the game is started. Some of the main points are as follows:

1. Scooter hockey accomplishes two objectives: It develops the large muscle groups and presents an enjoyable, relaxing recreation.

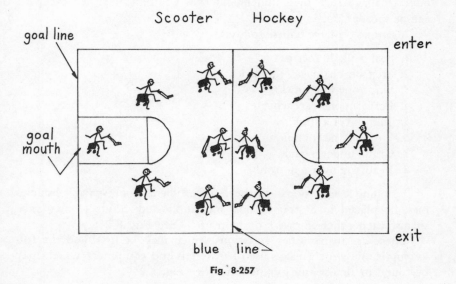

Fig. 8-257

2. This game is used to familiarize the students with the game of hockey, which is rapidly becoming a great spectator sport.

3. All rules of hockey are used, with the exception of line violations due to the elimination of the blue line. In place of the blue line, the center line of the basketball floor is used.

4. During the demonstration an assistant explains to the audience rule enforcements, etc.

5. On entering, all students carry their scooters to the center of the floor and line up for the face off. They are also responsible for their scooters after the demonstration. (See Fig. 8-257.)

SIMPLE OBSTACLE COURSE

Any type of obstacle course provides excitement and laughs to both spectator and participant. It is particularly adaptable to a demonstration. The one presented here is very simple, but provides enough of a challenge to be interesting to all.

Any number of participants may be used. The instructor may use any of the activities already learned, or others that these may suggest. Equipment should be simple, and at least five different actions should be required. Though speed is important, skill should not be sacrificed. The group should be permitted to "walk through" all actions once to make sure they understand the requirements; then the pace can be speeded up.

A sample obstacle course follows:

1. Seal walk 20 feet.
2. Step on chair and jump down.
3. Skip rope five times.
4. Perform one cart wheel.
5. Jump over a stick.
6. Hop on one foot along a line.
7. Crawl under a stick.
8. Leapfrog over a person.

Teaching Suggestions: If there is sufficient floor space, obstacles may be placed in a straight line and duplicated. Students may race against each other in two's or in teams. (See Fig. 8-258.)

There are many other variations which may be used and the following is one which makes use of materials and equipment which may be found in almost any gymnasium. (See Fig. 8-259.)

Simple Obstacle Course

Fig. 8-258

PROCEDURE

Mat I—The participants approach the mat and do a forward roll.

Mat II—The participants crawl under the chairs that have been placed on the mats in such a way that they form a tunnel or bridge.

Mat III—After crawling under the chair backs the participants approach this mat, turn around facing in the same direction from which they came, and do a backward roll.

The participants, after doing a backward roll on Mat III, run between the pins, as shown in the figure, jump over the hurdles and cross the finish line.

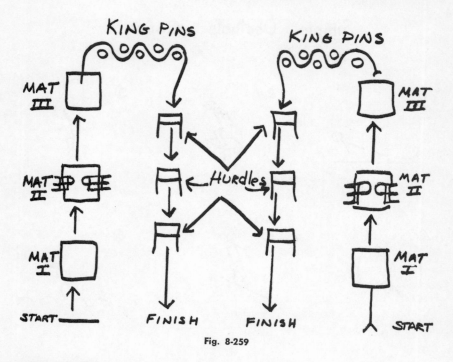

Fig. 8-259

WALL SCALING

There are various ways in which wall scaling can be demonstrated in an exhibition. It may be used as a race between classes, or purely for show, or it can be worked into a drill on timing, precision, and execution.

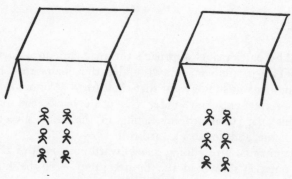

Fig. 8-260

One demonstration would be to run races between the junior gym classes of the high school. A wall 8 feet high should be used with a step about 2 or 3 feet up to help the student.

If competition is going to be used in wall scaling, two 8-foot walls should be placed side by side with protective nets underneath. The contestants line up in two lines, with an equal number of contestants in each line. (See Fig. 8-260.) At a designated signal the first contestant in each line runs to the wall, scales it, and continues on to the finish line. The winner is determined when all the players on a team have finished scaling the wall and have crossed the finish line.

HORSE VAULTING

Gymnastic activities play an important part in the demonstration because they lend themselves well to it. The simplest movements on any piece of apparatus can be made to look spectacular to the untrained and inexperienced person. The horse vault in its various forms —the difficulty of which, of course, depends upon the ability of the performers—falls into this category. The following vaults may be used in a demonstration because they are not difficult and yet they show the fundamental vaults most used on the horse and those that are necessary to learn before progressing to the more difficult types. At the same time, the vaults shown are both interesting and spectacular if the performers have the ability to execute them properly, and the average physical education class should be able to do this. From 15 to 30 boys may participate in this activity. (See Fig. 8-261.)

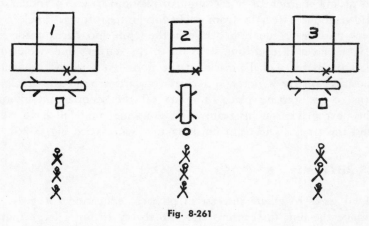

Fig. 8-261

Equipment

> 1. Three side horses with pommels removed
> 2. Two beat boards
> 3. One springboard or mini-tramp
> 4. Enough mats to safely cover the area

Vaults to Be Used

Lines 1 and 3

1. Squat mount to stand and jump off
2. Straddle mount to stand and jump off touching toes
3. Squat vault
4. Straddle vault
5. Flank vault
6. Neck or headspring
7. Handspring
8. All finish with a fast-squat vault, then form a circle facing outward as a finish.

Line 2

1. Same
2. Straddle vault
3. Squat vault
4. Straddle vault with one-half turn
5. Squat mount to stand and jump off with one-half turn, land, and backward roll
6. Stoop vault
7. Cart wheel

Difficulty of the vaults will be determined by the ability of the performers.

RACE TRACK RACE

There should be four teams, of equal number, each taking a position at one corner of a rectangular playing area. An Indian club is placed about 4 feet in from each corner to form a "track." The players must ride scooters between the club and the outside line. The first player in each line steps up to the starting line, which may be designated by a chalk mark on the floor. At a signal, he assumes his position on the scooter and rides forward around the track and returns to his starting place, jumping off the scooter and giving it to the next player on his team. This continues until all have ridden around the track. The team finishing first wins. (See Fig. 8-262.)

GIRLS' RHYTHMS

Two ways to create interest in physical education for girls is to introduce the unit in rhythms and also to try to use a large number

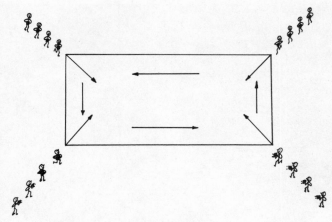

Fig. 8-262

of girls in the physical education demonstration. One of the new methods of teaching rhythms, and one which will fit in well in the demonstration because of its appeal to both spectator and participant, is a dance which originated in the Vissayan Islands and is a national favorite throughout the Philippines.

This dance is called the tinkling dance and it received its name from the tinkling bird. The bird has a long neck and long legs and the dance imitates the movements of the bird as it flits through the grass and tree branches which are represented by bamboo poles.

The bamboo poles are approximately 9 feet long. Two boards approximately 3 inches high and 3 feet long are placed on the floor in front of the two persons manipulating the poles. These two sit or kneel at either end of the poles and grasp the ends, one in each hand. The poles are struck together and against the pieces of board which are placed about 1 foot from the ends of the poles.

The movement of the poles and of the dancers are all done to music. The trick, of course, is for the performers to dance in, out, and between the bamboo poles in time to the music without catching the feet in the poles. There must be perfect coordination between the dancers and the two persons manipulating the bamboo poles. (See Figs. 8-263 and 8-264.)

Different rhythms may be worked out. Following are two examples:

Fig. 8-263

Fig. 8-264

Rhythm I

The dancers stand at the left side of the poles, and the rhythm or count is three beats to a measure or three-quarter time. The poles are placed on the boards about a foot apart in preparation for the rhythm.

To begin the rhythm, the poles are struck together by sliding them along the boards (count 1) or lifting them an inch or so (count 1) and striking them twice against the boards (count 2, 3). This procedure may be repeated in rhythm as many times as desired.

Rhythm II

Strike the poles as above (count 1), then open the poles about one foot apart and strike them three times against the boards. (counts 2, 3, 4) with right, left, right hands of player No. 1 and with left, right, left hands of player No. 2. The maneuver is as follows:

Player No. 1 — right, left, right — lift-strike-strike-strike
Player No. 2 — left, right, left — 1st beat-2nd beat-3rd beat

The dance or tinkling step has many variations, one of which is as follows:

The dancers line up on the left side of the poles. They begin by hopping on the left foot outside the poles (count 1) and on the right foot between the poles (count 2), then on the same spot as the first hop (count 3), raising the right foot. The above maneuver would enable the dancer to hop outside when the poles are struck together (count 1) and make the two hops inside when the poles are apart (counts 2, 3). Another dance may be done by having the dancers line up on the right side of the poles and do the same as in the preceding dance, except that it is started with the right foot.

The dance may be varied by placing the hands on the person in front in various ways. The dances may also be on a competitive basis, one player against another, or team competition. All contestants who miss are eliminated. The greatest number remaining on one team in a certain time limit is declared the winner.

ROLLER SKATING

Roller skating is a skill that will add variety to the demonstration as well as to the physical education curriculum. The fiber-wheel skate will not harm the gymnasium floor if the floor is properly sealed and taken care of. The type of skills presented will be dependent upon the ability of the participant. This, of course, will also depend upon the teaching program and how much time is spent on this particular skill. Skating, like other physical skills, may be learned faster by one individual than another.

The benefits derived from skating, such as improved coordination, balance, poise, etc., should be made known to the audience.

Due to the fact that some students will be better skaters than others, three groups may be formed in order to show progression in teaching the skill. The first group may perform the simple or elementary skills as follows:

Stopping

The drag stop is performed by pointing the toe of the left or inside foot straight forward and placing the right foot behind the left foot. The right foot should be perpendicular to the left foot and the heels should be touching. The four wheels of the right skate should be dragged on the floor with as much pressure as is needed to stop properly. All four wheels should be in contact with the floor.

The Reverse Stop

The reverse stop is performed by pointing the toes of both feet outward with the right foot slightly forward. The body is swung backward and the right leg is projected forward. The body should lean forward with the weight well distributed on both feet. The turn should be made in the form of a half-circle, and the skater should end up facing in the opposite direction, with the toes pointed out, the body leaning forward, and legs slightly bent.

Skating Forward

The body should lean forward slightly with arms swinging and elbows slightly bent. One foot is placed ahead of the other in a walking-gliding motion. The other foot pushes off to provide the forward momentum. After the glide or forward motion is accomplished the other foot is brought forward in a walking motion and the push-off is done with the gliding foot which now is the back foot. This procedure is repeated.

Skating Backward

The body should lean forward with the toes pointing in. The push-off should be done as in skating forward. One foot is placed backward in a backward walking-gliding motion with the push-off coming from the other foot. Turns may be accomplished by placing the inside foot across the outside foot.

Turning

Several methods of turning may be shown, the most popular of which is done by crossing the outside foot over and across the inside foot in a continuous motion while the turn is being made.

Another method of turning is by placing the left or inside foot ahead and in direct line with the right or back foot. The body leans to the inside and the forward momentum carries the skater through the turn. He then assumes a skating position. Still another method is gliding on the inside foot with the outside foot raised behind the body. The skater should lean forward. The back foot should be brought forward, and back to skating position after the turn has been made.

Skating with a Partner

The boy and girl begin by standing side by side with right hands joined. Different skating positions may be assumed.

Skills for Better Skaters

Skating may be done in groups of four, or two couples. Two boys and two girls perform, keeping in step. The arms may cross, or the arms may be linked together.

Better skaters may also demonstrate turning in groups of three. Several groups of three skate around the outside of the skating area. The three link their elbows and at a given signal the inside skater pivots to his left, or inside, with the other two skaters turning to their left, or inside. After changing direction the group continues to skate forward in the opposite direction.

The waltz step is not difficult, yet if done correctly to music, it is very impressive. Partners are formed with the boy and girl facing each other. The girl skates backward with the boy skating forward.

Skills for the Best Skaters

One skill would be balancing on one leg with the other leg and the body parallel to the floor. This may be done singly or by partners. The partners may go into this from the waltz step.

Another skill may be balancing on the front wheels of the back skate and the back wheels of the front skate.

Another skill would be for partners, as they hold hands, to balance on one foot, with the other leg and the body parallel to the floor. One of the partners, of course, must be skating backward.

Another skill while in skating position could have the girl cross the left foot over the right foot with the boy doing the same. The right would then be crossed over the left foot.

There are many other skills that can be used in a demonstration, depending upon the ability of the students and the stress placed on the skating program in the curriculum.

WEIGHT LIFTING

The weight lifting demonstration should show only the types of exercises engaged in during the regular class period. Care should be taken to show that the program in the school involves more than just lifting weights and trying to build muscles. It should be emphasized that the program is for general conditioning. The demonstration should show the gradual progression from the light weights to the heavier weights. It should be emphasized that the starting weight is important and should be determined for each performer before the demonstration. Every precaution should be taken to prevent the problem that might result if a student were permitted to lift too heavy a weight, or if people are led to believe that the program is strictly a muscle building activity. The purpose of the course should be fully explained.

Mats should be used so that the weights do not touch the floor. These mats should be placed far enough apart so that there will be no chance for injury should more than one exercise be performed at the same time.

A discussion on the physiology of exercise will add to the demonstration. When the exercise is being demonstrated, a description of the muscles involved and the value of the exercise may be stated.

The program should include a demonstration of the correct way to lift a bar bell, accompanied by a verbal explanation as to what part of the body is being benefited.

The demonstration should include the following exercises. Others may be added if desired.

The Military Press

In performing this exercise, bar bell is brought from floor to chest in one quick, smooth movement. Performer stands perfectly

Fig. 8-265

Fig. 8-266

Fig. 8-267

still with feet about shoulder-width apart and even with each other. Hands should be placed on bar a little farther apart than shoulder-width to give better balance. Weight is pressed overhead to full arm's length, using only arms and shoulders. Bar bell is returned to chest and this is repeated. This movement may be continued for as many times as is deemed necessary to complete demonstration. Bar bell need not be placed back on floor once it has been brought to chest. Repeating of exercise should be from chest to overhead position. (See Figs. 8-265 through 8-267.)

Shoulder Shrug

Feet are placed together and bar bell is grasped with a fairly wide grip. Ears should be merely touched with shoulders, and performer should be careful not to bend elbows, as arms should not help at all except to hold weight. Shoulders must not be allowed to slump when they are dropped down, as they should be parallel to floor. (See Fig. 8-268.)

Exercise should not be continued for too long a period of time. Bar should be gripped with palms facing in and should not be too heavy.

Fig. 8-268

Three-Quarter Squat

In beginning to perform squat, performer should keep knees locked and slightly flexed. Back should be straight while squatting. Bar bell is placed behind neck and held by hands and arms, but should rest lightly on shoulders and neck. Feet should be approximately shoulder-width apart. Body is lowered to squatting position, but care should be taken not to squat farther than three-quarters of the way down or there might be a tendency to injure knees. This precaution should be emphasized, since a full squatting position is not recommended as an exercise, even without added weight. (See Fig. 8-269.)

Fig. 8-269

Toe Raises

Bar bells are kept in same position as for three-quarter squat. Performer merely raises up on balls of feet as far as possible. Exercise is repeated several times to give audience an idea of what is being done. Exercise may be emphasized by having performer place balls of feet on small raised piece of wood so that audience may better observe feet as exercise is being performed. (See Fig. 8-270.)

Fig. 8-270

Press Behind the Neck

Weight is brought to chest in same manner as in military press and then raised overhead. Instead of returning weight to chest, it should be lowered behind neck to shoulders and pressed up again.

This movement should be continued as long as is necessary to complete demonstration. Hands grasp bar with palms toward performer

Fig. 8-271

Fig. 8-272

and backs of hands face outward. Care should be taken not to allow bar bells to be lowered too far below neck and shoulders, as this could result in injury. (See Figs. 8-271 and 8-272.)

Two-Hand Underhand Curl

Back should be kept straight. Hands should be shoulder-width apart on bar. Weight should be held with arms fully extended and in front of thighs. Weight should be curled all the way up to chest just below neck, with elbows kept to sides at all times. (See Fig. 8-273.)

Fig. 8-273

Supine Press

In performing supine press, performer lies on back with feet about 6 inches apart and legs straight. Bar bell is grasped slightly wider apart than shoulder-width and rests lightly on chest. Bar bell is pressed straight up until arms are fully flexed and is then returned to starting position. Extreme care should be taken by performer not to drop weights as he presses them upward. Severe injury may result if bar bell is dropped on face or chest. (See Fig. 8-274.)

Fig. 8-274

Sit-Ups

A weight should be used that is not too heavy. A 10-pound weight should be maximum, and number of repetitions should be limited.

This exercise is performed in same way as regular sit-ups, but with added weight. Boy lies on back on mat with knees straight and feet together. Hands are placed behind head. A companion sits perpendicular to him with legs on top of legs of boy that is being tested. Exercise is begun as soon as both boys are ready and continues as long as it is deemed necessary to demonstrate exercise satisfactorily.

REBOUND TUMBLING

Rebound tumbling is a new activity which has been included in many physical education programs and will add a great deal to the gymnasium demonstration. It is important that the safety element be stressed in the rebound tumbling program. It is necessary that each side and the ends of a trampoline be protected by spotters. The responsibility of the students standing by the frame is to watch the performer at all times and to direct him back to the center of the bed by talking to him. If necessary, mechanical aids should be used.

To keep the spotters alert and aware of the fact that their turn is coming up, some form of rotation around the trampoline should be worked out. One end of the "tramp" should be designated as the mounting end and, as the performer mounts, each spotter should move one position clockwise around the apparatus. Each performer should dismount at a designated corner so that he may take his position as a spotter and help his teammates who will take their turn as performers. Proper mounting and dismounting should be taught and practiced before the demonstration. The value of correct spotting should be emphasized. The students should be taught to stand at the ends and sides while anyone is bouncing.

If possible, the demonstration should include the stunts in order on the skills list. The explanation should be brief and to the point. The skills should be demonstrated quickly, and will add much to the program. Audiences will be astounded by the complexity of some of the apparently simple routines performed by the high school students.

Hand and Knee Bounce

This exercise is begun from an "all fours" position. Performer rests on hands and knees in a position which must be well coordinated, or a rocking motion will result. Performer bounces up and down increasing height of bounce each time. (See Fig. 8-275.)

Fig. 8-275

Front Bounce

Exercise is begun from a medium-height foot bounce. Legs are lifted up and back with body leaning slightly forward as performer reaches height of bounce. Body is straightened out so that it is parallel to bed. Belt of performer should strike point on bed that was last

Fig. 8-276

touched by feet. It is absolutely essential that performer land flat. (See Fig. 8-276.)

Fig. 8-277

402

Seat Bounce

This exercise is performed from a medium foot bounce. Feet are lifted up in front of body with legs forming right angles to trunk. Performer lands flat on legs and seat with hands at sides. Fingers should point toward feet. Hands should be used to push up from sitting position to regain standing position on bed. (See Fig. 8-277.)

Back Bounce

Performer lifts legs and drops to back from a low foot bounce. Chin should be held to chest and performer should be careful not to drop too far on back of neck. This exercise may be done from a high leg bounce. (See Fig. 8-278.)

Fig. 8-278

Doubles or Alternate Bouncing

This exercise must not be attempted unless performers have had considerable experience. Routine is begun by having one performer start bouncing. Other performer times jump so that he is going up while first performer is coming down. Various landings may be used but at no time should performers be in unison on jumps or landings. While not too difficult, this type of bouncing is rather spectacular. (See Fig. 8-279.)

Fig. 8-279

Foot Bounce

Performer begins exercise by placing feet about shoulder-width apart. Arms should be swung up in front of face, with toes pushing into bed of rebounding tumbling unit. Eyes should be focused upon end of bed to make it easier for performer to stay in center. Body should be kept in erect position.

Bounce may be stopped by flexing knees upon contacting bed. (See Fig. 8-280.)

Knee Bounce

This exercise is begun from a low foot bounce. Feet are lifted so that legs are extended backward at right angles to body. Toes should be pointed backward to avoid landing on them. Body should be kept straight from head to knees. (See Fig. 8-281.)

PHYSICAL FITNESS

A demonstration of physical fitness activities which are being conducted in the high school program will create an awareness of the necessity of youth fitness and will inform the public as to what is being done. Many states have made an all-out effort in stressing

Fig. 8-280

Fig. 8-281

fitness in the schools. Criteria for self-evaluation in physical education have been developed. Norms have been established for comparative purposes and tests have been devised. School people and laymen have been alerted to the fact that physical fitness is an important phase in the overall program of health and physical education.

The test battery presented here includes pull-ups, squat jumps, sit-ups, push-ups, broad jumps, vertical jumps, softball throw, 600-yd. run and 1-mile swim. (See Fig. 8-282.)

Name_____

PHYSICAL FITNESS TEST

	SOPHOMORE				JUNIOR				SENIOR			
SCHOOL YEAR	FALL		SPRING		FALL		SPRING		FALL		SPRING	
AGE												
WEIGHT												
HEIGHT												
DATE OF TEST												
	NO.	SCORE	NO.	SCORE	NO.	SCORE	NO.	SCORE	NO.	SCORE	NO.	SCORE
PULL-UPS												
SQUAT-JUMPS												
SIT-UPS												
PUSH-UPS												
BROAD JUMPS												
VERTICAL JUMPS												
SOFTBALL THROW												
600-YARD RUN												
1-MILE SWIM												
TOTAL SCORE												

Fig. 8-282

The program described here is a representative one and can be changed to meet the needs of a particular school system or community. The terms used may be different from the usual ones. The implications and meanings are the same.

The physical fitness norms as shown in the chart are national norms. In scoring the results on the physical fitness score card, the actual number of times the activity was performed is placed on the card under the "No." heading. The number is then checked on the "norm" chart under the activity to establish the points scored by the individual, according to the national norm. These points are placed on the physical fitness card under "score." The scores are then added and averaged to establish a final result. A full description of the activities will thus be presented. (See Fig. 8-283.)

PHYSICAL FITNESS NORMS

Points	Chins	Standing Broad Jump	Squat Jumps	Push-ups	2 min. Sit-ups	600 yd. Run	Vertical Jump	14'' Softball Throw	Bonus Swim by Laps	Points
1000	35	10' 6''	24-1/2	71	94	1:13	31	250	22	1000
990	32	10' 3''	24	68	91	1:15	30	245		990
980	29	10' 0''	23-1/2	65	88	1:17	29	240		980
970	26	9' 9''	23	62	85	1:19	28	235		970
960	23	9' 6''	22-1/2	59	82	1:21	27	230	21	960
950	20	9' 3''	22	56	79	1:23	26	225		950
940	18	9' 0''	21-1/2	53	76	1:25	25	220		940
930	16	8' 9''	21	50	73	1:27	24	215		930
920	14	8' 6''	20-1/2	47	70	1:29	23	210	20	920
910	12	8' 3''	20	44	67	1:31	22-1/2	205		910
880	11	8' 0''	19-1/2	41	64	1:34	22	195		880
840	10	7' 9''	19	38	61	1:37	21	185	19	840
760	9	7' 6''	18-1/2	35	58	1:40	20	175	18	760
670	8	7' 4''	18	32	56	1:43	19	165	17	670
590	7	7' 2''	17-1/2	29	54	1:46	18-1/2	155	16	590
500	6	7' 0''	17	26	52	1:48	18	145	15	500
410	5	6' 10''	16-1/2	23	50	1:50	17-1/2	135	14	410
330	4	6' 8''	16	20	48	1:53	17	125	13	330
270	3	6' 6''	15-1/2	17	46	1:56	16	115	12	270
210	2	6' 4''	15	14	44	1:59	15	105	11	210
160	1	6' 2''	14-1/2	11	41	2:02	14	95	10	160
120		6' 0''	14	8	38	2:05	13-1/2	85	9	120
90		5' 9''	13-1/2	5	35	2:07	13	75	8	90
80		5' 6''	13	3	32	2:09	12	70	7	80
70		5' 3''	12-1/2	2	29	2:11	11	65	6	70
60		5' 0''	12	1	26	2:13	10	60	5	60
50		4' 9''	11-1/2		23	2:15	9	55	4	50
40		4' 6''	11		20	2:17	8	50	3	40
30		4' 3''	10-1/2		17	2:19	7	45	2	30
20		4' 0''	10		14	2:21	6	40	1	20
10		3' 9''	9-1/2		11	2:23	5	35		10

Fig. 8-283

Pull-Ups

This activity is done on high bar. Boy grasps bar with palms out and pulls himself up so that chin comes over bar. Body is then lowered until arms are straight. Body must not swing during performance. It will be counted as a chin if act is more than three-fourths completed, providing it is last attempt. Feet must be kept together. Boy must not stop action until he has done as many pull ups as he is able to do. (See Fig. 8-284.)

Fig. 8-284

Squat Jumps

This activity is performed by first standing up straight with feet together. Hands are placed on top of head with fingers entwined.

Fig. 8-285

Boy will start exercise by jumping off floor and returning with heel of one foot parallel with toe of other foot, and with feet about 6 inches apart. The return to floor continues with full squat. Boy will recover from squat by again jumping into the air as at first. While in the air, he will change position of feet so that right foot will be in opposite position of left foot and execution of skill may be performed second time. Exercise is continued until boy can no longer perform. Count is kept of number of times boy is able to do exercise. Count begins after boy has gone into squatting position and returns to upright position. It will be counted as a squat jump if skill has been more than three-fourths completed. Boy is not allowed to stop at any time. He must go all the way down so that rump touches heel of back foot and he must come all the way up to an erect position, with knees completely straight and feet off floor on jump. Hands must remain on head during exercise. (See Fig. 8-285.)

Sit-Ups

Boy lies on back on floor with knees straight and feet together. Hands should be clasped behind head. A companion sits perpendicular to him with legs on top of legs (near ankle) of boy being tested. Instructor gives signal to begin exercise and counts number of sit-ups boy does in two minutes. Tester must watch that boy does exercise correctly. He should be stopped if it is not being done in accepted manner. Count begins when boy touches right knee with left elbow. Procedure should be alternated on each touch with

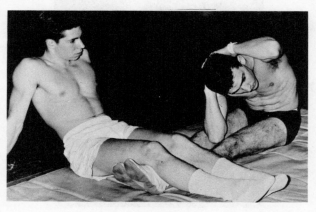

Fig. 8-286

left knee being touched by right elbow. Boy must touch floor with both shoulder blades. Count is continued until two minutes are up at which time instructor calls a halt. Boy is given credit for a completion if exercise is three-fourths completed. (See Fig. 8-286.)

Push-Ups

Boy lies on floor face down, with legs straight and feet together. Hands are placed palms down directly under shoulders. Boy pushes body upward until arms are completely straight, at which time he is resting on hands and toes of both feet. Entire body and legs must be straight, although a slight bend is permissible, but not a sag. He must lower body, allowing chest to touch floor, and this only lightly. No other part of body should touch floor. This procedure is continued without interruption for as many times as is possible. Boy should not be allowed to stop and rest. Exercise must be continuous. (See Fig. 8-287.)

Fig. 8-287

Broad Jumps

This is a standing broad jump. A line is drawn on floor. Boy stands with toes on line and jumps out as far as he can. Distance he jumps is measured from line to heel of foot that is closest to line. If boy falls back he is allowed another try. (See Fig. 8-288.)

Vertical Jumps

This exercise is a test of leg strength and is accomplished in following manner: Boy stands next to a wall with a piece of chalk in

Fig. 8-288

hand. He jumps as high as he possibly can and makes a mark with chalk as high on wall as he can reach. Measurement of jump is taken from mark on wall to floor. Measurement procedure may be simplified and a great deal of time may be saved by making a scale on wall which will indicate feet and inches boy has jumped without measuring each jump. Points scored may be found by checking chart.

Softball Throw

This is a throw for distance using a 14-inch ball. A line is drawn and boy must stay behind line. He may take a run before throw. Ball is thrown overhand and distance is measured from line to spot where ball lands.

600-Yard Run

This is a run against time and should be done outside on track under as ideal conditions as possible. It is timed as any other running event is timed.

One-Mile Swim

This is not a swim against time. Boy may take as long as he needs, providing he keeps swimming and does not stop to rest. Chart shows 22 laps as one mile.

Posting of Scores

The posting of scores is a tremendous motivating force and serves as an added incentive for the boy to improve on his score. He is competing not only against his companion, but also against himself.

A score of 900 and up would be considered excellent; 760 to 900, good; 500 to 760, fair; and below 500, poor.

GYMNASTIC CYCLE

Gymnastic activities always make an interesting part of a program. By combining several activities, combinations may be worked into an interesting gymnastic demonstration cycle. The equipment necessary for this activity will include floor mats, parallel bars, still rings, spring box, long horse, and a large tumbling mat.

The participants should line up in single file in front of the mats with the first student in line assuming the role of leader, and the rest of the group performing the same acts that he does on the various pieces of apparatus.

The cycle will begin by having the leader, followed by the other participants, do a series of forward rolls from one end of the mat to the other. From here he would proceed to the parallel bars, walk on his hands to the middle of the bars, swing into a shoulder stand, and follow up with a dismount. After dismounting from the parallel bars, participants will move to the next piece of equipment, the still rings. Each member of the group performs an inverted hang from the rings. The group then proceeds to the spring box and, using this piece of equipment, each participant vaults over the long horse. From here the group goes to the mat, where the group will take turns doing a handspring. (A rolled-up mat may be used to aid the boys in this.) After the handspring, the group lines up in preparation for dismissal or for another cycle.

There are various ways in which the interest of the audience may be held throughout the demonstration, one of which is to make every cycle or round more difficult. This will gradually reduce the size of the group into a few boys upon whom the audience may center their attention. (See Fig. 8-289.)

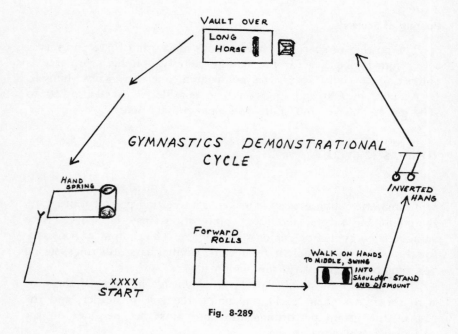

Fig. 8-289

CIRCUIT TRAINING

Introduction:

Circuit training is a physical fitness activity in which a number of exercises are selected and arranged in the form of a circuit in the gymnasium. The purpose of circuit training is twofold: one, to present an environment for activity of large muscles, and two, to individualize each student's work on a self-competitive basis rather than in group competition.

Exercises to be done:

Cable chest pull
Dumbbells
Wrist developer
Climbing rope
Push-ups
Jump rope
Sit-ups
Bridging
Bar bells
Step-ups
Four-counts

Procedure:

Squad leaders assemble across the center line of the gym for calisthenics. The other students take their place behind the leader they choose, providing there are not more than three in a squad. The squads, which number 11 in all, correspond to the number of exercising stations involved in the circuit. (See Fig. 8-290.) The purpose

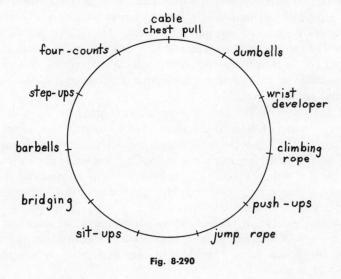

Fig. 8-290

of calisthenics in a program such as circuit training is to emphasize mental discipline more than muscle activity, although the latter is sought also.

Squads are assigned to one of the 11 stations to begin exercising. Each station is named according to the piece of equipment that is being used. In order that each squad has all its members exercising at the same time, three pieces of the same equipment are provided at each station.

Each student exercises 30 seconds at the various stations after which time a whistle is blown. The squad then rotates clockwise to the next station to begin a new exercise. The procedure continues until the circuit is completed by each squad. (See Fig. 8-290.)

SUMMARY

Physical education is a necessary part of the school curriculum. It is a part of everyday living for it is necessary to be physically fit to perform our daily tasks. Man must be physically fit to take his place in a democracy that places emphasis on the well-being and happiness of all its constituents. To accomplish this, one needs robust health and radiant vitality. A well-organized physical education program which promotes the health and happiness of its students through activities which are both creative and enjoyable should be as much a part of the school curriculum as the study of "the three R's."

A physically fit nation is a strong nation. A physically fit person is constantly striving to move forward. He is not afraid of the future. He has the will to win and the strength to perform the tasks required to be a contributor to the nation's progress. If our nation is to maintain its role of world leadership, its leaders must be physically fit and not sick men.

By and large, educators have now recognized, at least in theory, the great value of health, physical education, and recreation in the total curriculum and the entire educational process, and have provided in no small measure the necessary facilities to nurture and promote this value. Physical educators are still confronted with the task of overcoming some of the prejudices and inhibitions inherent in the minds of a few doubters.

Physical education, therefore, needs to establish itself as a vital force for giving meaning to the concept of education for responsibility. It should be integrated and identified with other phases of the school curriculum. The benefits that come from vigorous activities are needed in education in order to make it complete. These benefits have not been generally recognized, and educational authorities must be shown how to acquaint the public with them. The physical education demonstration is one means of accomplishing this objective. Too few people know the purpose of physical education and its place in the total school program. We must identify its contributions to the education of our youth in many areas and in many ways.

We have been entrusted by the public with the task of developing physically educated youth. This is our responsibility, and in general terms it is being accomplished. But is the general public aware of what is being done or is it aware of the athletic program only? People tend to support the things they believe in. They should then be given the opportunity of observing first hand what is being done in the physical education program.

We can try to convince the school administration of the need for physical education. We can talk to the boards of education about the value of such a program, but the real power lies in the parents. The school administration will listen and respond to the demands of the parents. When the parents are convinced that their children need a program of physical education the school administrators will take the appropriate steps.

The purpose, therefore, of the demonstration should be the same as that of any other school function. The goals should compare with those set up for the entire school curriculum, because the educational objectives and opportunities are commensurate with other educational agencies within the school.

The values attached to the demonstration are many and varied. Perhaps the outstanding value of the demonstration is that it affords an opportunity for students and teachers to work together cooperatively, democratically, and creatively on a group project. This is the American way of life, and anything that can be done to develop this democratic attitude is furthering democracy which in turn will develop the human personality and improve the American way of life.

It is important that the general public be given a true picture of the physical education program. The demonstration, therefore, must be a direct outgrowth of the curriculum. The program should not be measured by stellar performances, but rather by experiences gained by many students through participation in the demonstration.

This entails both long- and short-range planning, which should not, of course, take precedence over the actual teaching of the class. All the students should have some part in the program in order to give everyone a chance to gain recognition and prestige. The demonstration provides an opportunity for the student who may not have any other chance to gain group acceptance and approval. He learns to work cooperatively as a member of a group that is striving for a common goal. This will help in the development of the social-emotional growth, which can be an important outcome of the demonstration.

There is no substitute for good planning, and there is no magic formula. Wise and thoughtful planning of every detail can do a great deal to make the demonstration a success. In order to justify the demonstration, it should be in keeping with the educational values and goals considered important for the entire school.

When properly conducted, the demonstration can be a potent force in the education of both participants and spectators. It presents an opportunity for all the students to participate in an all-school activity where many of the prime objectives of education can be brought out and emphasized. It provides an opportunity for those not actively engaged as a participant to realize what is being done in the physical education program to accomplish the aims and objectives as set forth by education in general.

All the duties need not fall upon the shoulders of one or two individuals; other departments in the school should be asked to cooperate in one way or another. The demonstration should reflect the work of the entire school program. There should be an overlapping of interests so that each department within the school system may derive values from participating in the demonstration.

Care should be taken in the selection of activities for the program so that the talent in other departments may be used. An attempt should be made to obtain the good will of parents, administrators, and other teachers. In order to do this, committees should be set up, the members of which will include personnel from every department within the school. The people placed on these committees should be those who have indicated a keen interest in the demonstration and are willing to work diligently. The success of the demonstration depends upon each committee's fulfilling its obligations on time. The smoothness with which the demonstration is run off will be in direct proportion to the efficiency of the committees. These committees should be under the direction of a planning committee. This committee, in planning the program, should establish a basic philosophy and should list specific objectives prior to actual organization.

The director of the demonstration assumes the responsibility for major decisions. Selection of personnel, making sure they are instructed properly as to their assigned duties and responsibilities, and generally directing their efforts constitute the bulk of his duties.

The demonstration supervisor serves as a go-between from the director to staff personnel. He should be classified as a special advisor to the director.

The announcer will be the direct contact between the audience, staff, and participants. His position is very important. It is the responsibility of the announcer to see that each aspect of the program fits into its proper place time-wise.

The ticket committee personnel and duties will depend to a large extent upon the school policy regarding charges for school events. Large schools may have a ticket manager who is responsible for handling tickets to all school activities.

The committees on ushering and changing of scenery have a responsibility that may mean the difference between a successful demonstration or a failure. Students can be trained for ushering. Varsity club members are sometimes used for this purpose. The ushers should be responsible for enforcing the rules and regulations of the building. Organizing the changing of scenery entails changing of props, backdrops, spotlighting, decorations, and floor equipment such as ropes, mats, apparatus, etc.

The program committee should work hand-in-hand with the publicity committee, inasmuch as both are attempting to do the same thing—inform the public. The program committee, however, will be more concerned with the actual printing, cost, distribution, advertising, and design of the program rather than the information contained therein.

The duties of the concession committee are concerned mainly with the purchasing and selling of various food and souvenir items. The arrangements will vary from school to school, and the extent of the enterprise will be determined by the attendance and by the school regulations.

One of the most important committees from the standpoint of public welfare is the first-aid committee. It will be concerned with all safety matters in regard to the demonstration. A nurse or physician should be present at the demonstration, and first-aid supplies should be available. A room should be set aside for emergency purposes. Emergency equipment and transportation should be provided.

The maintenance committee should work closely with all the custodians. The custodian in charge of the gym area should be a member of this committee, since much of the responsibility will of necessity fall upon his shoulders. Much of the actual clean-up can be done by the students if they have proper supervision.

The publicity committee must be very active, because the publicity given the demonstration will do much to determine its success or failure. It should be the duty of this committee to determine what methods will be used to inform the public about the demonstration. This committee should compose and release all information in relation to the demonstration. There are many ways in which the demonstration can be brought to the attention of the general public, among them being talks, newspaper stories, radio, television, assembly programs, handbills, banners, surveys, signs, posters, window displays, and parades.

It should be made clear that a concerted effort should be made to establish a basic philosophy and a list of objectives prior to the organization of the demonstration. This should be adhered to throughout the demonstration. The activities selected should be a direct outgrowth of the physical education program as it is being taught every day of the school year. There should be no attempt to camouflage the program by selecting those activities which will portray only the best of the regular program. It is important that the general public be made aware of the fact that the demonstration is a direct outgrowth of the curriculum.

The central theme which has been chosen should be a determining factor in the selection of the activities which are to be presented. Another determining factor is the fact that an effort is always made to include all the students in the demonstration. Therefore, activities which can be performed reasonably well by everyone will need to be selected. Care must be taken to avoid the belief by the spectators that the demonstration is an exhibition where only the better students are performing.

The success of the demonstration depends upon how well the basic objectives have been met. The most important outcome is that an opportunity has been provided for every student to engage in an educational experience which he may not otherwise have had. The demonstration can be justified only on this basis, because it will show that every student is trained in a physical education program.

This training will help to give us a nation with the physical and mental health to carry on the traditions which have made this the greatest nation on earth. The demonstration will show the public what our schools are doing and encourage them to support our physical education programs.

In conclusion, it should be remembered that all the information included in this book cannot be used in every physical education demonstration. Every situation is different and the physical educator should select the material that will fit his own particular situation.

BIBLIOGRAPHY

American Association for Health, Physical Education and Recreation, "Physical Education for High School Students," 1960.

American National Red Cross, *First Aid Text Book*, Garden City, New York: Doubleday and Company, Inc., 1957.

Anderson, C. F., "Practical Hints on Demonstrations," *Journal of Health and Physical Education*, March, 1936.

Aurora, Edra Cox, "Informing the Public We Serve," *School and Community*, December, 1962.

Baker, Joseph J., and Jon S. Peters, *School Maintenance and Operation*, Danville, Illinois: The Interstate Printers & Publishers, Inc., 1963.

Barrow, Harold M., Marjorie Cresk and James Long, *Physical Education Syllabus*, Minneapolis: Burgess Publishing Company, 1961.

Bender, Jay A., Harold Kaplan, and Alex Johnson, "Isometrics—a Critique of Faddism vs. Facts," *Journal of Health, Physical Education and Recreation*, 1963.

Benjamin, Harold, *Emergent Conceptions of the School Administrator's Task*, Stanford: Stanford University Press, 1942.

Bennett, Bruce L., "Tell It to Mom and Dad," *Journal of Health, Physical Education and Recreation*, March, 1962.

Bennett, Henry Eastman, *School Efficiency*, Boston: Ginn and Company, 1917.

Bent, Rudyard Kipling, *Administration of Secondary Schools*, New York: McGraw-Hill, 1960.

Bishop, Thelma, "Values in Sports," *Journal of Health, Physical Education and Recreation*, September, 1962.

Blake, William O., and Anne Volp, *Lead-Up Games to Team Sports*, Englewood Cliffs, New Jersey: Prentice Hall Inc., 1964.

Bookwalter, Karl W., *Physical Education in the Secondary Schools*, Washington: The Center for Applied Research in Education, Inc., 1964.

Boydston, Donald N., "P.E. Can Boost Your School's P.R.," *Illinois Education*, October, 1956.

Bradford, Jean K., "How to Shine as Madam Chairman," *Parents Magazine*, August, 1961.

Brown, Camelle, and Rosalind Cassidy, *Theory in Physical Education*, Philadelphia: Lea and Febiger, 1963.

Bucher, Charles A., *Administration of School Health and Physical Education Program*, St. Louis: The C. V. Mosby Co., 1963.

Bucher, Charles A., Constance Koeney, and Milton Barnhard, *Methods and Materials for Secondary School Physical Education*, St. Louis: The C. V. Mosby Co., 1961.

Bucher, Charles A., *Foundations of Physical Education*, St. Louis: The C. V. Mosby Co., 1964.

Bullington, R. A., "First Aid in High Schools," *Illinois Education*, Springfield, Illinois, April, 1940.

Campbell, Bruce J., "No Longer Unaccustomed," *National Parent Teachers*, October, 1960.

Cassidy, Rosalind, *Curriculum Development in Physical Education*, New York: Harper and Brothers, 1954.

Cowell, Charles C., and Helen Hazelton, *Curriculum Designs in Physical Education*, Englewood Cliffs, New Jersey: Prentice Hall, 1955.

Davis, Elwood Craig, Earl L. Wallis, *Toward Better Teaching in Physical Education*, Englewood Cliffs, New Jersey: Prentice Hall, 1962.

Donnelly, Richard J., William Helms, and Elmer Mitchell, *Active Games and Contests*, New York: The Ronald Press, 1958.

Duggan, Anne S., "The Place of Dance in the School Physical Education Program," *Journal of the American Association for Health, Physical Education and Recreation*, March, 1951.

Duke, Wayne, "Public Relations and Athletics," *Journal of Health, Physical Education and Recreation*, October, 1959.

Duncan, Ray O., and Helen B. Watson, *Introduction to Physical Education*, New York: Ronald Press Co., 1960.

Elkow, Duke J., and Herbert Stack, *Education for Safe Living*, Englewood Cliffs, New Jersey: Prentice Hall, Inc., 1957.

Erdman, Bernard P., "Selling Physical Education," *School Activities*, January, 1950.

Evans, Ruth, and Leo Gans, *Supervision of Physical Education*, New York: McGraw-Hill, 1950.

Fait, Hallis F., John Shaw, Grose Fox, and Cecil Hallengsworth, *A Manual of Physical Education Activities*, Philadelphia: W. B. Saunders Co., 1956.

Fait, Hallis F., and Mary Vannier, *Teaching Physical Education in Secondary Schools*, Philadelphia: W. B. Saunders Co., 1964.

Fine, Benjamin, *Education Publicity*, New York: Harper and Brothers, 1943.

Florio, A. E., and Stafford, G. T., *Safety Education*, Second Edition. New York: McGraw-Hill Book Co., 1962.

Forsythe, Charles E., and Ray Duncan, *The Administration of Physical Education*, New York: Prentice Hall, Inc., 1951.

Forsythe, Charles E., *The Administration of High School Athletics*, Englewood Cliffs, New Jersey: Prentice Hall, 1962.

Forsythe, Charles E., *The Athletic Directors Handbook*, Englewood Cliffs, New Jersey: Prentice Hall, 1954.

Foster, Catherine, and Rolland Langerman, "Physical Education on the Air," *School Activities*, November, 1949.

Gray, Miriam, *Physical Education Demonstration*, New York: A. S. Barnes and Company, 1947.

Harlow, Rex F., and Marvin Block, *Practical Public Relations*, New York: Harper and Brothers, 1947.

Harral, Stewart, *Tested Public Relations for Schools*, Norman, Oklahoma: The University of Oklahoma Press, 1952.

Havel, Richard C., and Emery Seymour, *Administration of Health, Physical Education and Recreation for Schools*, New York: The Ronald Press Company, 1961.

Healey, William A., *The Administration of Athletic Events*, Danville, Illinois: The Interstate Printers & Publishers, Inc., 1961.

Hendman, Darwin A., *Handbook of Active Games*, New York: Prentice Hall, 1951.

Henneke, Ben Graf, and Edward S. Dumit, *The Announcer's Handbook*, New York: Holt, Rinehart and Winston, 1960.

Hinton, L. W., "School Fire Safety Inspections," *Illinois Education*, April, 1962.

Hoaks, Gene, *Application of Weight Training to Athletics*, Englewood Cliffs, New Jersey: Prentice Hall, Inc., 1962.

Howard, Glenn W., and Edward Masonbrink, *Administration of Physical Education*, New York: Harper and Row, 1963.

Hughes, William L., Esther French, and Nelson G. Lehsten, *Administration of Physical Education for Schools and Colleges*, New York: The Ronald Press, 1962.

Hughes, William L., and Esther French, *The Administration of Physical Education*, New York: A. S. Barnes, 1954.

Hughes, William L., and Jesse Williams, *Sports—Their Organization and Administration*, New York: A. S. Barnes and Company, 1944.

Hull, Henrich J., "Public Relations Can Make or Break," *Nations Schools*, October, 1947.

Hunsicker, Paul, "AAHPER Physical Fitness Test Battery," *Journal of Health, Physical Education, and Recreation*, September, 1958.

Jackson, C. O., "Suggested Programs for Demonstrations and Exhibitions," *Journal of Health and Physical Education*, February, 1937.

Jackson, C. O., "Ten Principles for Good Public Relations," *Physical Education and School Athletics Newsletter*, New London, Connecticut: Crafts Co., 1957.

James, Charles S., *A Frontier of Municipal Safety*, New York: Stratford Press, Inc., 1955.

James, Charles S., *Police and Fire Integration in the Small City*, California: Public Administration Service, 1955.

Johnson, Granville B., Warren Johnson, and James Humphrey, *Your Career in Physical Education*, New York: Harper and Brothers, 1957.

Jones, Violet D., "Physical Education Exhibit," *Journal of Health, Physical Education and Recreation*, February, 1960.

Kindred, Leslie W., *School Public Relations*, Englewood Cliffs, New Jersey: Prentice Hall, 1957.

Kirkpatrick, Marion, "School Publicity Should Reach All People," *School Activities*, March, 1954.

Kleendeenst, Viola, and Arthur Waston, *Intramural and Recreational Programs for Schools and Colleges*, New York: Appleton-Century-Crofts, 1964.

Kraus, Hans, and Ruth Herscheand, "Muscular Fitness and Health." *Journal of the American Association for Health, Physical Education and Recreation*, December, 1953.

Kraus, Richard, *Play Activities for Boys and Girls*, New York: McGraw-Hill Company, 1957.

LaPorte, William R., *The Physical Education Curriculum*, Los Angeles: Parker and Company, 1951.

Lippincott, Gertrude, "Mechanics and Materials of the Demonstration Lesson," *Journal of Health, Physical Education and Recreation*, January, 1961.

Lovelace, Walter B., "How to Get School News Published," *Phi Delta Kappan*, November, 1955.

Lucia, Mary Sister, "Our Illustrated Activity Calendar," *School Activities*, March, 1962.

Mason, Bernard S., and Elmer Mitchell, *Active Games and Contests*, New York: A. S. Barnes and Company, 1935.

McCloskey, Gordon, *Education and Public Understanding*, New York: Harper and Brothers, 1959.

McCloskey, Gordon, "Planning the Public Relations Program," *National Education Association Journal*, February, 1960.

McCoy, Raymond F., *American School Administration*, New York: McGraw-Hill, 1961.

Means, Louis E., *Physical Education Activities, Sports and Games*, Dubuque: Wm. C. Brown Company, 1963.

Melby, Ernest O., *Administering Community Education*, Englewood Cliffs, New Jersey: Prentice Hall, Inc., 1955.

Menke, Frank G., *The Encyclopedia of Sports*, New York: A. S. Barnes and Company, 1953.

Miano, Louis E., *Intramurals: Their Organization and Administration*, Englewood Cliffs, New Jersey: Prentice Hall, Inc., 1963.

Michael, Lloyd S., "New Directions for the High School Curriculum," *California Journal of Secondary Education*, October, 1958.

Miller, Harold, "Physical Education a la Roller Skating," *School Activities*, January, 1957.

Mitchell, Elmer D., and Bernard Mason, *The Theory of Play*, New York: A. S. Barnes and Company, 1948.

Moss, Bernice, and Harold Areon, "The Public School Program in Health, Physical Education and Recreation." *Journal of Health and Physical Education*, October, 1939.

Mueller, Pat, and Elmer D. Mitchell, *Intramural Sports*, New York: The Ronald Press, 1960.

Nash, Jay B., Frances Moenih, and Jeannette Sourborn, *Physical Education: Organization and Administration*, New York: A. S. Barnes, 1951.

National Safety Council, *Safety in Physical Education and Recreation*, Chicago, Illinois: National Safety Council, Inc., 1963.

Nulton, John E., "We Are on Display," *Journal of Health, Physical Education and Recreation*, April, 1963.

Oberteuffer, Delbert, *Physical Education*, New York: Harper and Brothers, 1951.

Oberteuffer, Delbert, "Some Contributions of Physical Education to an Educated Life," *Journal of Health and Physical Education*, January, 1945.

O'Conner, John, "Organizing a Variety Show," *School Activities*, October, 1958.

Oermann, Karl C., Carl Young and Gary Mitchell, *Conditioning Exercises, Games, Tests*, Annapolis: United States Naval Institute, 3rd ed., 1960.

O'Keefe, Ruth P., and Anita Aldrich, *Education Through Physical Activities*, St. Louis: C. V. Mosby Company, 1959.

Page, Milton S., "Roller Skating for Schools," *School Activities*, November, 1956.

Pape, Laurence A., and Louis Means, *A Professional Career in Physical Education*, Englewood Cliffs, New Jersey: Prentice Hall, 1962.

Reeder, W. G., *The Fundamentals of Public School Administration*, New York: The Macmillan Company, 1958.

Rider, John F., *Installation and Servicing of Low Power Public Address Systems*, New York: John F. Rider Publications, Inc., 1948.

"Royal Canadian Air Force Exercise Plans for Physical Fitness," Mount Vernon, New York: *This Week Magazine*, 1962.

Ryan, Allan J., *Medical Care of the Athlete*, New York, Toronto, and London: McGraw-Hill Book Co., Inc., 1962.

Salt, E. Benton, Grace I. Fox and B. K. Stevens, *Teaching Physical Education in the Elementary School*, New York: The Ronald Press, 1960.

Sapora, Allan V., and Elmer Mitchell, *The Theory of Play and Recreation*, New York: The Ronald Press Company, 3rd ed., 1961.

Scott, Harry A., *Competitive Sports in Schools and Colleges*, New York: Harper and Brothers, 1951.

Scott, Harry A., "The Society of Directors of Physical Education in Colleges," *Journal of Health and Physical Education*, April, 1932.

Sellers, Mary V., "Opportunities for Guidance in the School Program," *Journal of American Health, Physical Education and Recreation*, February, 1949.

Shepard, Natalie M., *Foundations and Principles of Physical Education*, New York: The Ronald Press Company, 1960.

"Show and Explain Your Program to the Public by Presenting a Physical Education Demonstration This Year," *Physical Education Newsletter*, January 1, 1966.

Staley, Steward C., *Games, Contests, and Relays*, New York: A. S. Barnes and Company, 1938.

Staley, Steward C., *Individual and Mass Athletics*, New York: A. S. Barnes, 1928.

Staley, Steward C., *Physical Education Programs*, St. Louis: The C. V. Mosby Company, 1953.

Stanley, D. K., and Irwin Woglaw, *Physical Education Activities Handbook*, Boston: Allen and Bacon, 1966.

The National Committee on Safety Education and the AAHPER., *Safety in Physical Education for the Classroom Teacher*, The National Education, 1951.

Traina, Aubrey, "Talent Show," *School Activities*, October, 1949.

Vannier, Mary Helen, and Hollis F. Fait. *Teaching Physical Education in Secondary Schools*, Philadelphia: W. B. Saunders Co., 1964.

Viles, Nelson, *The Custodian at Work*, New York: The University Publishing Company, 1941.

Voltmer, Edward F., and Arthur Eslinger, *The Organization and Administration of Physical Education*, New York: Appleton-Century-Crofts, Inc., 3rd ed., 1958.

Williams, Jesse F., *The Principles of Physical Education*, Philadelphia: W. B. Saunders Company, 8th ed., 1964.

Williams, Jesse F., Clifford Brownell, and Elmon Vernier, *The Administration of Health, Physical Education and Recreation*, Philadelphia: W. B. Saunders and Company, 1964.

Yeager, William A., *Administration of the Noninstructional Personnel and Services*, New York: Harper and Brothers, 1959.

Young, Jean M., "Four-Wheeled Fun in Pontiac, Michigan," *Journal of Health, Physical Education and Recreation*, March, 1959.

Zeigler, Earle S., *Human Relations and Administration in Physical Education and Athletics*, Englewood Cliffs, New Jersey: Prentice Hall, Inc., 1959.

INDEX

A

Back to back wrestling
  Description of, 297
Backward-all-fours relay
  Description of, 258
Backward handspring
  Description of, 205
Backward pull-away
  Description of, 288
Backward push away
  Description of, 298
Backward roll
  Description of, 204
Backward-run-relay
  Description of, 257
Backward scooter relay
  Description of, 247
Bag boxing
  Description of, 276
Ball fight
  Description of, 280
Balloon fight
  Description of, 281
Balloon squash
  Description of, 301
Band
  Arrangements for, 42
  Duties of, 155
  Importance of, 154
  Positioning of, 154, 157
  Practice of, 155
  Provision for, 42
  Recognition of, 156
  Rehearsal with, 42
  Size of, 156
  Type of, 156
  Use of, 97, 100, 154, 306
Band director
  Cooperation of, 154
  Duties of, 154
  Use of, 154
Banner
  Use of, 98
Baseball batter
  Description of, 202
Baseball pitching
  Description of, 201
Basketball
  Drills for, 275
Basketball circle dribbling drill
  Description of, 214
Basketball court
  Use of, 300
Basketball drills
  Kinds of, 214

Bat pull
  Description of, 291
Bear hug wrestle
  Description of, 312
Bend and reach exercise
  Description of, 220
Bend the arm
  Description of, 282
Bills
  Collection of, 73
  Payment of, 73
  Sending of, 73
Bird fight
  Description of, 296
Boat relay
  Description of, 265
Body twists
  Description of, 222
Bone of contention
  Description of, 307
Bookcovers
  Provision of, 185
  Use of, 185
Book markers
  Information on, 187
  Making of, 187
  Use of, 187
  Value of, 187
Books
  Access to, 188
  Acquisition of, 187
  Arrangement for display
    of, 185-186
  Ordering of, 188
  Use of, 187
Bowling
  Effects of, 375
  Efficiency of, 375
  Interests in, 376
  Techniques of, 376
  Use of, 376
Boy Scouts
  Use of, 82
Boys and girls, 13
  Characters of, 49
  Placement of, 13
Broad jumps
  Description of, 409
Bronco busting
  Description of, 273
Broom relay
  Description of, 262
Budget
  Administration of, 179
  Adoption of, 179

N

O